Windows Telephony
Programming

Windows Telephony Programming

A Developer's Guide to TAPI

Chris Sells

Addison-Wesley

An imprint of Addison Wesley Longman, Inc.

Reading, Massachusetts • Harlow, England • Menlo Park, California
Berkeley, California • Don Mills, Ontario • Sydney
Bonn • Amsterdam • Tokyo • Mexico City

The publisher offers discounts on this book when ordered in quantity for special sales. For more information, please contact:

AWL Direct Sales
Addison Wesley Longman, Inc.
One Jacob Way
Reading, Massachusetts 01867
(781) 944-3700

Library of Congress Cataloging-in-Publication Data

Sells, Chris.
    Windows telephony programming : a developer's guide to TAPI /
    Chris Sells.
        p.   cm.
    Includes index.
    ISBN 0-201-63450-3
    1. Computer interfaces—Standards.   2. Telephone systems.
    3. Internet programming.   4. Microsoft Windows (Computer file)
    I. Title.
    TK7887.5.S43   1988
    005.7′1268—dc21   98-20433
                                                          CIP

ISBN 0-201-63450-3
Text printed on recycled and acid-free paper.
1 2 3 4 5 6 7 8 9 10—MA—0201009998
First printing, July 1998

Contents

t Monitor

+ Usefull Sample

Preface

This Book

This book has been a part of my life for the last four years. It started as an outline when I was working at Intel. Herman D'Hooge had produced the first version of the TAPI (Telephony API) specification, and Paul Drews was leading its implementation. I was working in a group building telephony boards and telephony applications. I remember it was quite a challenge debugging early TAPI applications that were using alpha versions of TAPI 0.9 through first-try TSPs running in VxDs acting as a multi-tasking OS below single-tasking Windows 3.1 communicating with another OS running on a preproduction DSP mounted on a prototype telephony board. If you think the Telephony API hard to program now, you don't know what you missed.

Which brings me to the purpose of this book. The Telephony API is a fundamental piece of the communications architecture of the modern versions of Windows, that is, Windows 9x, Windows NT 4+, and even Windows CE. However, it's fairly large and somewhat daunting to the uninitiated. Still, there is an underlying architecture and a philosophy that, once understood, makes TAPI, if not especially easy, at least approachable. As one of the world's first TAPI programmers, I feel I have a TAPI story to tell that will help ease you into the world of Windows Telephony. This book tells that story.

Who This Book Is For

This book is for any C or C++ developer interested in building telephony applications under Windows. This may include human-assisted applications such as call control, call monitoring, and predictive dialing or human-free applications such as audiotex, voicemail, and automatic call directing. The range of telephony applications includes really anything you can do when you hook a telephone or telephone line to a computer. This book is also useful for the TAPI Service Provider developer, as an example of both how typical TAPI applications are written as well as how to write an actual TSP.

Simplifying TAPI

This book will be especially useful to the C++ and Microsoft Foundation Classes programmer. In the course of developing TAPI applications, I found myself doing the same things over and over. So, like any C++ programmer, I built a class library. And then I threw it away. I built another one, and I threw that one away, too.[1] Finally, I built the Telephony Framework (TFX). The TFX provides a set of C++ classes that, while leveraging the object model built into TAPI, removes much of the grunt work of developing TAPI applications. Since I was using the TFX to build MFC applications, it has been designed to work well in MFC applications. In addition, many of the samples in this book use the TFX in MFC applications to demonstrate how TAPI is used.

That's not to say that this book is useful only to MFC programmers. In fact, only half of the chapters of this book mention MFC. Those that do *always* describe and show how the underlying TAPI functions work *before* they show the TFX equivalent. If you never want to use the TFX or MFC or even C++, I believe this book still provides a good starting place for any TAPI developer.

The TFX itself is really just a repository for a set of classes that I find useful when developing telephony applications in C++. I present them so that the sample applications, and therefore the concepts, are a little cleaner. If you want to use the TFX to build telephony applications, feel free. If you'd rather just use it as a set of code to copy and paste from or as an illustration of the concepts of TAPI, that's OK, too.

Who I Am

Whenever I pick up a technical book of any kind, I always wonder what makes the author qualified to write the book. I assume you do the same, so I wanted to tell you a little bit about myself. I've done telephony work of one kind or another for about nine years as of the time of this writing. I started at Spanlink Communications building small- to medium-sized multicaller voicemail, audiotex, and host

---

[1] However, pieces of this second TAPI class library were used in Intel's ProShare line of products.

access systems. Those 386 systems, at their peak, handled about 50 simultaneous calls at a rate of 1,200 calls/day.[2] After about three years at Spanlink, I moved to Intel to help with their telephony efforts. Although the telephony boards I helped to build never saw the light of day, they did spawn the current crop of video conferencing boards that Intel still makes. While at Intel, I developed a bunch of TAPI applications, provided many bug reports, submitted a telephony-related patent,[3] and wrote the original outline of this book . . . which I then filed in a drawer.

I left my software engineering job at Intel to become an instructor at Develop-Mentor. There, I began hanging out with the cream of the crop of the Windows community. These were the guys who spoke at the conferences, wrote the magazine articles, and authored the books that I knew and loved. What can I say? I was inspired. A couple of e-mails later and this book was born.

TAPI has evolved since I first put fingers to keyboard composing that original outline. It's moved from 16-bit TAPI 1.3 running under Windows 3.x, to half 16-bit/half 32-bit TAPI 1.4 running under Windows 95, to full 32-bit TAPI 2.0 running under Windows NT 4.0, to the latest COM-based TAPI 3.0 slated to run under Windows NT 5.0. While I have drawn the line at covering any 16-bit versions of TAPI, I've tried to cover the basics of writing both TAPI applications as well as TAPI Service Providers for all 32-bit versions. The last chapter provides an advance preview of TAPI 3.0.

Need More?

This book is not an encyclopedia of TAPI. Instead, I have emphasized its architecture and philosophy with the idea that anything else you need to learn will fit more easily into your newfound understanding. I can recommend several additional resources. First, I recommend the online documentation. The overviews of both TAPI and the TSPI included with the platform SDK are excellent. They were an immensely helpful resource in my understanding some of the more obscure parts of TAPI, as well as helping to track the changes from one version to another.

I also recommend several resources on the Internet. Two public newsgroups, *microsoft.public.win32.programming.tapi* and *microsoft.public.win95.commtelephony,* have many excellent people answering questions. If your local USENET provider doesn't have these newsgroups, Microsoft maintains a public news server at *msnews.microsoft.com.*

---

[2] I think it's ironic that I feel I need an entire 266MHz Pentium II all to myself just to run the copy of Microsoft Word I used to prepare this book.
[3] Patent #5,471,522, *Telephone Line Sharing for a Personal Computer System,* was awarded on November 28, 1995.

Microsoft maintains a World Wide Web ("Web") site dedicated to the communications infrastructure of Windows that includes the latest news on TAPI. That address is *http://www.microsoft.com/communications*. It also maintains an FTP site with some tools and samples at *ftp://ftp.microsoft.com/developr/TAPI*.

If you'd like answers to some questions about TAPI that I didn't cover enough in the book and you suspect that they have been asked before, I recommend the two TAPI Frequently Asked Questions pages that I'm aware of:

> *http://ourworld.compuserve.com/homepages/schenck/tapifaq.txt*
>
> *http://ourworld.compuserve.com/homepages/bruce_pennypacker/tapifaq.htm*

Both are well-maintained by long-time TAPI developers Bruce Pennypacker and Grant Schenck. If you post a question on one of the newsgroups, it's likely that one of these two guys will be providing the answer.

If you'd like more information from me, the Web site for this book is maintained at *http://www.sellsbrothers.com/telprog* and will include any updates that I need to make after the book is published. Finally, if you'd like to comment to me about this book, you may send me e-mail at *csells@sellsbrothers.com*.

The Source

The source code for all of the samples provided with the book as well as the entire TFX is provided on the Web site *http://www.sellsbrothers.com/telprog*. I thought long and hard about providing the source as a set of appendices for this book and ultimately decided against it. Printed source is sometimes useful for understanding specific implementation details. As these details come up, I tried very hard to put the significant source into the text of the chapters themselves. On the other hand, having the full source printed at the end of the book performs no real service except to puff up the size (and potentially the perceived coverage) of the book. As my favorite books are of the thin, focused variety, I found this unnecessary bloating unappealing to me. Plus, I may save a few trees in the bargain.

Acknowledgments

This book is the concentrated effort of many individuals. First, I want to thank my wife, Melissa. She tolerates me and my work. What could be more helpful to a telephony nerd than that? And I'd like to thank my kids, John and Tom, for bringing me back to reality when I needed it most. You guys give meaning and perspective to everything I do.

I'd like to thank my publishing team at Addison-Wesley. Because I'm such a sloth of an author, this has included several people who have come and gone during the life of this project, as well as others who have stuck it out the whole time, including Mike Hendrickson, Ben Ryan, J. Carter Shanklin, Alan Feuer, and Rachel Beavers.

I'd also like to thank the folks who invented, implemented, evangelized, and supported this technology, including Herman D'Hooge, Raman Srinivasan, Paul Drews, Guy Blair, Toby Nixon, Dan Knudson, Charles Fitzgerald, and Mitch Goldberg.

As they're the guys in the trenches battling it out over my clumsy prose, the reviewers need a great deal of thanks. They are Jon Flanders, Tim Ewald, Raman Srinivasan, Alan Moffet, Bruce Pennypacker, Grant Schenck, R. Keith Cox, and Erik Gilbert. I'd really like to thank Tim specifically. He had no telephony background before reading this book, but he has such great insight into the flow of any story that his feedback was indescribably valuable.

I'd like to thank Brett Shockley, Todd Parentau, and Skip Singer for the job at Spanlink Communications, where I got my start in telephony. I'd like to thank Matt Katzer for hiring me at Intel, where I was allowed to play with TAPI before nearly anyone else. Finally, I'd like to thank Mike Abercrombie and Don Box for hiring me at DevelopMentor. DevelopMentor has really given me the skills to tell this story. Don specifically showed me what the term "expert" means and why no one can ever truly be one (with the possible exception of Don himself).

These people have made the book as good as it is. Of course, all mistakes and omissions are mine.

Prologue

Intel has one of the largest research and development (R&D) budgets in the personal computer (PC) industry. R&D has one purpose at Intel: to make the Intel PC the best computer it can be. Don Dennis is a big thinker at Intel in Oregon who is in charge of spending his share of the R&D money. In late 1990, Don noticed that the PC had almost no support for sound. He was comparing it to the Apple Macintosh, which had good support for sound built in. Each PC had a speaker, but it was good only for beeps and boops. To hear anything else, one had to open the PC and add an expansion card. At the time, this was typically a SoundBlaster card from Creative Labs, a company dedicated to building high-quality sound cards for games.

Unfortunately, Andy Grove, the CEO of Intel, had a standing order to fire anyone who mentioned the word "game" in his presence. Games were for the Macintosh; PCs were for business applications. The question Don had to answer was, how do you add support for sound in a business setting?

The Story of Windows Telephony

About then, Herman D'Hooge, a member of Don's group, returned from a sabbatical. Every seven years, each Intel employee—from the lowest technician to the most exalted VP—gets a two-month paid vacation. When combined with normal vacation time, this means three months of paid time to goof off. The purpose of a sabbatical is to clear the mind for newer, deeper thoughts. When Herman returned to work, Don set him to work to enable "audio annotation," a general-purpose way to associate voice messages with documents and the "killer application" for sound in a business environment.

Herman noticed that there was already an audio input/output (I/O) device right next to the PC in every office—the telephone. The telephone didn't produce high-quality sound, like a home stereo, but it was far better than the PC speaker. So Herman got a SatisFAXtion board (an internal fax/modem that Intel produced at the time) and tried to connect his telephone to his PC. He failed.

The Telephony Connection

Around the world, in every business larger than a garage start-up, you will find the need for multiple telephone lines. Instead of each telephone line being hard-wired like so many Bat-Phones, lines are shared between the office telephones. This arrangement is managed by a centralized telephone line switching system kept in the office called a PBX (Private Branch eXchange). A PBX is connected to a public switch held in the local telephone company Central Office (CO). The local CO is then connected, eventually, to all other COs in the world.

The connection between a CO and a PBX has been standardized in both digital and analog formats. However, the connection between a PBX and the telephone on a desk is proprietary and determined by the PBX make and model. The telephone line Herman was trying to connect to was connected to a PBX made by Rolm. The Rolm PBX used digital communication with its telephones to allow special features like Caller ID. The SatisFAXtion board, like nearly every other fax machine and modem, was built to understand the analog standard used to connect residential telephones to COs in the United States—POTS (Plain Old Telephony Service). The details of how a Rolm PBX talks to its telephones is still a closely held secret, but it is definitely not POTS. This was why Herman was unable to make his Satis-FAXtion board work on his office telephone line. A SatisFAXtion technical support person explained to Herman that to use any modem or fax machine, one must use a standard POTS line. That meant two telephone lines at Herman's desk, one digital and one analog.

Herman was stunned. "You mean I have to use an analog line to send digital information from my digital PC, but the digital line I have sitting right next to me can be used only for analog voice conversations?"

At that time, Intel had been asking focus groups what kinds of features they expected from a telephone-PC connection. It learned that people wanted more than just a microphone and a speaker. They wanted to see their voicemail messages on the screen. They wanted to dial people by name instead of by strings of digits. They wanted to unlock all of the hidden secrets of their telephones, such as how to perform a conference call or transfer a call (and thereby avoid the use of the classic phrase, "Hold on and I'll try to transfer you. Here's the telephone number in case I lose you . . .").

This extra functionality would use the entire network behind the telephone, not just the telephone itself. So, Herman needed to find an interface between the computers and the telephone lines on everyone's desks. What he found was that many PBX vendors—for example, AT&T, Rolm, Northern Telecom—already had connections between their switches and a PC. However, all of these vendors were in the process of taking their products off the market—they just weren't selling. It didn't take Herman long to figure out why.

In mid-1991, the Intel SatisFAXtion board cost less than $500 and could be used with hundreds of ISV (Independent Software Vendor) software packages. On the other hand, each telephony board from a switch vendor cost in the neighborhood of $2,000 and came with the single software package it supported. This software was usually DOS-based and always horrible. While some of the boards had an SDK (Software Development Kit), most ISVs wouldn't use it to create applications.

Telephony Drivers

In the telephony market, the only ISVs to build applications for switch vendor telephony boards were those that had been paid by the switch vendors to do so. No ISVs were building applications to work across the range of telephony boards. The problem was that each telephony application was intimately tied to a specific switch vendor's telephony equipment. For an ISV to support more than one board, many hours of development time would have to be spent building telephony board drivers, just like in the old days with printers. But now the market was moving too fast to spend that kind of time developing drivers, so ISVs moved on to other projects.

What ISVs needed, Herman realized, was a way to separate an application from a specific telephony board. This would separate the ISV from a specific switch vendor and open up the market. "That's why they're called Independent Software Vendors, because they can develop independently," he said. Clearly, the industry needed a standard API for telephony application development. If there was a standard, ISVs could develop software, people would buy telephony boards, and switch vendors would manufacture boards and write driver software for their switches. And finally, Herman would be able to connect his Rolm telephone to his PC. (I know it seems like a stretch, but people think big at Intel.)

Existing Telephony Standards

Herman began looking at telephony conferences for a standard API. After attending a few, he felt he knew most of what there was to know about telephony standards. There wasn't much. "It was always the same guy, with the same story, the same slides, and the same suit," he said. By then, Herman had worked up a set of requirements needed to fulfill the requests of the focus groups. He was looking for a standard API that was call-control focused, that allowed access to media (like sound and fax data) via standard APIs, that was network-, platform-, and connection-model independent, and that allowed line sharing between applications.

Herman found that the telephony industry already had several standards. Hayes had the AT (Attention) command set for modems, and Europe had the CSTA (Computer Supported Telephony Application) for call centers. Some switch vendors supported SCAI (Switch Computer Adjunct Interface) for controlling PBXs from a computer. AT&T and Dialogic each had their own APIs for IVR (integrated-voice response, for example, voicemail) applications. But none of these standards was driving the industry towards a standard that attracted ISVs or met Herman's requirements.

Herman noticed that Charles Fitzgerald, a marketing manager from Microsoft, also attended the telephony conferences. It turned out that Microsoft was looking for the same kind of standard API as Intel. Instead of competing, Intel and Microsoft decided to work together to bring a telephony standard to the Windows PC.

Windows Telephony

The winter weather in Oregon is usually mild, but in December 1992, Herman made his way to the airport in one of the worst snowstorms in Portland's history. He was headed for the headquarters of Microsoft in Seattle with two goals in mind. The first was to meet Toby Nixon, a telephony engineer at Microsoft, newly hired away from Hayes. The second was to present the first draft of TAPI (the Telephony API) in a private meeting with more than 40 of the companies that controlled the telecommunications industry. The first draft of TAPI was so simple—it contained only about 25 function calls—but its presentation lasted a full day. Because the audience had few comments about the proposed standard, Herman and Toby felt that TAPI would be quickly ratified. How wrong they were.

The silence that met the presentation of TAPI didn't indicate overwhelming agreement. Instead, the members of the telephony industry were secretly composing their comments so as to keep them from their competitors. After Herman returned to Portland, the faxes started coming in. And they continued to come in for weeks. At one point, Herman had a stack of flimsy faxes over a foot thick—all with comments about TAPI. It was clear that there was much work left to do. In fact, Herman said that had he known just how much was needed to meet the seemingly contradictory requirements of the telecommunications industry, he would never have begun the project in the first place. He finally understood why there had never been a standard.

Over the next few months, Herman and Toby wrote an errata document to address the issues raised about TAPI. TAPI 1.0 was presented to the public at the Computer Telephony Exposition in Dallas, Texas, in May 1993. Again, the fax machine started spitting out comments. Herman and Toby went back to work.

Meanwhile, beginning in January 1993, Paul Drews and Raman Srinivasan at Intel began to implement TAPI. Paul did the internal design specification and the

Telephony Service Provider Interface (TSPI) specification, and Raman did most of the development of TAPI. The purpose of the TSPI was to provide a layer for the telephony hardware provider to implement. ISVs would program to TAPI, and telephony hardware vendors would implement the TSPI; TAPI would be left in the middle to connect the two. Engineers at Microsoft did the initial TSP (TAPI Service Provider) for a standard modem and the first shipping TAPI application. Eventually, these two projects became the Unimodem TSP and the Phone Dialer application that ship with Windows 95.

At Microsoft, Toby's group was running each build of TAPI through an extensive testing and validation suite. The TAPI engineers kept stomping bugs until TAPI could pass the tests. Then one day in November 1993, Herman got a call. The current release candidate of TAPI had passed, and the TAPI SDK was shipping.

Evangelizing TAPI

After the TAPI development had been completed, Herman, Paul, and Guy Blaire (in marketing at Intel) began the process of evangelizing TAPI. What good was a standard unless everyone adopted it? Because TAPI did such a good job of separating the hardware from the applications, developers needed to be sure that their applications would work across telephony hardware that was still under development. To further this end, the first in a series of compatibility testings between TAPI applications and TSPs was done in August 1994. The first TAPI Bake-Off (named after the famous Pillsbury Bake-Off) was held at Intel in Hillsboro, Oregon. At each station, a vendor would set up its telephony hardware and TSP. Once an hour, the lights would be turned off and on, signaling each application vendor to move to another station and install and test their TAPI applications. That was what Herman had been looking for: "Competitors were working together to build an industry to compete in."

Several other TAPI Bake-Offs have been held since then. The first saw about a dozen hardware and software telephony products. By May 1996, when the fourth was held in Hawaii, there were nearly ten times that many.

Microsoft has built TAPI into every one of its operating systems. When TAPI 1.3 was released, it was supported under Windows 3.*x*. In August 1995, Microsoft shipped Windows 95 with support for TAPI 1.4. In September 1996, Windows NT 4.0 was delivered with TAPI 2.0. It was clear that Intel and Microsoft had cracked the nut and built the standard for Windows Telephony. Finally, Herman could get back to work connecting his PC to his telephone.

Windows Telephony Overview

Telephony—Isn't that when you know what someone
on the phone is going to say before they say it?
Ted Pattison
DevelopMentor

The term "telephony" refers to any of a number of technologies that are used to transmit voice from one person to another across a distance. With the growing popularity of Internet Telephony, it can't be said to involve only actual telephones anymore. The subject of this book, Computer Telephony Integration (CTI), is all about connecting together computers and telephones. This kind of connection is useful for all kinds of tasks, including the placing, answering, routing, and monitoring of phone calls and the taking of information from a caller via touch-tones, voice recordings, or voice recognition. Many different kinds of applications can be built using telephony features. Personal Information Managers (PIMs) and productivity applications such as word processors and spreadsheets can provide support for dialing selected phone numbers. A call manager application can provide help for those of us who can never remember how to transfer a call or set up a conference call. A call manager can be especially smart and use Caller ID information to show who was calling, even if you are already on another call.

Several kinds of applications don't require a human on both sides of the call. You can install an application on your computer that will answer the phone when you call and provide access to what I like to call "Excel from Abroad." By using touch-tones or your voice, you can access the data on your computer from any phone in the world. Also, several programs on the market allow you to access data via a telephone when normally, to access the data you would have to be sitting in front of your computer using an application such as Microsoft Excel. Further, a computer with multiple phone lines can provide an IVR application. IVR applications include auto-attendants to route phone calls, voicemail systems to take messages, and audiotex systems to provide information from your local bank or newspaper.

The Telephone Network

The existing Public Switched Telephone Network (PSTN) is usually represented as shown in Figure 1.1. Most homes are connected to the CO of the local telephone company via an analog POTS line. If you disconnect the wire from the back of your home telephone, you'll likely see four wires held in place by a plastic RJ-11

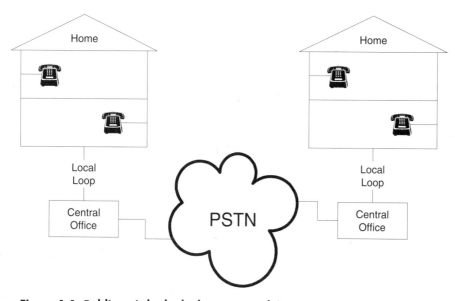

Figure 1.1: Public switched telephone network.

connector. The inner pair of wires is for line one, and the outer pair is for line two. Each wire in the pair has a name (tip and ring), and the two together provide a complete connection to the local CO, thereby giving rise to the name of this connection, the *local loop*. Each pair of wires transmits voice, tones, and power. The tones consist of both Dual-Tone Multi-Frequency (DTMF) tones you send by pressing the keys on your touch-tone keypad and information tones from the CO. The power is used to ring your telephone and keep it working when your home's power is out (otherwise, how could you call and complain?). Even data from a fax machine or a modem is translated into voice energy—which sounds like static—before it's sent over the line.

The connection between the COs around the world inside of the PSTN cloud has long since been converted from analog to digital. There's just too much information being sent to leave it in analog format. Instead, the voice energy on the line is sampled, turned into 1s and 0s, and sent digitally. Once the data reaches the CO on the other end of the connection, the data is turned back into voice and sent down the final mile of the local loop.

Because the PSTN is all digital and a digital connection has so much more bandwidth and capability than an analog connection, businesses for years have used various flavors of digital connections in the local loop. These are connections with names like T1, T3, and Switched-56. For businesses with lots of telephone lines and lots of money, these are wonderful inventions. For homes in the 90s with

To Modulate or Not To Modulate? That Is the Question.

The word "modem" stands for modulation-demodulation. Modulation happens when digital data is translated into analog signals for your POTS telephone line. Demodulation happens on the receiving side to translate the analog signals back into digital data. Modem speeds have continued to rise over the years because engineers at various telephony companies, such as Lucent Technologies, Rockwell, and US Robotics, have found ways to increase the speed of the modulation-demodulation process.

The irony is that because the PSTN cloud is now digital, the local CO must turn the modulated data back into bits before sending it to the remote CO. The remote CO must then turn it back into an analog signal, send it down the line to the modem, which then demodulates it back into bits. It's no wonder modern modems have so many fancy error-correction protocols.

So, why have the phone engineers been spending all of their time making modems faster? Shouldn't they be replacing the analog local loop and thereby save all of the unnecessary translating back and forth between analog and digital? Unfortunately, it's currently cheaper for them to leave the existing copper wire than to replace it with fiber optic cabling. Maybe the cable company can help. . . .

PCs, and limited spending capacity, these solutions have been out of reach. However, one affordable solution has been available for quite a while: the Integrated Services Digital Network, or ISDN (this is sometimes expanded, by the bitter proponents of other standards, to It Still Does Nothing or I Still Don't kNow).

ISDN is an international standard with two major flavors: BRI-ISDN (Basic Rate Interface) and PRI-ISDN (Primate Rate Interface). BRI-ISDN consists of 2B + 1D—two bearer channels and one data channel. Each bearer channel is for data sent at up to 64 Kbps (kilobits per second), including voice, fax, video, and network packets. Combined, the two B-channels can provide up to 128 Kbps, more than four times as much as the 28.8 Kbps analog modem. In addition, the D-channel can provide 16 Kbps. However, it is usually used only for call-related information, for example, announcing a new call or placing a new call. BRI-ISDN is great for a small business or a well-wired home. It's fairly well-supported by computer and telephone manufacturers and is relatively inexpensive (at least when compared to other options). For larger businesses, and more money, PRI-ISDN provides 23B+1D.

POTS provides the capability to answer and receive a call and has provided for Caller ID, call forwarding, call hold, and three-way conferencing. To be able to do anything more heavy-duty—for example, uniform dialing plans, class of service distinctions, and Direct Inward Dialing (DID)—you need more than POTS. Most COs provide an additional set of advanced call capabilities grouped into a service called CENTREX (which stands for "CENTRal office acting as the customer's EXchange"). This service extends the advanced functionality found on larger business telephone lines to your home or small business. When these features are provided on their own switch equipment, the CO can often provide them more cheaply and more easily than you can with your own switch.

A switch provides the brains of any telephone connection. When you pick up a telephone receiver and hear a dial tone, that's the switch's signal that it's ready to do your bidding. With POTS, ISDN, and CENTREX, the switch is located at the CO. However, you can have your own switch. Owning your own switch means that you control it completely. If you want an analog connection between your switch and the telephones it supports, you'll be using a *Key System.* A Key System is very much like having your own personal CENTREX. However, because it is analog, and typically doesn't support many telephones, it is fairly limited. If, instead, you want a digital connection between the switch and the phones it supports, and you want to support more telephones, you want a PBX. Because a PBX is digital, it's more flexible and more full-featured.

Each of the switches involved in any of the types of telephone networks I've mentioned is—surprise, surprise—a computer. These computers typically have a closed architecture, which means that the only one who can add features or fix bugs is the manufacturer of the switch. However, the features provided by switches are limited because they are implemented on proprietary computers by a fairly limited number of engineers. Other companies are beginning to realize this and provide switches based on general-purpose computers, that is, PCs. The number of engineers available for PCs far outweighs that for proprietary computers, so there can be more software for switches based on PCs. As PCs become more powerful, more and more switches will be based around them.

Using standard interfaces for hardware and software, switches can be controlled via network protocols of all kinds. These include traditional telephone networks like POTS, ISDN, and CENTREX, as well as PC networks using protocols like TCP/IP (the language of the Internet) and IPX/SPX (the protocol used by Novell's Netware product). The software programming standard that makes all of these protocols available for telephony applications under Windows is TAPI, the Telephony Application Programming Interface.

Windows Open Services Architecture

TAPI is based on the principles of the Windows Open Services Architecture (WOSA). It provides some central services and holds some global state. Its main purpose, however, is to provide connections between TSPs and TAPI applica-

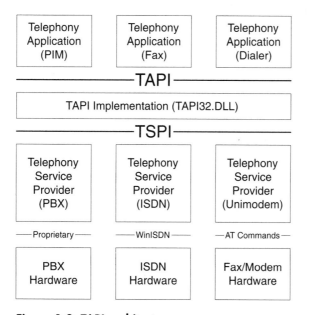

Figure 1.2: TAPI architecture.

tions. Applications are programmed using TAPI. TSPs implement the TSPI functions that are used by the TAPI implementation. Each TSP then uses whatever interface is appropriate to control its telephony hardware. Figure 1.2 shows the TAPI architecture.

This layered approach makes it possible for an application to be developed without the developers having to worry about the specific hardware provided on a particular machine. Any telephony hardware vendor can then implement the appropriate parts of the TSPI without worrying about what telephony applications have been installed. This separation makes applications and hardware independent of each other. Applications and hardware can come and go without directly affecting each other.

The WOSA model is used to achieve the goals of the TAPI:

1. Call control focus

2. Access to data via existing standard APIs

3. Network independence

4. Connection-model independence

5. Platform-independence, where possible

6. Sharing of lines between multiple applications

These each are discussed in the following sections.

Call Control Focus

TAPI was designed to establish connections between endpoints on a telephone network. These endpoints are called *addresses.* Think of an address as a telephone number. It's possible to have more than one address on a single line. On a business telephone system, where you're allowed to have multiple calls at once (although you can talk on only one at a time), an address with an active call is a *call appearance.* The *line* is the physical connection between each endpoint and the CO switch. Of course, you're allowed multiple lines at any location. All businesses of any size have multiple telephone lines. Most homes have one, although some have two or more.

> ### The Third Line Is the Charm
> Most homes built within the last twenty years are wired internally for two or three lines even if they use only one. For example, my house is wired for three lines. This means that at every telephone outlet in my house, I've got six copper wires, or three pair. Currently, the telephone company has connected only two pair to the CO. At any time, however, I could spend the money (usually between $35 and $75) to have the third pair activated. I'd love this, of course, being a telephony nerd, but it was hard enough to talk my wife into two. . . .

The physical connections between each endpoint and a CO and the telephone network between each CO allows a logical connection to be made from any endpoint to any other endpoint. This logical connection is a *call.* You make a call, of course, by providing the switch with another address, that is, by dailing a telephone number.

When establishing a call, an address can take any of several forms, depending on where the call's receiver is located. If you're connecting to another person on your key system or PBX, you can dial an abbreviated version called an extension number. This is usually the last three, four, or five digits of the full telephone number. If you're dialing someone in your area code, you dial just the telephone number without the area code. If you're dialing long distance within the United States, you first have to dial 1 and then the area code. If you're dialing an international number, you first have to dial the prefix string that identifies an international number—011 in the United States—and then the country code, the area code, and then the number. As you can see, the further away the call's receiver is, the more complicated the telephone number becomes.

For example, say you want to dial Addison-Wesley to order this book for a friend (it makes a lovely Christmas gift). Table 1.1 shows the digits you'll have to dial based on where you're calling from.

Table 1.1: Example of dialing various locations.		
Dialing From	Number to Dial	Digits
Inside Addison-Wesley.	4-3700	5
In same area code.	944-3700	7
Inside the United States.	1-781-944-3700	11
From Germany.	001-781-944-3700	13
From a PBX in Germany using an AT&T credit card.	9-0130-0010-781-944-3700-xxx-xxxx-xxxx	30

According to the psychology classes I took in college, people are able to group together about five things, give or take a couple, in a single thought. The typical telephone number is seven digits long, which is pushing it. Dialing long distance is about all I can manage. When I have to dial internationally using a calling card and some number to get an outside line first—well, I'll just say I don't usually get it right the first time.

Wouldn't it be great if we could just give the computer a telephone number and let it figure out what digits to actually dial? TAPI has support for doing just that. To transform a telephone number into a *dial string,* TAPI needs two things: a telephone number in *canonical address format* for a specific country and a description of a *dialing location.* Following is the canonical address format.

+ *country-code space* [*(area-code) space*] *subscriber-number* [*more*]

country-code   Identifies the country of the address. One or more digits followed by a space.

area-code   Identifies the area code of the address. Zero or more digits. If there are digits, they're surrounded by parentheses, which are followed by a space.

subscriber-number   The rest of the telephone number. One or more digits, dialing control characters, or formatting characters.

more   Optional delimiter character and one or more characters denoting an ISDN subaddress, name information, or another address. Multiple addresses are used in ISDN to combine multiple data channels.

Therefore, the canonical format of Addison-Wesley is + 1 (781) 944-3700.

Since I know to where I'm calling, all I need now is a description of the location from which I'm dialing. The Telephony Control Panel allows access to the

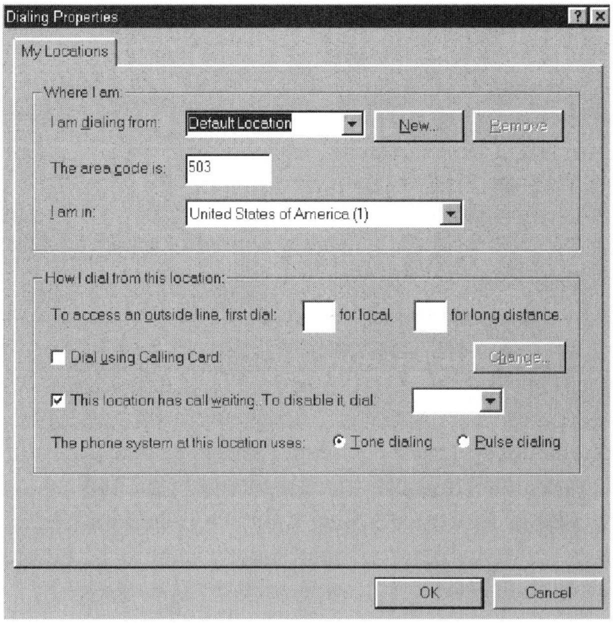

Figure 1.3: Dialing Properties settings.

Dialing Properties available on your system. The "My Locations" tab allows you to set up one or more dialing locations. See Figure 1.3. The Default Location applies to desktop computers. You set up the dialing rules for your computer once—what country you're in, what to dial to get an outside line, and so on—and they will be used by every TAPI application. Configuring multiple locations applies to laptop computers. For example, I take my laptop to hotels all over the United States. Invariably, hotels require me to dial either an 8 or 9 to get an outside line and a 1 for long distance calls. For each hotel, I set up a separate dialing location. When I want to access my Internet Service Provider (ISP) from the road, I simply choose the location from which I'm dialing. This means I can enter telephone number information once and the dial string will be properly composed based on my location.

When you are dialing a number, every good TAPI application will let you enter the area code, the subscriber number, the country you're dialing, and the location from which you're calling. For example, HyperTerminal has a dialog like that shown in Figure 1.4.

In this case, the telephone number, country, area code, and subscriber number can be changed by clicking the Modify button and the location can be changed in the "Your location" drop-down box. To access the Dialing Properties dialog, as in the Telephony Control Panel, click the Dialing Properties button. HyperTerminal uses this information to form the canonical address of the telephone number you're

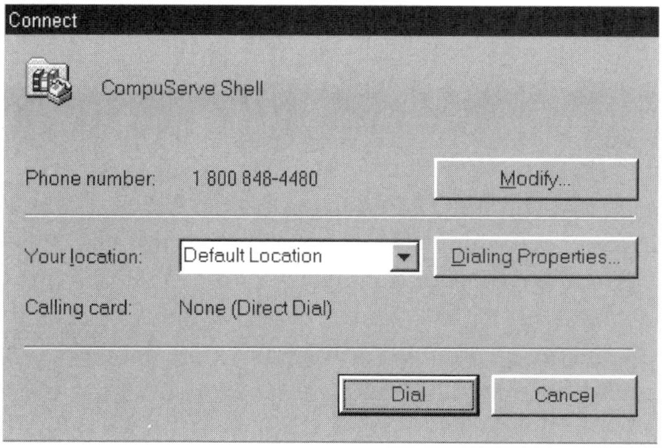

Figure 1.4: Dialing a TAPI telephone number from HyperTerminal.

dialing. It then asks TAPI to translate this address into *dialable address format.*
A dialable address is the actual string of numbers and control characters needed to
dial the address from your location. Following are the possible characters.

0–9 and A–D	Dial digits. A–D are special tones used for telephony maintenance and are not available on most telephone keypads.
!	*Flash hook* (500 ms on-hook, 500 ms off-hook). Most telephones have a *hook switch* that the receiver rests on when you hang up. The action of depressing this switch for a short time is called a *flash.*
P or p	Dial digits using pulses.
T or t	Dial digits using tones.
,	Pause (time based on device settings).
W or w	Wait for the dial tone before proceeding.
@	Wait for *quiet answer* (a ring followed by several seconds of silence).
;	Indicates the end of a partial dialing string. Another dial string will follow subsequently.

For example, on a line supporting tone dialing, the dial string for Addison-
Wesley in the United States from a home in another U.S. area code is
T17819443700. This is the string that will actually be sent to TAPI to dial
the telephone.

   After a canonical address is translated into a dialable address and dialing is
initiated, a call begins. Before the call is connected, it will go through a number
of *call states.* These states include dialing, proceeding, and ringing. If the call is

picked up on the other end, it will then transition into the connected state. If the other end is busy or there is a network error ("Doo-doo-do. I'm sorry, your call could not be connected . . ."), the call will transition into the appropriate state. Once the call has been disconnected, it transitions into its final state: idle. It's the responsibility of a Full TAPI application to properly handle these states. (See Chapter 2 for a discussion of the difference between Full TAPI and Assisted TAPI.)

TAPI provides programming access to three objects for call control: lines, addresses, and calls. As I said earlier, one location can have multiple lines and one line can have multiple addresses. In addition, one address can have multiple calls. You can switch between calls by placing one on *hold* before activating another. You can place a call on hold, establish another call, and *transfer* the initial call to the new address. You can join two or more calls together and have a *conference*. These and many other advanced call control techniques are supported by TAPI.[1]

One other telephony object supported by TAPI is the telephone—the hunk of hardware you use for its convenient placement of speaker, microphone, and keypad. TAPI enables call control to occur independently of the phone. To connect input and output to a line, TAPI allows a *terminal* to be established. Often, the default terminal will be the telephone. However, this facility allows a sound card, speakers, and a microphone to be used instead of a telephone. It also allows the telephone to be used as an I/O peripheral without its being connected to a line.

Media Access via Existing APIs

TAPI was designed from the ground up for call control, but it has no facility for direct access to the *media* available on a call, address, line, or telephone. The media is the data available, for example, modem, fax, network, and voice. The designers of TAPI had several options from which to choose when deciding how to provide access to media via TAPI. One was to add whole subsets of functionality to the API for each kind of media. This would have required ISVs to learn these media access sub-APIs. It also would have required that TAPI be updated every time a new kind of media appeared.

Another option—the one they chose—was to provide a way of getting at a specific *API handle* for use with an existing or future media API. The API handle could then be used in subsequent calls to the media API. This doesn't require ISVs to learn new APIs. Nor does it require TAPI to change when a new media type is

---

[1] Unfortunately, the TSP that ships with Windows—Unimodem—does not expose this kind of advanced call control. However, many third-party service providers do.

Table 1.2: Device classes defined for TAPI.	
Device Class Name	*Description*
comm	Communications port.
comm/datamodem	Modem through a communications port.
comm/datamodem/portname	Name of the device to which the modem is connected.
wave/in	Wave audio device for input only.
wave/out	Wave audio device for output only.
midi/in	Midi sequencer for input only.
midi/out	Midi sequencer for output only.
ndis	Network device.
tapi/line	Line device.
tapi/phone	Phone device.
tapi/terminal	Terminal device.

developed. Instead, if a device supports a specific kind of media, it simply provides an API handle for that media type when asked.

Media types are described by *device classes*. A device class is a description of a device that provides access to a specific type of media. A *device class name* is a string that identifies a specific device class. The device classes[2] defined for TAPI are given in Table 1.2.

If a telephony device doesn't support a specific class of media, it will simply fail when asked to provide an API handle. If a telephony vendor wants to support a device class other than those shown in the table, it can do so and provide documentation for that device class.

Network Independence

For an ISV to be able to cover enough of a market to make a difference, all of the telephone network communication protocols had to be covered with a single API: POTS, PBX, ISDN, Key Systems, wireless, cellular, and even the LAN (local area network). TAPI provides a superset API to functionality provided for all of these

---

[2]For a complete description of the device classes and the returned API handles, see Appendix A.

networks, abstracted in a way that isn't tied to a specific one. Telephony devices provide access to the various features of their networks without requiring the application to have specific knowledge related to each one.

Unfortunately, because TAPI must be a superset of the functionality of every kind of telephone network, the API is rather large. All telephony devices can't support all of the functionality accessible via TAPI. Developers need to be aware of this and write applications that provide subsets of functionality based on the capabilities of the target system's telephony devices. The good news is that TAPI allows an application to get a complete description of telephony device capabilities at runtime.

Connection-model Independence

The layer of abstraction between applications and hardware that TAPI provides allows for a single programming model no matter how the hardware has been connected to the user's PC. The TAPI Specification lists several possible examples of connection models. Ultimately, however, as long as the programming model remains consistent, a hardware vendor is free to provide a connection in any way that makes sense. Several of the popular connection models are described in the following subsections.

Phone-centric Connection

The phone-centric model, depicted in Figure 1.5, is the one most liked by people in the telephone hardware business. The focus of this model, as the name states, is the telephone. The telephone line from the wall is connected to the desktop telephone. The telephone is then connected to the PC via some kind of digital connection. The telephone controls the calls, and the PC directs the telephone. For

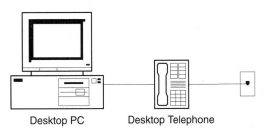

Desktop PC   Desktop Telephone

Figure 1.5: Phone-centric connection model.

example, the Mitel 9120i is a single-line telephone that connects to the PC via a serial cable. It comes with a TSP that provides access to the telephone line. However, the telephone has a lot of features that are available without help from the PC, including Caller-ID display, speed dial memory, hold, mute, and volume.

This model works equally well for whatever kind of phone the computer is connected to—POTS, CENTREX, ISDN, PBX-specific, or cellular. To get most of the functionality out of the telephone in this model, the PC doesn't even have to be on.

Computer-centric Connection

PC manufacturers like the computer-centric connection model, depicted in Figure 1.6. In this model, the telephone line is connected directly to the computer via some telephony hardware like a modem or an ISDN adapter card. The computer is the brains of this model; the telephone (sometimes called the *down-line phone*) simply acts as a microphone and speaker. In this model, the PC essentially replaces the telephone. Of course, for this to work, the PC has to be on.

Windows 95 and Windows NT 4.0 come with a built-in TSP called Unimodem. This TSP has a giant database of modem-specific AT commands to direct a modem through a telephone call. Most modem hardware is limited when it comes to voice calls, however, so Unimodem makes a poor TSP. Some modems provide voice support via proprietary extensions or by implementing an AT command extension set called AT+1V (AT plus Voice). At least one, Rockwell, provides its own proprietary extension, called AT#V. The TSP Unimodem/V[3] provides special support for these voice modems.

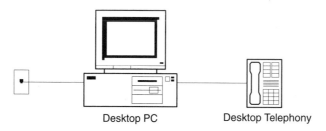

Desktop PC   Desktop Telephony

Figure 1.6: Computer-centric connection model.

---

[3] At the time of this writing, Unimodem/V ships only with Windows 95, OSR2 and Windows 98. For plain vanilla Windows 95, it is available for download from *http://www.microsoft.com*. Unimodem/V won't be supported under Windows NT until version 5.0.

LAN Connection

In the LAN connection model, depicted in Figure 1.7, the desktop PC and the telephone aren't even directly connected. Instead, a server on the LAN connects to the telephone switch—a PBX—via some kind of digital link. The desktop PC connects to the server via the LAN and directs it to control calls. The server passes this command to the switch, which controls the telephone located on the same desktop as the PC. Unlike the previous two models, which use first-party call control, this is a third-party call control model.

For the LAN connection model, the TSP provided on the desktop PC is not talking to a telephone, but rather to the server PC on the LAN. This model typically limits access to the data on the call. Little bandwidth is required to send data or voice between the switch and the server PC and between the server PC and the desktop PC. However, when access to the data on a telephone call is multiplied by the number of people on the phone, and combined with existing LAN traffic, it is a luxury most LAN and switch managers are not willing to provide.

This model's main benefit is that no additional hardware is required on the desktop PC to make it work. A desktop PC connected to the LAN can control the desktop telephone by using some additional software, specifically, a TSP. Once the server PC is connected to the switch, everyone can control his or her telephone from the desktop.

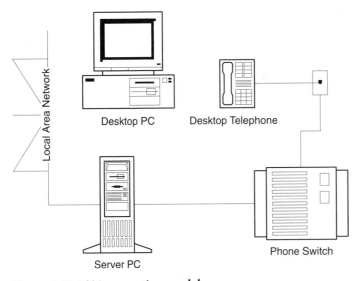

Figure 1.7: LAN connection model.

What Happened to the Second Party?

Each connected telephone call has at least two parties, one on each end. Each party, whether a person or a computer, has control of one end of the call. First-party call control means that the control of the call rests solely with the parties participating in the call. If the call is transferred somewhere else, control is given to the transferee. Third-party call control means that the endpoints of the call share control. Third-party call control allows a computer to request that calls are made, dropped, conferenced, etc, without the computer being involved as an endpoint of the call.

For example, in the LAN connection model, an endpoint of the call is the desktop telephone, which has first-party control. The desktop PC has third-party call control by talking to the switch, via the server PC, to control the call. This means that you could disconnect your end of the call by hanging up the telephone (first-party call control) or by sending a hang-up signal to the switch from your desktop PC (third-party call control).

What about second-party call control? There is no such thing.

Client/Server Connection

The client/server connection model, shown in Figure 1.8, is used for IVR applications. For example, a bank that needs to provide account information to its customers or an automated operator run by the local telephone company will use this model. The server PC is connected to the switch by several telephone lines. The server PC controls the calls on these lines by using first-party call control. It can play messages, take input, and provide information. Think of this system as you would any other kind of PC server, except that instead of using a LAN connection to communicate with its clients, it uses a telephone network connection.

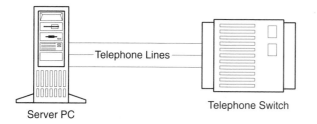

Server PC · Telephone Lines · Telephone Switch

Figure 1.8: Client/server connection model.

Platform Independence

There are developers for every existing computer platform and every operating system. Ideally, the TAPI designers wanted to create a PC standard for telephony programming that worked across computers and operating systems. However, because it was Intel and Microsoft that were designing the standard, they wanted to solve the problem for Windows first. Unfortunately, TAPI hasn't yet made it to other platforms, but it works on Windows 3.x, Windows 95 (or better), Windows NT 4.0 (or better), and Windows CE 1.0 (or better).

Line Sharing

The Windows 3.x Communications API for accessing serial and parallel ports didn't allow multiple applications to share a single telephone line. This makes it impossible, for example, for one application to wait for an incoming fax call while another application makes an outgoing voice call. TAPI, on the other hand, provides extensive support for this kind of sharing (even under Windows 3.x). Any number of applications can share a single-line device by opening it with one of several privileges, given in Table 1.3.

A line owner application needs to specify one or more *media modes* that it is interested in for inbound calls. A media mode describes the type of media available on the call. The media modes and who or what might be interested in them are shown in Table 1.4.

Table 1.3: Privileges for sharing a single-line device.	
Privilege	*Meaning*
None	Application can make outbound calls only.
Monitor	Application can watch inbound and outbound calls only.
Owner	Application can make outbound calls and will be given inbound calls that match requested media modes.
Owner + Monitor	Application wants to monitor calls other than those it owns.

Table 1.4: Media modes and who/what may be interested in them.	
Media Mode	*Who/What May Be Interested*
Interactive Voice	Person or call control application.
Automated Voice	Automated application such as an answering machine.
Data Modem	Communications application.
Group 3 Fax	Fax application.
Group 4 Fax	Fax application.
Digital Data	Communications application or network driver.
Telephony Devices for the Deaf (TDD)	Display application.
Teletex	Display application.
Videotext	Display application.
Telex	Display application.
Mixed	ISDN application.
Analog Display Services Interface (ADSI)	Mixed voice and data application.
VoiceView	Mixed voice and data application.
Unknown	Any application looking for incoming calls for which the media mode has yet to be determined.

An application can ask to handle one or more types of media mode. When an incoming call is available, TAPI has the unfavorable job of working with the applications to determine the media mode of the incoming call. For the vast majority of calls, which are analog, the call type can't be determined until the call has been answered. However, a call can't be answered until it has been given to an application, which will then answer the call. Therefore all analog calls come in as media mode unknown.

Once the call type has been determined, the answering application has a couple of options. It can handle the call itself or it can *handoff* the call to TAPI, specifying the new media mode. TAPI will then attempt to give the call to an application that can handle that media type. When an application performs a handoff, it can either give up the call altogether or maintain access to it for later use.

For more information about line ownership and media modes, see Chapter 5.

Summary

The Telephony API was designed to provide call control and media access to line, telephone, address, and call objects over multiple telephone networks that are using many different kinds of connection models. It was designed to be platform-independent, but it has been implemented only for various flavors of Windows. To overcome specific device-sharing problems encountered in Windows 3.x, TAPI provides extensive support for sharing by using line ownership privileges.

Assisted Telephony

Direct access to the phone line is
unethical. It's a felony in Oregon.
Herman D'Hooge
Intel Corporation

Before TAPI, any application that wanted to dial a telephone had to access the telephone line directly via a COM port and the Windows COMM API. This required complicated setup on the user's part and complicated code on the developer's part. These complications stopped personal information managers, databases, and productivity applications from providing a universal Dial command for a selected phone number. Why should dialing be limited to only a select few applications? Why can't there be a simple programming interface just to dial a phone number? With TAPI there is a simple way: Assisted Telephony.

Assisted Telephony Functions

Assisted Telephony is a tiny subset of the Windows Telephony API. In fact, under Win32, it's only the following two functions:

`tapiRequestMakeCall`	Request the placement of a voice phone call.
`tapiGetLocationInfo`	Get the current country code and city/area code.

Windows 3.*x* had two additional Assisted Telephony functions that are no longer supported under Win32, as follows:

`tapiRequestMediaCall`	Request the placement of a media phone call based on a device class.
`tapiRequestDrop`	Request a media call to be dropped.

The intent of the Assisted Telephony functions is for an application with a phone number to pass it to a telephony application willing to place the call. The telephony application that volunteers for this duty will be a Full Telephony application and it will actually handle the call as it progresses through its various states. Windows 95 and Windows NT 4.0 ship with the Phone Dialer, an Assisted Telephony *request recipient* that can make and track a phone call on behalf of an Assisted Telephony application.[1]

---

[1] For a description of what it takes for an application to become a request recipient, see Chapter 6.

An application can request that a call be made on its behalf by calling
`tapiRequestMakeCall`:

```
LONG
tapiRequestMakeCall(
   LPCSTR lpszDestAddress,  // telephone number to dial
   LPCSTR lpszAppName,      // Requesting application
   LPCSTR lpszCalledParty,  // Person being called
   LPCSTR lpszComment)      // Misc. comment
```

When `tapiRequestMakeCall` is called, TAPI will check for a running request recipient. If there is one, it will pass on the request. If there isn't one, it
will try to start one and then pass on the request. If both of these fail or there is a
problem with the phone number itself, the call to `tapiRequestMakeCall` will
return one of four possible errors, shown in Table 2.1. A return of zero indicates
success.

To prevent an invalid address error, the `lpszDestAddress` can be in either
canonical address format or dialable address format.[2] The canonical address format
is preferred, as some request recipients assume it (although the Phone Dialer does
a pretty good job with phone numbers not in canonical format). By far the easiest
way to get a phone number in canonical format is to require the user to enter the
country code, area code, and phone number separately. Because people are more
likely to place calls in their own area, setting reasonable defaults for the country
code and area code make the user's life easier when entering phone numbers.

Table 2.1: Possible errors from the call to `tapiRequestMakeCall`.	
Error	*Meaning*
`TAPIERR_NOREQUESTRECIPIENT`	There is no registered request recipient.
`TAPIERR_REQUESTQUEUEFULL`	The request recipient hasn't removed enough call requests from TAPI's queue to handle another request.
`TAPIERR_INVALDESTADDRESS`	The request recipient has declared the phone number invalid.
`TAPIERR_INVALPOINTER`	TAPI has detected an invalid pointer.

---

[2] Recall the description of the canonical address and dialable address formats from Chapter 1.

These defaults are part of the current location that is set in the Telephony Control Panel and are available by calling `tapiGetLocationInfo`:

```
LONG tapiGetLocationInfo(
   LPCSTR lpszCountryCode, // 8-byte buffer
   LPCSTR lpszCityCode)    // 8-byte buffer
```

If either the country code or the area code isn't available, the buffer will be set to an empty string. If location information isn't available, the `TAPIERR_REQUEST-FAILED` error code will be returned.

The last two Assisted Telephony functions, `tapiRequestMediaCall` and `tapiRequestDrop`, were meant to help communications programs like WinFax and ProComm. These kinds of programs don't need to do any call management operations such as hold or transfer. Instead, they just need to establish a connection to a modem or a fax machine. Unfortunately, `tapiRequestMediaCall` didn't provide enough flexibility to set line parameters (speed, error correction, and so on) before the call is placed, so it was pretty useless. `tapiRequestDrop` was valid only on a call placed with `tapiRequestMediaCall`, so when the latter was removed from the API, so was the former.

Assisted Telephony Example

The CustoDial example, found on the web site provided with this book, is a simple Assisted Telephony application developed using MFC. It allows you to enter a name, country code, area code, and phone number. Once you're satisfied with your choices, you can dial the number. Filled in, CustoDial's singular UI looks like Figure 2.1.

The code for the dialog box itself does nothing but take input, show the About button, and return `IDOK` or `IDCANCEL`. The meat of the application is contained in the `InitInstance` member function of the `CCustoDialApp` class, shown next. Specifically, notice the calls to `tapiGetLocationInfo` and `tapiRequestMakeCall` and how the phone number is formatted into its canonical form:

```
BOOL CCustoDialApp::InitInstance()
{
    // Standard initialization
    CCustoDialDlg dlg;
    m_pMainWnd = &dlg;
```

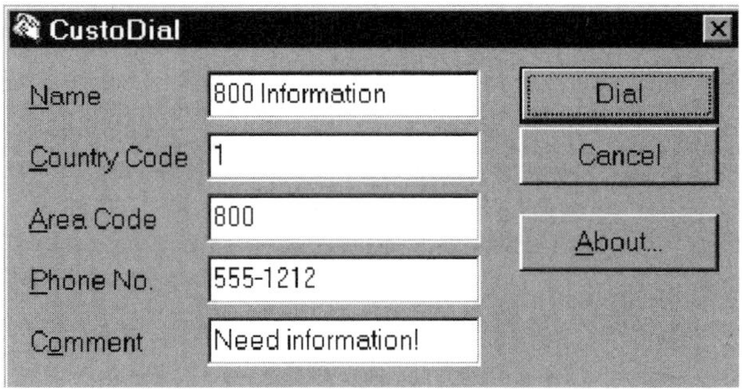

Figure 2.1: Assisted Telephony's CustoDial sample.

```
// Initialize the dialog
dlg.m_sName = "A. Nonymous";

// Get default location info
LONG    r;
r = ::tapiGetLocationInfo(
        dlg.m_sCountryCode.GetBuffer(8),
        dlg.m_sAreaCode.GetBuffer(8));
dlg.m_sCountryCode.ReleaseBuffer();
dlg.m_sAreaCode.ReleaseBuffer();

if( r < 0 )
{
    ::AfxMessageBox(IDS_NOLOCATIONINFO);
}

// Run the dialog.
if( dlg.DoModal() == IDOK )
{
    // Init arguments to tapiRequestMakeCall()
    LPCSTR szName = dlg.m_sName;
    LPCSTR szAppName = ::AfxGetAppName();
    LPCSTR szComment = dlg.m_sComment;

    // Try to make a canonical telephone number.
    CString sDestAddress;
    if( !dlg.m_sCountryCode.IsEmpty() &&
        !dlg.m_sPhoneNo.IsEmpty() )
    {
```

```
        if( !dlg.m_sAreaCode.IsEmpty() )
        {
            sDestAddress.Format("+%s (%s) %s",
                                dlg.m_sCountryCode,
                                dlg.m_sAreaCode,
                                dlg.m_sPhoneNo);
        }
        else
        {
            sDestAddress.Format("+%s %s",
                                dlg.m_sCountryCode,
                                dlg.m_sPhoneNo);
        }
    }
    // Can't make it canonical easily,
    // so let the request recipient deal w/ it.
    else
    {
        sDestAddress.Format("%s %s %s",
                            dlg.m_sCountryCode,
                            dlg.m_sAreaCode,
                            dlg.m_sPhoneNo);
    }

        // Remove WM_QUIT the queue
        MSG msg;
        ::PeekMessage(&msg, 0, WM_QUIT, WM_QUIT,
                    PM_REMOVE);

        // Dial the number
        r = ::tapiRequestMakeCall(sDestAddress, szAppName,
                                    szName, szComment);

        switch( r )
        {
        case TAPIERR_NOREQUESTRECIPIENT:
            ::AfxMessageBox(IDS_NOREQUESTRECIPIENT);
        break;

        case TAPIERR_REQUESTQUEUEFULL:
            ::AfxMessageBox(IDS_REQUESTQUEUEFULL);
        break;
```

```
        case TAPIERR_INVALDESTADDRESS:
            ::AfxMessageBox(IDS_INVALDESTADDRESS);
        break;

        case TAPIERR_INVALPOINTER:
            TRACE("TAPIERR_INVALPOINTER\n");
            ASSERT(FALSE);
        break;
        }
    }

    // Since the dialog has been closed, return FALSE
    // so that we exit the application, rather than
    // start the application's message pump.
    return FALSE;
}
```

Compiling for TAPI

The CustoDial sample, like all TAPI applications, requires you to include the proper header file and link with the proper library. All of my samples are 32-bit and have been tested under Windows 95 and Windows NT 4.0. Table 2.2 shows TAPI support for each major Windows platform.

Later implementations of TAPI are backward-compatible with earlier versions. If you're developing a Windows 3.1x TAPI application under Windows 95 or Windows NT 4.0, use the Windows 3.1x header file and include file (and a 16-bit compiler).

Table 2.2: TAPI support for Windows platforms.			
Platform	TAPI Version(s)	Include File	Header File
Windows 3.1x	1.3	tapi.h	tapi.lib
Windows 9x	1.3, 1.4, 2.0	tapi.h	tapi32.lib
Windows NT 3.x	(No TAPI support.)	N/A	N/A
Windows NT 4.0	1.3, 1.4, 2.0	tapi.h	tapi32.lib

While support for 32-bit TAPI is integrated into the Win32 SDK, support for 16-bit TAPI is not integrated into the Windows 3.1*x* SDK. Instead, it's usually provided separately on the same set of CDs.

There's one other detail to be aware of when building your TAPI applications, especially if you've got an existing TAPI application that you're porting to a newer version of TAPI. Beginning with version 2.0, the TAPI header file started with the following define:

```
#ifndef TAPI_CURRENT_VERSION
#define  TAPI_CURRENT_VERSION 0x00020002
#endif
```
use 00020000

The implementers of TAPI decided that if you were recompiling an application under a new version of TAPI, you would want access to new functionality, for example, functions and data structure elements. However, the behaviors of existing TAPI functions and TSPs change based on the version of TAPI with which your application is compiled. If it seems that your TAPI application is no longer working after compiling with the newest version of TAPI, you may want to define the `TAPI_CURRENT_SYMBOL` yourself before including `tapi.h`, for example,

```
// stdafx.h
#define TAPI_CURRENT_VERSION 0x00010004
#include <tapi.h>
```

This will give your application the TAPI environment that you expected when you developed the application. Once this is working, you should probably port your application to the latest behavior so that it can use the latest features of TAPI. In the rest of this book, I'll point out the differences between revisions of TAPI as they arise.

Assisted Telephony from Visual Basic

I've duplicated CustoDial in Visual Basic (VB) to show you how to use Assisted Telephony from another language. Using a function from a DLL in VB requires the use of a `declare` statement. It also requires setting up any auxiliary constants that might be needed to understand the results of the function. Following is the code required to use the Assisted Telephony functions from VB.

Unimoden/V is only supported under Windows 95/98 with TAPI 1.4
∴ Voice TAPI apps must use TAPI 1.4 (not 2.0), and not on NT4.

```
Private Const TAPIERR_REQUESTFAILED = -16&
Private Const TAPIERR_NOREQUESTRECIPIENT = -2&
Private Const TAPIERR_REQUESTQUEUEFULL = -3&
Private Const TAPIERR_INVALDESTADDRESS = -4&
Private Const TAPIERR_INVALPOINTER = -18&

Private Declare Function tapiGetLocationInfo Lib
    "TAPI32.DLL" (ByVal lpszCountryCode As String,
                  ByVal lpszCityCode As String) As Long
Private Declare Function tapiRequestMakeCall Lib
    "TAPI32.DLL" (ByVal lpszDestAddress As String,
                  ByVal lpszAppName As String,
                  ByVal lpszCalledParty As String,
                  ByVal lpszComment As String) As Long
```

Once declare statements are in place, the complete telephony code for the VB
version of CustoDial looks like this:

```
Private Sub Form_Load()
    ' Initialize the form.
    txtName = "A. Nonymous"
    Dim sCountryCode As String * 8
    Dim sAreaCode As String * 8

    ' Get default location info.
    Dim r As Long
    r = tapiGetLocationInfo(sCountryCode, sAreaCode)
    If r = TAPIERR_REQUESTFAILED Then
        MsgBox "No location information available."
    Else
        txtCountryCode = sCountryCode
        txtAreaCode = sAreaCode
    End If
End Sub

Private Sub cmdDial_Click()
    ' Init arguments to tapiRequestMakeCall().
    Dim sAppName As String
    Dim sComment As String
    sAppName = "CustoDial, VB"
    sComment = txtComment
```

```vb
Dim sDestAddress As String
' Try to make canonical telephone number.
If txtCountryCode <> "" And txtPhoneNo <> "" Then
    If txtAreaCode <> "" Then
        sDestAddress = "+" & txtCountryCode & " (" & _
                    txtAreaCode & ") " & txtPhoneNo
    Else
        sDestAddress = "+" & txtCountryCode & " " & _
                    txtPhoneNo
    End If
' Can't make it canonical easily,
' so let the request recipient deal w/ it.
Else
    sDestAddress = txtCountryCode & " " & _
                    txtAreaCode & " " & txtPhoneNo

End If

' Dial the number.
Dim sName As String
sName = txtName

Dim r As Long
r = tapiRequestMakeCall(sDestAddress, sAppName, _
                    sName, sComment)

Select Case r
Case TAPIERR_NOREQUESTRECIPIENT
    MsgBox "No Telephony request recipient."
Case TAPIERR_REQUESTQUEUEFULL
    MsgBox "Request recipient says no."
Case TAPIERR_INVALDESTADDRESS
    MsgBox "Invalid telephone number."
Case TAPIERR_INVALPOINTER
    MsgBox "VB screwed up."
End Select

End
End Sub
```

> ## Too Much Telephony
>
> The name of this sample, CustoDial, could have one of several meanings. It could mean "<u>Custo</u>mer <u>Dial</u>." It could mean "<u>Custom</u> <u>Dial</u>er." It could mean something else equally clever. It doesn't.
>
> One evening at a certain large microprocessor corporation, I was working with an early version of TAPI way past quitting time. On the way to the restroom, I noticed a door with a label that I pronounced in my head as "cust-o-dial." I wandered back to my cube and asked my colleagues what the heck a "cust-o-dial" was. They didn't know but asked me to spell it. After I'd written it on my white-board, one of the more clever of them said, "Custodial? You mean like janitorial?"
>
> At that point, I packed up my stuff and went home to spend some time with my family. There really is such a thing as too much telephony.

Phone Numbers

Phone numbers are unusual beasts. Recall from Chapter 1 the difference between a displayable phone number and a canonical phone number. A displayable phone number is something that is easy to recognize (by a human), while a canonical phone number is something that is easy for TAPI to recognize. Canonical phone numbers use a formal string format to distinguish the country code, the area code, and the subscriber number. Specifically, TAPI uses phone numbers in canonical format to produce the actual digits to dial. In the proper management of phone numbers, one of two things can happen:

1. To make the developer's life easy, the user is often forced to enter a phone number as three parts.
2. If the user is allowed to enter a phone number in a single field, the developer is forced to write string parsing code that takes user input and turns it into canonical format.

It would be best if the parsing code was separated out for the developer's use so that life is easy for both the user and the developer. That's what CtPhoneNo[3] is for.

CtPhoneNo is a class I built for dealing with phone numbers. It manages the buffers for each of the three parts of a phone number as well as the buffers for each

---

[3] CtPhoneNo should not be confused with an even more popular C++ class developed by Steven Spielberg: EtPhoneHome. (Thanks to Alan Moffet for that joke!)

of the various translations that the `CtPhoneNo` class can perform. Here is the declaration of the `CtPhoneNo` class:

```
class CtPhoneNo
{
public:
    // Set default country code and area code.
    CtPhoneNo();

    // Will pass szWholePhoneNo onto SetWholePhoneNo()
    CtPhoneNo(LPCSTR szWholePhoneNo);

    // These are the easy constructors
    CtPhoneNo(LPCSTR szCountryCode, LPCSTR szAreaCode,
            LPCSTR szPhoneNo);
    CtPhoneNo(DWORD nCountryCode, LPCSTR szAreaCode,
            LPCSTR szPhoneNo);

    // Copy constructor & assignment operator
    CtPhoneNo(const CtPhoneNo& pno);
    CtPhoneNo& operator=(const CtPhoneNo& pno);

    virtual ~CtPhoneNo();

    LPCSTR  GetCountryCode();
    DWORD   GetCountryCodeNum();
    LPCSTR  GetAreaCode();
    LPCSTR  GetPhoneNo(); // No area code

    // Will leave letters alone.
    // Format: "+CC [(AC) ]PN"
    virtual LPCSTR  GetCanonical();

    // Will leave letters alone.
    // Format: "[CC ][(AC) ]PN"
    virtual LPCSTR   GetDisplayable();

    // Chooses canonical if available or
    // displayable otherwise
    // (pass an alternate string to change mapping or
    // NULL to prevent mapping).
```

```
      virtual LPCSTR  GetTranslatable(
            LPCSTR pszMap = "2223334445556667777888999");

      // Given an arbitrary telephone no., will split out
      // parts if it can (will test for canonical format)
      virtual void SetWholePhoneNo(LPCSTR szWholePhoneNo);

      // Given a phone no. in canonical format,
      // will split it up.
      // Assumes rigid format "+CC [(AC) ]PN"
      virtual void      SetCanonical(LPCSTR szCanonical);

      // Sets canonical format if everything's been broken
      // out already.
      virtual void      SetCanonical(LPCSTR szCountryCode,
                                     LPCSTR szAreaCode,
                                     LPCSTR szPhoneNo);
      virtual void      SetCanonical(DWORD nCountryCode,
                                     LPCSTR szAreaCode,
                                     LPCSTR szPhoneNo);

      // Clear telephone no. and set country code and area code
      // to current location defaults.
      void      ResetToLocation();

      // Set individual pieces.
      void      SetCountryCode(LPCSTR szCountryCode);
      void      SetCountryCode(DWORD nCountryCode);
      void      SetAreaCode(LPCSTR szAreaCode);
      void      SetPhoneNo(LPCSTR szPhoneNo);

      ... // private implementation removed for clarity
};
```

To create a telephone number from the area code, country code, and phone number, you can create a **CtPhoneNo** object using the three-part constructor:

```
CtPhoneNo    pno(pszCountryCode, pszAreaCode, pszPhoneNo);
```

Or, if the parts are available after the object has been created, the parts can be set collectively or separately:

```
CtPhoneNo    pno;
pno.SetCanonical(pszCountryCode, pszAreaCode, pszPhoneNo);
// or
pno.SetCountryCode(pszCountryCode);
pno.SetAreaCode(pszAreaCode);
pno.SetPhoneNo(pszPhoneNo);
```

To set the `CtPhoneNo` object to the current location's country code and area code, use the default constructor or the `ResetToLocation` method:

```
CtPhoneNo pno;
// or
pno.ResetToLocation();
MessageBox(0, pno.GetCountryCode(), "Current C.Code", 0);
MessageBox(0, pno.GetAreaCode(), "Current Area Code", 0);
```

The real power of the `CtPhoneNo` class is that it knows how to parse various phone number formats and make reasonable assumptions about what parts are present in the phone number:

```
const const* pszWholePhoneNo = "1 (503) 555-1212";
CtPhoneNo pno(pszWholePhoneNo);
// or
pno.SetWholePhoneNo(pszWholePhoneNo);
pno.SetWholePhoneNo("503-648-2609");
pno.SetWholePhoneNo("911");
```

Once a `CtPhoneNo` object has been initialized, the three parts are available separately:

```
MessageBox(0, pno.GetCountryCode(), "Country Code", 0);
MessageBox(0, pno.GetAreaCode(), "Area Code", 0);
MessageBox(0, pno.GetPhoneNo(), "Phone No.", 0);
```

The phone number as a whole is available in several formats:

```
MessageBox(0, pno.GetCanonical(), "+CC [(AC) ]PN", 0);
MessageBox(0, pno.GetDisplayable(), "[CC ][(AC) ][PN]",0);
lineTranslateAddress(..., pno.GetTranslatable(), ...);
```

The translatable format[4] tries to pull together enough information to provide canonical format, but if there is not enough information to build a canonical string, it will fall back on displayable format. The translatable format will also perform letter-to-number translation based on the letters on the keypad of a U.S. touch-tone phone. The map is the first argument to the `GetTranslatable` function and can be replaced either with another map or with an empty string, which means perform no translation at all:

```
virtual LPCSTR GetTranslatable(
// Letters:      ABCDEFGHIJKLMNOPQRSTUVWXYZ
  LPCSTR pszMap="2223334445556667778889999");
```

If you'd like to play around with phone numbers, the CustoDial2 sample uses a `CtPhoneNo` object to take a whole phone number and pull out the three parts as well as the translations. CustoDial2 is shown in Figure 2.2.

The translation is done every time the content of the Phone No field changes:

```
void CCustoDialDlg::OnChangePhoneNo()
{
    if( UpdateData(TRUE) )
    {
        CtPhoneNo    pno = m_sPhoneNo;
        m_sCountryCode = pno.GetCountryCode();
        m_sAreaCode = pno.GetAreaCode();
        m_sSubscriberNo = pno.GetPhoneNo();
        m_sCanonical = pno.GetCanonical();
        m_sDisplayable = pno.GetDisplayable();
        m_sTranslatable = pno.GetTranslatable();
        UpdateData(FALSE);
    }
}
```

---

[4] The phone number's translatable format is used to call `lineTranslateAddress`, discussed in Chapter 3.

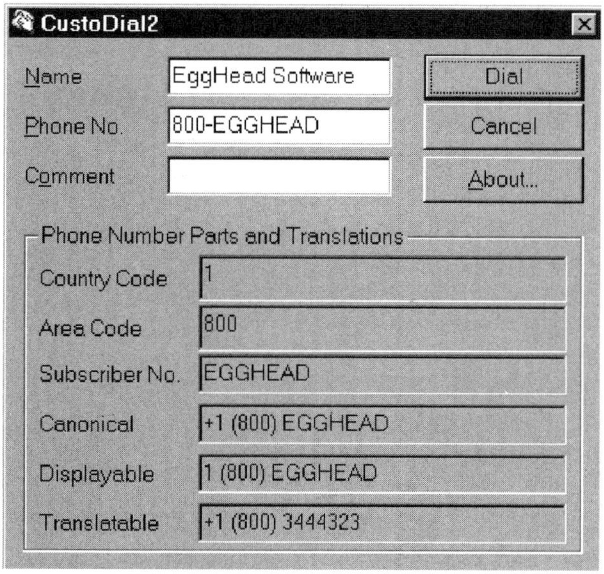

Figure 2.2: CustoDial2 sample using CtPhoneNo.

Summary

Assisted Telephony was developed for those applications that couldn't justify the code overhead needed for Full TAPI support. With a single function call, any Windows application, using any language, can dial the phone. An Assisted Telephony application under Win32 is no longer allowed to dial anything but a voice call, but since the media call function turned out to be useless, this is no great loss.

Making a Call

*TAPI is the assembly language
of telephony.*
Paul Drews
Intel Corporation

Assisted Telephony is great for PIMs, word processors, and spreadsheets. But if your application needs control of your end of the telephony universe, you need more. When it comes to TAPI, you need *a lot* more.

TAPI was designed to contain the collective features of all of the telephony equipment and all of the telephony communications protocols on the planet. This makes for quite an impressive API. As of version 2.0, TAPI includes 696 flags, 143 error messages, 128 functions (not including the Unicode equivalents), 49 structures, 27 notification messages, 5 handles, and 2 callbacks. The benefit is that any telephony device can be exposed and manipulated via TAPI. The hard part is navigating your way through the API to do it.

The Sample

The sample application discussed in this chapter is a very simple dialer called tDial. It is a dialog-only MFC application that looks like Figure 3.1. The tDial sample can't do much. It initializes and shuts down the line part of TAPI, takes a phone number, opens a line, places a call, displays call status, and allows the user to hang up a call. In the grand scheme of telephony, these are baby steps. Still, a lot of ground needs to be covered to do these simple things.

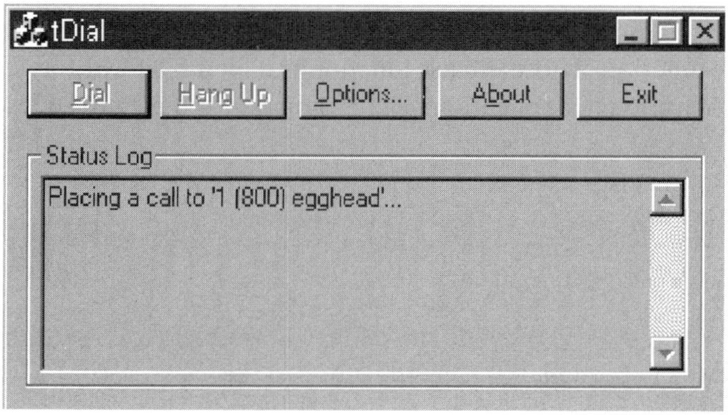

Figure 3.1: tDial main window.

This sample is the last in which I use raw TAPI calls. In the next chapter, I present a series of MFC classes for wrapping TAPI that I call the TFX (Telephony Framework). I will always describe all of the raw TAPI functions, structures, and events, but the samples in subsequent chapters will use the TFX to make the concepts stand out more clearly from the code. In this chapter, however, I use raw TAPI in the sample so that you can see exactly what's going on under the hood.

Initialization

Before using TAPI, you must initialize the parts of the API you need. TAPI has two parts: the line and the phone. Each is initialized separately via `lineInitialize` and `phoneInitialize`, respectively. Since this chapter is about making a call, the line part of TAPI needs to be initialized. The `lineInitialize` function looks like this:

```
LONG
lineInitialize(
    LPHLINEAPP   lphLineApp,    // Line usage handle
    HINSTANCE    hInstance,     // App's instance handle
    LINECALLBACK lpfnCallback,  // Callback function
    LPCSTR       lpszAppName,   // App's friendly name
    LPDWORD      lpdwNumDevs)   // Available devices
```

The `hLineApp` that is returned from this call is the application's license to use the line part of the API, that is, the TAPI functions with the "line" prefix. The friendly application name is for use in other applications if they are interested in where a call was originated. The final parameter is a pointer to a `DWORD` to hold the number of line devices available on the system. The most important parameter is the pointer to the line callback function. This callback function is called by TAPI for any telephony event of concern to the application. The prototype for the callback function looks like this:

```
void
lineCallbackFunc(
    DWORD hDevice,              // Line or call device
    DWORD dwMsg,                // Line or call message
    DWORD dwCallbackInstance,   // App-defined data
    DWORD dwParam1,             // Message specific param.
    DWORD dwParam2,             // Message specific param.
    DWORD dwParam3)             // Message specific param.
```

Inside TAPI Events

This callback function is the Windows Procedure of the telephony API. It translates hardware events into telephony events. Calling `lineInitialize` causes a window to be created for the calling process. Events are posted to this window when a telephony device notifies TAPI of an event. To receive the events, the application must service the Windows message queue (via `GetMessage/DispatchMessage`).

A TSP is really just a Windows DLL. Under 16-bit Windows, a TSP is often called back in *interrupt context*, that is, when an event is generated by some piece of telephony hardware. To remove certain restrictions on what can happen in interrupt context (that is, no memory can be allocated while in interrupt context), TAPI will post a message to the window created during `lineInitialize`. When one of these messages is pulled off the application's message queue (via the `GetMessage` function), the TAPI window receives the message and turns it into a call to the application's callback function.

32-bit Windows applications using TAPI 2.0 are still allowed to use `lineInitialize`. However, they are encouraged to use `lineInitializeEx` instead, as follows:

```
LONG
lineInitializeExA(
    LPHLINEAPP    lphLineApp,
    HINSTANCE     hInstance,
    LINECALLBACK  lpfnCallback,
    LPCSTR        lpszFriendlyAppName,
    LPDWORD       lpdwNumDevs,
    LPDWORD       lpdwAPIVersion,
    LPLINEINITIALIZEEXPARAMS
                  lpLineInitializeExParams)
```

The `LINEINITIALIZEEXPARAMS` structure allows an application to receive telephony events via a Win32 Event or an Asynchronous Completion Port, as well as a hidden window. This gives applications that don't have windows or message queues an opportunity to use TAPI as well.

API Negotiation

The first part of proper TAPI initialization is to call `lineInitialize`. The second part is to negotiate version numbers for all of the lines the application is going to use. This is done via the `lineNegotiateAPIVersion` function:

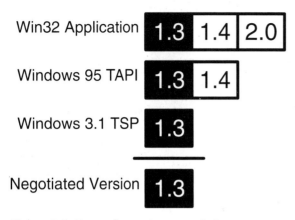

Win32 Application 1.3 1.4 2.0

Windows 95 TAPI 1.3 1.4

Windows 3.1 TSP 1.3

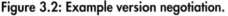

Negotiated Version 1.3

Figure 3.2: Example version negotiation.

```
LONG
lineNegotiateAPIVersion(
    HLINEAPP          hLineApp,      // Line usage handle
    DWORD             dwDeviceID,    // Line ID
    DWORD             dwAPILowVer,   // Minimum version
    DWORD             dwAPIHighVer,  // Maximum version
    LPDWORD           lpdwAPIVer,    // Negotiated version
    LPLINEEXTENSIONID lpExtID)       // Available ext. ID
```

The identifiers used to uniquely identify each line device range between zero and the number of devices (minus one) returned by the lineInitialize function. The low and high version numbers are included to maintain backward compatibility as TAPI grows to support additional functionality. The version number is made up of a major and a minor version stored in the high- and low-order words, respectively. The lineNegotiateAPIVersion function looks at the range of functionality that the application supports and tries to match it with the TSP that controls the line (as specified by the dwDeviceID parameter) and TAPI itself. For example, a Windows 3.x TSP installed on Windows 95 will support only TAPI 1.3 functionality. TAPI under plain Windows 95 supports versions 1.3 and 1.4. A Win32 telephony application could support versions 1.3, 1.4, and 2.0. The result of this negotiation would be the highest version that all three parties support, that is, 1.3. See Figure 3.2.

An application should negotiate the API version on all lines and cache them for later use. This tells TAPI the version of the application (so it can send version-specific telephony events) and allows the application to use the cached API versions for later TAPI calls. Following is an example of initializing the line part of TAPI and negotiating the API version for all available lines:

Extended Line Services

The Windows Open Services Architecture, or WOSA, was designed to separate applications from specific devices by inserting a middleman. In the current case, the middleman is TAPI32.DLL (the Win32 implementation of TAPI). TAPI, in turn, relies on a TSP to implement the TSPI. The benefit of this is that the application never has to talk directly to the underlying device. The disadvantage is that *the application can never talk to the underlying device.* The layer of abstraction between the application and the TSP makes it extremely difficult for a TSP to expose functionality that isn't provided for in TAPI.

A TSP vendor that wants to provide extra functionality has two options. The first is to wait for Microsoft and Intel to jointly revise the TAPI and the TSPI specifications and implementations. This has happened a few times and, frankly, it took a while.

The second option is for a TSP to provide extended services. TAPI can expose this additional functionality via the lineDevSpecific() and the lineDevSpecificFeature() functions and the LINE_DEVSPECIFIC and LINE_DEVSPECIFICFEATURE callback events. An application can detect and negotiate a version number with a TSP that provides extended services via the lineNegotiateExtVersion() function. While it's a bad idea for an application to depend on extended services, there's no crime in taking advantage of them if they're available.

```
LONG CtDialDlg::InitializeLines(
    DWORD dwLoVersion,
    DWORD dwHiVersion)
{
    LONG tr = lineInitialize(&m_hLineApp,
                             AfxGetInstanceHandle(),
                             MyLineCallback,
                             AfxGetAppName(),
                             &m_nLines);

    if( tr == 0 )
    {
        // Negotiate the API versions
        if( m_nLines &&
            (m_aApiVersions = new DWORD[m_nLines]) )
        {
            LINEEXTENSIONID extid;
```

```
for( DWORD nLineID = 0;
        nLineID < m_nLines;
        nLineID++ )
{
    tr = lineNegotiateAPIVersion(m_hLineApp,
                                 nLineID,
                                 dwLoVersion,
                                 dwHiVersion,
                                 m_aApiVersions +
                                     nLineID,
                                 &extid);
    if( tr < 0 )
    {
        m_aApiVersions[nLineID] = 0;
        tr = 0;
    }
    }
    }
}

return tr;
}
```

The sample caches the negotiated API version for later calls to TAPI that require them. However, not all TAPI functions that take a version number require the negotiated version; some require the highest version the application supports (called the *application version*). If you read the documentation carefully, you can figure out which is which, but the distinction is subtle. So, for your convenience, I've provided in Table 3.1 a list of the TAPI line functions that take an API version and whether the version is the negotiated version or the application version.

TAPI Function Returns

Notice that the TAPI functions in the previous examples returned zero to indicate success or a negative number to indicate failure. The lineInitialize and lineNegotiateAPIVersion functions are both *synchronous*. A synchronous TAPI function is one that finishes completely and returns either a zero to indicate success or a negative error code. A complete list of possible error codes is provided in the online documentation for every TAPI function.

Table 3.1: TAPI line functions that take an API version.	
TAPI Function	*API Version Type*
`lineGetAddressCaps`	Negotiated.
`lineGetCountry`	Application.
`lineGetDevCaps`	Negotiated.
`lineGetProviderList`	Application.
`lineGetTranslateCaps`	Application.
`lineNegotiateAPIVersion`	Application.
`lineNegotiateExtVersion`	Negotiated.
`lineOpen`	Negotiated.
`lineTranslateAddress`	Application.
`lineTranslateDialog`	Application.
`phoneGetDevCaps`	Negotiated.
`phoneNegotiateAPIVersion`	Application.
`phoneNegotiateExtVersion`	Negotiated.
`phoneOpen`	Application.

An *asynchronous* TAPI function, on the other hand, is a function that begins an operation and returns a positive request identifier or a negative error code. The request identifier uniquely identifies the pending operation. Some telephony operations can take up to several seconds to complete. For example, `lineMakeCall` is an asynchronous function that won't return until there has been some response from the underlying telephony hardware. This response time can be long for a user waiting to regain control of the user interface.

When the request has been completed, a `LINE_REPLY` event will be sent to the line callback function. The `dwParam1` parameter will be the request identifier, and the `dwParam2` parameter will be either zero to indicate success or a negative error code (just like a synchronous TAPI function).

All TAPI functions are either synchronous or asynchronous and are marked as such in the TAPI Specification. This means you don't have to worry about a synchronous function returning a request identifier or an asynchronous function returning success immediately.

Discovering Line Capabilities

Once TAPI has been initialized, a suitable line for a call must be found. To discover the capabilities of a line, an application calls the `lineGetDevCaps` function to fill in the `LINEDEVCAPS` structure:

```
LONG
lineGetDevCaps(
    HLINEAPP      hLineApp,      // Line usage handle
    DWORD         dwDeviceID,    // Line ID
    DWORD         dwAPIVersion,  // Negotiated API version
    DWORD         dwExtVersion,  // Optional ext. version
    LPLINEDEVCAPS lpLineDevCaps) // Variably-sized struct.

typedef struct linedevcaps_tag
{
    DWORD         dwTotalSize;
    DWORD         dwNeededSize;
    DWORD         dwUsedSize;
    ...
    DWORD         dwBearerModes;
    DWORD         dwMediaModes;
    DWORD         dwLineFeatures;
    ...
} LINEDEVCAPS, FAR *LPLINEDEVCAPS;
```

The `lineGetDevCaps` function takes the line usage handle, the line device identifier, the negotiated API version (which was cached as a result of the `line-NegotiateAPIVersion` function), the optional Extended Services version, and a pointer to a `LINEDEVCAPS` structure. Under TAPI 1.3 and 1.4, this structure has over 50 fields—not counting substructure fields. To make a voice call, however, we care about only three of them: `dwBearerModes`, `dwMediaModes`, and `dwLineFeatures`. Each of these fields is a bit set with several possible `#defined` flags with the pattern `LINEBEARERMODE_*`, `LINEMEDIAMODE_*`, and `LINEFEATURE_*`, respectively. To make a voice call, an application can use a line only if it supports `LINEBEARERMODE_VOICE`, `LINEMEDIAMODE_INTERACTIVEVOICE`, and `LINEFEATURE_MAKECALL`. If these bits are set in their appropriate fields, we know we can make a call using that line device.

Don't be confused by how similar the concepts of bearer mode and media mode seem. *Bearer mode* is a measure of quality provided by the underlying telephony network. The `LINEBEARERMODE_VOICE` means a line that provides a sampling rate of no less than 3.1kHz. This is adequate for a voice call as well as a modem or fax call. *Media mode,* on the other hand, refers to the type of data currently being transmitted over a line. `LINEMEDIAMODE_INTERACTIVE-VOICE` means that the application plans on placing a call for the purpose of facilitating a human voice conversation. Other media modes are used for modem and fax calls. (For more information about media modes, see Chapter 1.)

Variable-length Structures

The `LINEDEVCAPS` structure, like nearly every structure in TAPI, is of variable length. This means that an application can't just have a variable of type `LINEDEV-CAPS`, pass it to `lineGetDevCaps`, and expect to get all of the device capabilities information. The designers of TAPI could have put hard limits on things like the length of the line name or the TSP name (both pieces of information are available from the `LINEDEVCAPS` structure). However, to obtain maximum flexibility, they allowed information of nearly unlimited length to be put into a TAPI variable-length structure (which I call a VLS).

A VLS always starts with the following three fields:

```
DWORD dwTotalSize;   // Current VLS size (bytes)
DWORD dwNeededSize;  // Required VLS size (bytes)
DWORD dwUsedSize;    // Bytes that contain useful info.
```

As a TAPI application developer, it's your job to write an application that allocates memory using `new` or `malloc` to some size not less than the size of the base structure, for example, `sizeof(LINEDEVCAPS)`. The application must then mark the VLS size in the `dwTotalSize` field before calling the VLS filling function, for example, `lineGetDevCaps`. If the filling function succeeds and the `dwNeededSize` field is less than or equal to the `dwTotalSize` field, the amount of memory allocated was right. The application has retrieved a snapshot of the current VLS information and can use it for whatever it likes.

Suppose instead that the result of the VLS filling function is a success code but the `dwNeededSize` is greater than the `dwTotalSize`. In this case, the application must reallocate the amount of memory indicated in the `dwNeededSize` field, reset the `dwTotalSize` field to `dwNeededSize`, and call the VLS filling function again.

One could suppose that two round trips should be enough to figure out how much memory is needed and then to allocate the memory and fill the field. Unfortunately, this just isn't so. Since we're dealing with hardware, interrupts take priority and can change the size requirements of the VLS between one call and the next.

What the application really needs is a loop that keeps checking to make sure it's got enough memory and to keep trying to fill its memory needs.

To illustrate this procedure, here's an example of a function that fills in a LINEDEVCAPS structure:

```
// Caller responsible for freeing returned memory
LONG MyGetLineDevCaps(
    HLINEAPP        hLineApp,
    DWORD           nApiVersion,
    DWORD           nLineID,
    LINEDEVCAPS**   ppd)
{
    DWORD dwNeededSize = sizeof(LINEDEVCAPS);
    LONG  tr = 0;

    do
    {
        // Get some more memory if we don't have enough
        if( !*ppd || (*ppd)->dwTotalSize < dwNeededSize )
        {
            *ppd = (LPLINEDEVCAPS)::realloc(*ppd,
                                            dwNeededSize);
            if( *ppd )
            {
                (*ppd)->dwTotalSize = dwNeededSize;
            }
            else
            {
                return LINEERR_NOMEM;
            }
        }

        // Fill in the buffer
        tr = lineGetDevCaps(hLineApp,
                    nLineID,
                    nApiVersion,
                    0,
                    *ppd);

        // Check how much memory we need
        // (some TSPs succeed even if the
```

```
                  //  data size is too small)
                  if( tr == LINEERR_STRUCTURETOOSMALL ||
                      (tr == 0 &&
                        (*ppd)->dwTotalSize < (*ppd)->dwNeededSize) )
                  {
                        dwNeededSize = (*ppd)->dwNeededSize;
                        tr = LINEERR_STRUCTURETOOSMALL;
                  }
             }
             while( tr == LINEERR_STRUCTURETOOSMALL );

             return tr;
     }
```

[handwritten annotation, left margin] If this is true ⊕ neededsize will be ⏀

[handwritten annotation, right] Wrong!
If tris 't

Getting fixed-size information out of a VLS is simple. For example, each flag is just a bit in one of the DWORD members (of which dwBearerMode is one such field in LINEDEVCAPS). However, we have such a thing as a VLS for variable-length data and string information. This variable-length data is packed at the end of the fixed-length structure for easy marshaling between address spaces. Two DWORD fields in the structure—an offset and a size—represent each variable-length entry in a VLS. The offset is in bytes from the beginning of the structure and the size is the structure's length in number of bytes. Figure 3.3 is a picture of the LINEDEVCAPS structure illustrating offsets and sizes.

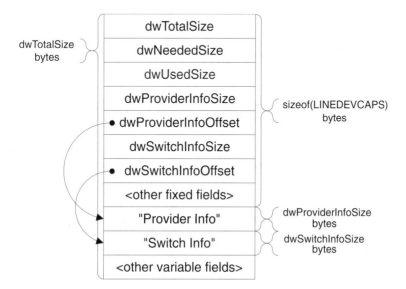

Figure 3.3: Sample variable-length TAPI structure.

As you might suspect, getting at the data referred to by the offset and the size requires some fun casting tricks. For example, here's how an application can get the NULL-terminated line name string from the LINEDEVCAPS structure:

```
LPCSTR MyGetLineName(
    LINEDEVCAPS*    pd)
{
    ASSERT(pd);

    // Note special handling of strings with zero size.
    return (pd->dwLineNameSize
            ? (LPCSTR)(BYTE*)pd + pd->dwLineNameOffset
            : "");
}
```

The dwStringFormat field of the LINEDEVCAPS structure or a VLS-specific dwStringFormat field (like in the VARSTRING structure) determines the format of the strings in all line VLS data. The dwStringFormat field has one of four values, set out in Table 3.2.

It's up to the application to properly handle strings of the first three types and convert them as needed. The last format, STRINGFORMAT_BINARY, is used to stuff raw data into a space normally held by a string. For example, sometimes this bit will be used in the VARSTRING structure when filled by the lineGetID function.

Table 3.2: The four values of dwStringFormat.	
dwStringFormat	*Meaning*
STRINGFORMAT_ASCII	NULL-terminated array of ASCII characters (1 byte each).
STRINGFORMAT_DBCS	NULL-terminated array of double-byte character set characters (1 or 2 bytes each).
STRINGFORMAT_UNICODE	NULL-terminated array of Unicode characters (2 bytes each).
STRINGFORMAT_BINARY	An array of unsigned bytes (not characters).

Structures of Unusual Size

It's possible to optimize the filling of VLS structures in two ways:

1. **The UNIX[1] Way:** Allocate a really big structure and hope it's enough. This reduces round trips (hopefully to one) and works fine if you've got a system with enough memory. If you're going to use this technique and you plan on holding onto the VLS structure for a while (for example, for the life of the application), use the dwUsedSize parameter of the returned VLS to reallocate just enough memory.
2. **The Fixed-Size-Only Way:** If you need only the fixed-size information (like the GetValidLines example in the next section), allocate enough memory to hold only the entire base structure and call the VLS filling function. While none of the variable-size string or data information will be returned, a successful return—zero—indicates that all of the fixed-size data has been filled in.

Checking For Valid Lines

Using the function MyGetLineDevCaps shown previously, the application can check for lines that allow voice calls:

```
void CtDialDlg::Dial(LPCSTR pszPhoneNo)
{
    // Get valid lines
    BOOL*    rgbValidLines = new BOOL[m_nLines];
    if( rgbValidLines )
    {
        LINEDEVCAPS*    pldc = 0;

        for( DWORD nLineID = 0;
             nLineID < m_nLines;
             nLineID++ )
        {
```

---

[1] Don't get me wrong—I like UNIX. But the guys who made virtual memory popular for the masses aren't exactly known for their careful memory management. For the ultimate in thrifty memory usage, ask a DOS or Win16 programmer. The memory management techniques they've been forced to adopt are perhaps the single biggest benefit of the segmented memory architecture (and the only one?).

```
        if( (::MyGetLineDevCaps(m_hLineApp,
                    m_aApiVersions[nLineID],
                    nLineID,
                    &pldc) == 0) &&
(pldc->dwBearerModes & LINEBEARERMODE_VOICE) &&
(pldc->dwMediaModes & LINEMEDIAMODE_INTERACTIVEVOICE) &&
(pldc->dwLineFeatures & LINEFEATURE_MAKECALL) )
        {
            rgbValidLines[nLineID] = TRUE;
        }
        else
        {
            rgbValidLines[nLineID] = FALSE;
        }
    }

    ::free(pldc);
}

// Show dialing options dialog...
}
```

Using Dialing Options

Once the application has determined the lines available for making a call, it is ready to take dialing options from the user. The user interface to do this can be fairly involved. Not only does the application have to be concerned about the phone number, it also has to know the location the user is dialing from and which line and address to use. Following is a list of the elements of the interface you'll want to consider.

- Separate fields for the country code, area code, and phone number. This makes it easier to build a canonical phone number.

- A list of known countries from which to choose.

- Sensible defaults for the area code and country code, when appropriate.

- An option whether to use the country code and area code information. This allows the user to turn off phone number translation for phone numbers like 911 or PBX extensions.

- A list of the available location settings and a way to let the user maintain those settings.
- A list of valid lines to dial on and their corresponding addresses.
- A way to set the properties of the currently selected line.
- Visual feedback to indicate what the dialing string will look like with the current settings. This allows users to determine if they've set their options properly.
- A way to allow the user to enter vanity numbers like 800-EGGHEAD or 976-FUNN. In my sample, I've assumed that letters in U.S. phone numbers translate directly into digits.
- Optionally, the icon associated with the currently selected line.

Figure 3.4 shows the Dialing Options dialog from the tDial sample for collecting phone number, location, and line information. You already know how to get the current country code and area code (the `tapiGetLocationInfo` function) and how to get the name of a line from the identifier (the `lineGetDevCaps`

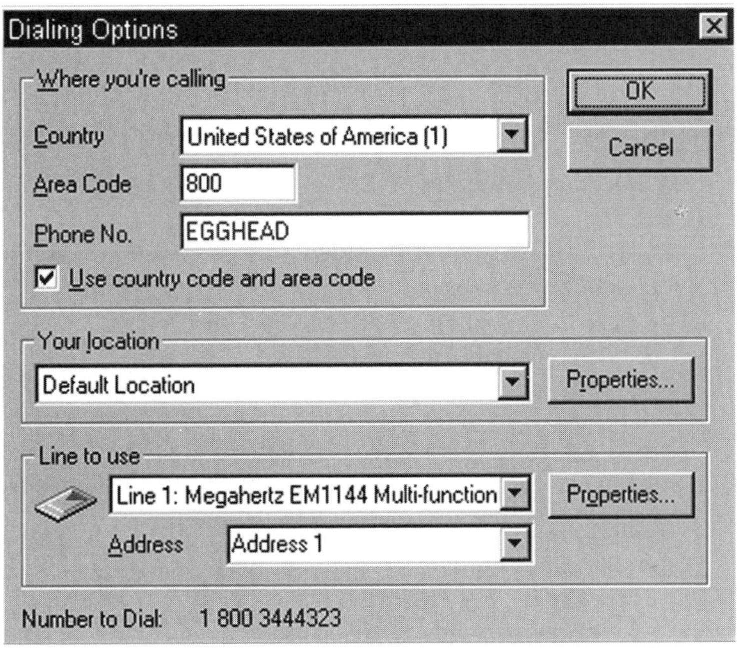

Figure 3.4: Sample dialog for gathering dialing options.

Instead of displaying separate line and address lists, how about amalgamating into a single "channel" list.

function). TAPI also provides direct support for getting a list of known countries, getting a list of locations, setting TSP specific line properties, and translating a phone number from canonical to displayable format.

The Country List

To populate the list of country names and country codes, use the `lineGet-Country` function to fill in the `LINECOUNTRYLIST` variable-length structure:

```
LONG
lineGetCountry(
    DWORD               dwCountryID,       // Arbitrary ID
    DWORD               dwAPIVersion,      // App. version
    LPLINECOUNTRYLIST lpLineCountryList)   // Returned VLS

typedef struct linecountrylist_tag
{
    DWORD        dwTotalSize;
    DWORD        dwNeededSize;
    DWORD        dwUsedSize;
    DWORD        dwNumCountries;
    DWORD        dwCountryListSize;
    DWORD        dwCountryListOffset;
} LINECOUNTRYLIST, FAR *LPLINECOUNTRYLIST;

typedef struct linecountryentry_tag
{
    DWORD        dwCountryID;
    DWORD        dwCountryCode;
    DWORD        dwNextCountryID;
    DWORD        dwCountryNameSize;
    DWORD        dwCountryNameOffset;
    DWORD        dwSameAreaRuleSize;
    DWORD        dwSameAreaRuleOffset;
    DWORD        dwLongDistanceRuleSize;
    DWORD        dwLongDistanceRuleOffset;
    DWORD        dwInternationalRuleSize;
    DWORD        dwInternationalRuleOffset;
} LINECOUNTRYENTRY, FAR *LPLINECOUNTRYENTRY;
```

When calling the `lineGetCountry` function, the application can specify that it would like the countries all at once or one at a time. The `dwNumCountries` field of the LINECOUNTRYLIST indicates how many countries have been returned. The dwCountryListOffset field is offset from the beginning of the LINE-COUNTRYLIST structure to an array of LINECOUNTRYENTRY structures of length dwNumCountries. For example, the country code for the *n*th entry of this array can be accessed using the following code:

```
DWORD MyGetCountryCode(
    LINECOUNTRYLIST*     pd,
    DWORD                nCountry)
{
    ASSERT(pd);
    ASSERT(nCountry < pd->dwNumCountries);

    LPLINECOUNTRYENTRY   alce =
        (LPLINECOUNTRYENTRY)((BYTE*)pd +
            pd->dwCountryListOffset);

    return alce[nCountry].dwCountryCode;
}
```

While it's easier to get all of the countries at once by passing 0 as the country identifier to the lineGetCountry function, this consumes more memory. The application can get one at a time by passing 1 as the initial country identifier. The country identifier for the next country in the list is kept in the dwNextCountry-ID field of the LINECOUNTRYENTRY array. When the dwNextCountryID goes to 0, the application has reached the end of the list.

The country identifier and the country code are not the same thing. The country code is for proper dialing and is not a unique identifier. Sometimes different countries share the same country code, for example, the United States and the Virgin Islands. The country identifier is unique and is used only for navigating the list of countries known to TAPI.

The Location List

The list of locations can be obtained via the lineGetTranslateCaps function, which fills in the LINETRANSLATECAPS variable-length structure:

```
LONG
lineGetTranslateCaps(
    HLINEAPP hLineApp,     // Line usage handle
    DWORD    dwAPIVersion, // App's version
```

```
                LPLINETRANSLATECAPS lpTranslateCaps) // Returned VLS

        typedef struct linetranslatecaps_tag
        {
            DWORD           dwTotalSize;
            DWORD           dwNeededSize;
            DWORD           dwUsedSize;
            DWORD           dwNumLocations;
            DWORD           dwLocationListSize;
            DWORD           dwLocationListOffset;
            DWORD           dwCurrentLocationID;
            DWORD           dwNumCards;
            DWORD           dwCardListSize;
            DWORD           dwCardListOffset;
            DWORD           dwCurrentPreferredCardID;
        } LINETRANSLATECAPS, FAR *LPLINETRANSLATECAPS;

        typedef struct linelocationentry_tag
        {
            DWORD           dwPermanentLocationID;
            DWORD           dwLocationNameSize;
            DWORD           dwLocationNameOffset;
            DWORD           dwCountryCode;
            DWORD           dwCityCodeSize;
            DWORD           dwCityCodeOffset;
            DWORD           dwPreferredCardID;
            DWORD           dwLocalAccessCodeSize;
            DWORD           dwLocalAccessCodeOffset;
            DWORD           dwLongDistanceAccessCodeSize;
            DWORD           dwLongDistanceAccessCodeOffset;
            DWORD           dwTollPrefixListSize;
            DWORD           dwTollPrefixListOffset;
            DWORD           dwCountryID;
            DWORD           dwOptions;
            DWORD           dwCancelCallWaitingSize;
            DWORD           dwCancelCallWaitingOffset;
        } LINELOCATIONENTRY, FAR *LPLINELOCATIONENTRY;
```

The list of locations is available via the dwLocationListOffset, which points to the first entry of a LINELOCATIONENTRY array of length dwNum-Locations. Each LINELOCATIONENTRY contains the location's name and its permanent identifier (among other things). One of these locations will be the current location. The permanent identifier for this system-wide location is in the `dwCurrentLocationID` of the `LINETRANSLATECAPS` structure.

When the user changes the location selection in the list box, the application should use the location's permanent identifier to call the `lineSetCurrent-Location` function:

```
LONG
lineSetCurrentLocation(
    HLINEAPP hLineApp,    // Line usage handle
    DWORD    dwLocation) // Permanent location ID
```

This will change the current location for the entire system and affect how the phone number is translated before dialing. To allow the user to maintain the settings for all of the locations as well as change the currently set location, the application can show the Dialing Properties dialog by calling the `line-TranslateDialog` function:

```
LONG
lineTranslateDialog(
    HLINEAPP hLineApp,        // Line usage handle
    DWORD    dwDeviceID,      // Line ID
    DWORD    dwAPIVersion,    // App's version
    HWND     hwndOwner,       // Dialog's parent window
    LPCSTR   lpszAddressIn) // Canonical format
```

The sample will show this dialog when the user clicks the Properties button of the "Your location" group. The current line identifier and the phone number entered so far are used to show the user the result of the settings changes. Remember, since the numbers and names of the system locations—as well as the currently selected location—can change as a result of this function, be sure to repopulate the locations list after a successful return.

The Line List

You've already seen how to populate the list of lines via the `lineGetDevCaps` function and the `LINEDEVCAPS` structure. To show the icon of the currently selected line, use the `lineGetIcon` function:

```
LONG
lineGetIcon(
```

```
    DWORD    dwDeviceID,       // Line ID
    LPCSTR   lpszDeviceClass,  // Optional device class
    LPHICON  lphIcon)          // Returned icon
```

The optional device class parameter allows a TSP to provide a special icon for each class of functionality it provides. The sample uses NULL in this parameter because we're just making a voice call.

To allow the user to set TSP-specific settings—data rate, data bits, stop bits, parity, and so on—the application can call the `lineConfigDialog` function:

```
lineConfigDialog(
    DWORD  dwDeviceID,        // Line ID
    HWND   hwndOwner,         // Parent window
    LPCSTR lpszDeviceClass)   // Optional device class
```

The sample does this when the Properties button in the "Line to use" group is clicked.

The Address List

To get the list of addresses available on a line, use the `lineGetAddressCaps` function to fill in the LINEADDRESSCAPS variable-length structure:

```
LONG
lineGetAddressCaps(
    HLINEAPP           hLineApp,     // Line usage handle
    DWORD              dwDeviceID,   // Line ID
    DWORD              dwAddressID,  // Address ID
    DWORD              dwAPIVersion, // Negotiated version
    DWORD              dwExtVersion, // Negotiated version
    LPLINEADDRESSCAPS  lpAddressCaps)// Returned VLS

typedef struct lineaddresscaps_tag
{
    DWORD       dwTotalSize;
    DWORD       dwNeededSize;
    DWORD       dwUsedSize;
    DWORD       dwLineDeviceID;
    DWORD       dwAddressSize;
    DWORD       dwAddressOffset;
    ...
} LINEADDRESSCAPS, FAR *LPLINEADDRESSCAPS;
```

The number of addresses for a line is kept in the `dwNumAddresses` field of the `LINEDEVCAPS` structure. This number will normally be 1, but for certain PBX systems, it will be more.

Displayable Format

The application can provide feedback to users about how the settings they've chosen affect the phone number being dialed. It does this by showing the phone number to be dialed as the settings change. The sample does that at the bottom of the Dialing Options dialog. Every time a setting changes in a way that might affect how the number is dialed—for example, changes to the country code, area code, phone number, location, or line—the "Number to dial:" field is updated by a call to `lineTranslateAddress`:

```
LONG
lineTranslateAddress(
    HLINEAPP hLineApp,          // Line usage handle
    DWORD    dwDeviceID,        // Line ID
    DWORD    dwAPIVersion,      // App. version
    LPCSTR   lpszAddressIn,     // Canonical format
    DWORD    dwCard,            // Override default
    DWORD    dwTranslateOptions, // Flags
    LPLINETRANSLATEOUTPUT lpTransOutput) // Returned VLS


typedef struct linetranslateoutput_tag
{
    DWORD        dwTotalSize;
    DWORD        dwNeededSize;
    DWORD        dwUsedSize;
    DWORD        dwDialableStringSize;
    DWORD        dwDialableStringOffset;
    DWORD        dwDisplayableStringSize;
    DWORD        dwDisplayableStringOffset;
    DWORD        dwCurrentCountry;
    DWORD        dwDestCountry;
    DWORD        dwTranslateResults;
} LINETRANSLATEOUTPUT, FAR *LPLINETRANSLATEOUTPUT;
```

The `lpszAddrIn` parameter is the canonical format of the number to be translated. If the user has decided not to use a country code and an area code, the application may not be able to construct a canonical phone number. In that case, the `line-TranslateAddress` function will not be able to do any translations.

The `dwCard` parameter overrides the credit card number associated with the currently selected location settings. The list of credit card numbers is available via the `dwCardListOffset` of the `LINETRANSLATECAPS` structure, which points to an array of `LINECARDENTRY` structures `dwNumCards` long. Your applications may decide to provide a handy list of available credit card numbers as well as location settings. For simplicity's sake, the sample doesn't do this.

The `dwTranslateOptions` is a set of flags you may find useful. Table 3.3 lists the flags and gives their meanings. The result of the `lineTranslate-Address` function is the `LINETRANSLATEADDRESS` variable-length structure. The displayable version of the translated address is available via the `dwDisplayableStringOffset` field. This string will not include private information like credit card numbers or PINs. When dialing the number, the

Table 3.3: `dwTranslateOptions` flags.	
Flag	*Meaning*
LINETRANSLATEOPTION_CARDOVERRIDE	This flag uses the dwCard parameter to override the current location's default credit card.
LINETRANSLATEOPTION_CANCELCALLWAITING	For modem or fax calls that can be interrupted by the call waiting beeps, this flag disables call waiting, if it was prepended to the dial string.
LINETRANSLATEOPTION_FORCELOCAL LINETRANSLATEOPTION_FORCELD	If a user is forced to dial what looks like a local call as long distance and vice versa, this flag allows the user to force a long distance call or force a local call.

application will use the `dwDialableStringOffset` field to access the full version of the number, which will include this private information. It's a good idea to show only the displayable version of the phone number in order to keep private information private.

Opening the Line

Before making a call, the application must open a line on which to make the call. This is done using the `lineOpen` function:

```
LONG
lineOpen(
    HLINEAPP hLineApp,              // Line usage handle
    DWORD    dwDeviceID,            // Line ID
    LPHLINE  lphLine,              // Returned line handle
    DWORD    dwAPIVersion,          // Negotiated API version
    DWORD    dwExtVersion,          // Option Ext. version
    DWORD    dwCallbackInstance,    // App-specific data
    DWORD    dwPrivileges,          // Answering privileges
    DWORD    dwMediaModes,          // Answering media modes
    LPLINECALLPARAMS const lpCallParams) // Optional
```

`lineOpen` is called to open the physical device represented by the line's unique identifier. The handle to the open line device (`HLINE`) is returned in the `lphLine` parameter. The `dwCallbackInstance` parameter is for application-supplied data. It will be returned in the `dwCallbackInstance` parameter of the line callback function for each event that occurs on the newly opened line device. This is a great place for an object's *this* pointer, and that's what it's used for in the sample.

The `dwPrivileges` and `dwMediaModes` parameters to `lineOpen` are used only to answer incoming calls and monitor calls happening in other applications. I discuss them in more depth in Chapter 5 and Chapter 6.

If the `dwDeviceID` parameter is set to the special value `LINE_MAPPER`, then the optional `lpCallParams` parameter is used to find a line that meets the requirements specified in the `LINECALLPARAMS` structure:

```
typedef struct linecallparams_tag
{
    DWORD       dwTotalSize;
```

```
    DWORD           dwBearerMode;
    DWORD           dwMinRate;
    DWORD           dwMaxRate;
    DWORD           dwMediaMode;
    DWORD           dwCallParamFlags;
    DWORD           dwAddressMode;
    DWORD           dwAddressID;
    LINEDIALPARAMS  DialParams;
    DWORD           dwOrigAddressSize;
    DWORD           dwOrigAddressOffset;
    DWORD           dwDisplayableAddressSize;
    DWORD           dwDisplayableAddressOffset;
    DWORD           dwCalledPartySize;
    DWORD           dwCalledPartyOffset;
    DWORD           dwCommentSize;
    DWORD           dwCommentOffset;
    DWORD           dwUserUserInfoSize;
    DWORD           dwUserUserInfoOffset;
    DWORD           dwHighLevelCompSize;
    DWORD           dwHighLevelCompOffset;
    DWORD           dwLowLevelCompSize;
    DWORD           dwLowLevelCompOffset;
    DWORD           dwDevSpecificSize;
    DWORD           dwDevSpecificOffset;

#if (TAPI_CURRENT_VERSION >= 0x00020000)
    DWORD           dwPredictiveAutoTransferStates;
    DWORD           dwTargetAddressSize;
    DWORD           dwTargetAddressOffset;
    DWORD           dwSendingFlowspecSize;
    DWORD           dwSendingFlowspecOffset;
    DWORD           dwReceivingFlowspecSize;
    DWORD           dwReceivingFlowspecOffset;
    DWORD           dwDeviceClassSize;
    DWORD           dwDeviceClassOffset;
    DWORD           dwDeviceConfigSize;
    DWORD           dwDeviceConfigOffset;
    DWORD           dwCallDataSize;
    DWORD           dwCallDataOffset;
    DWORD           dwNoAnswerTimeout;
```

```
        DWORD          dwCallingPartyIDSize;
        DWORD          dwCallingPartyIDOffset;
#endif
  } LINECALLPARAMS, FAR *LPLINECALLPARAMS;
```

If an application uses `LINE_MAPPER` to open a line based on its capabilities, it can discover the device identifier of the line it has opened. This is done by calling the `lineGetID` function using the `tapi/line` device class. Once the line is open, events are reported via the line callback function specified in your call to `lineInitialize`. Recall the prototype of this function:

```
void
lineCallbackFunc(
        DWORD hDevice,             // Line or call device
        DWORD dwMsg,               // Line or call message
        DWORD dwCallbackInstance,  // App-defined data
        DWORD dwParam1,            // Message-specific param.
        DWORD dwParam2,            // Message-specific param.
        DWORD dwParam3)            // Message-specific param.
```

Table 3.4 lists the events that can occur on a line that will be received via the line callback function. In this book, I describe the most important of these messages. However, for a voice call, the sample application handles a subset of these states: `LINE_CALLSTATE`, `LINE_CLOSE`, and `LINE_REPLY`.

Once the line has been opened, the application may call the `lineSetStatusMessages` function to narrow the range of line or address state change events that the application is sent by TAPI on that line:

```
LONG
lineSetStatusMessages(
        HLINE              hLine,
        DWORD              dwLineStates,
        DWORD              dwAddressStates);
```

The `dwLineStates` parameter is a bit field of the `LINEDEVSTATE_*` constants that represent the state changes in which the application is interested. Likewise, the `dwAddressStates` is a bit field of `LINEADDRESSSTATE_*` constants. Depending on how quickly the state of the telephony equipment changes, this may represent a significant decrease in the number of events that the application is sent.

Table 3.4: Events received via the line callback function.

Event (dwMessage)	Meaning
`LINE_ADDRESSSTATE`	The state of an address has changed.

`LINE_AGENTSTATUS`
`LINE_AGENTSPECIFIC`
`(TAPI 2.0)`
	The status of an ACD has changed.

`LINE_APPNEWCALL` `(TAPI 2.0)`	A call new to the application has been created.
`LINE_CALLINFO`	Call information has changed.
`LINE_CALLSTATE`	The state of a call has changed.
`LINE_CLOSE`	The line has been closed.
`LINE_DEVSPECIFIC`	Signifies a device-specific event.
`LINE_DEVSPECIFICFEATURE`	Signifies a device-specific event.
`LINE_GATHERDIGITS`	Digit gathering has completed.
`LINE_GENERATE`	Digit or tone generation has completed.
`LINE_LINEDEVSTATE`	The state of the line has changed.
`LINE_MONITORDIGITS`	A digit on a call has been detected.
`LINE_MONITORMEDIA`	The media mode of a call has been changed.
`LINE_MONITORTONE`	A tone on a call has been detected.
`LINE_PROXYREQUEST` `(TAPI 2.0)`	A proxy function handler has been requested.
`LINE_REMOVE` `(TAPI 2.0)`	A line device has been removed from the system.
`LINE_REPLY`	An asynchronous request has been completed.
`LINE_REQUEST`	An Assisted Telephony request has been made.

Making the Call

Well, it's taken a bit of setup, but we've finally done enough to be able to make a call using the `lineMakeCall` function:

```
LONG
lineMakeCall(
    HLINE   hLine,          // Open line handle
    LPHCALL lphCall,         // Returned call handle
    LPCSTR  lpszDestAddress, // Dialable phone no.
    DWORD   dwCountryCode,   // Called country code
    LPLINECALLPARAMS const lpCallParams) // Optional
```

The `lpszDestAddress` is the phone number to dial in dialable format. An example is the string found at `dwDialableStringOffset` in the LINE-TRANSLATEOUTPUT structure returned from `lineTranslateAddress`. The `lphCall` parameter is the handle to a call in progress. Since `lineMakeCall` is asynchronous, a successful call to `lineMakeCall` will return a positive request identifier. This request will either succeed or fail, but either way, a LINE_REPLY event will come in via the line callback function. The `dwParam1` parameter will be the request identifier, and the `dwParam2` will be the result of the request, either zero to indicate success or a negative error code.

The call handle referenced by the `lphCall` parameter isn't valid until (and unless) the request reply has completed successfully. No call operations can be made with that call handle until the LINE_REPLY has come in with a `dwParam2` of zero.

The `lpCallParams` parameter is an optional LINECALLPARAMS structure to determine the characteristics of the new call, make a call on a specific address, and provide monitoring applications with new call information. If it is left out, the fields have default values, given in Table 3.5. For a voice call, these values are exactly what we want. Following is an example of first opening a line using the `lineOpen` function and then making a call using the `lineMake-Call` function:

```
void CtDialDlg::Dial(LPCSTR pszPhoneNo)
{
    // Get valid lines...

    // Show the dialing options dialog...
```

Table 3.5: Default values of `LINECALLPARAMS`.	
LINECALLPARAMS Field	*Default Value*
dwBearerMode	LINEBEARERMODE_VOICE
dwMinRate	3100 (3.1hHz)
dwMaxRate	3100 (3.1hHz)
dwMediaMode	LINEMEDIAMODE_INTERACTIVEVOICE
dwCallParamFlags	0 (None)
dwAddressMode	LINEADDRESSMODE_ADDRESSID
dwAddressID	(Any available outgoing address)
(the rest)	0

```
if( dlg.DoModal() == IDOK )
{
    // Open the line for an outgoing call.
    if( ::lineOpen(m_hLineApp,
                dlg.m_nLineID,
                &m_hLine,
                m_aApiVersions[dlg.m_nLineID],
                0,
                (DWORD)this,
                LINECALLPRIVILEGE_NONE,
                LINEMEDIAMODE_INTERACTIVEVOICE,
                0) == 0 )
    {
        LONG    tr = ::lineMakeCall(m_hLine,
                    &m_hCall,
                    dlg.m_sDialable,
                    dlg.m_pno.GetCountryCodeNum(),
                    0);
        if( tr > 0 )
        {
            m_nMakeCallRequest = tr;
            LogStatus("Placing a call to '%s'...\r\n",
                    dlg.m_pno.GetDisplayable());
            UpdateStatus();
        }
        else
```

```
                {
                    ::AfxMessageBox(IDS_CANT_MAKE_CALL);
                }
            }
            else
            {
                ::AfxMessageBox(IDS_CANT_OPEN_LINE);
            }
        }

        delete[] rgbValidLines;
    }
```

When the call has been made, the line callback function will receive a LINE_ REPLY event:

```
void CALLBACK
MyLineCallback(
    DWORD    dwDevice,
    DWORD    nMsg,
    DWORD    dwCallbackInstance,
    DWORD    dwParam1,
    DWORD    dwParam2,
    DWORD    dwParam3)
{
    // dwCallbackInstance set in call to lineOpen()
    CtDialDlg*  pThis = (CtDialDlg*)dwCallbackInstance;

    switch( nMsg )
    {
    case LINE_REPLY:
        TRACE0("LINE_REPLY\n");
        pThis->OnReply(dwParam1, dwParam2);
    break;

    // Route other events...
    }
}

void CtDialDlg::OnReply(
    DWORD    nRequestID,
```

```
        DWORD    nResult)
    {
        if( nRequestID == m_nMakeCallRequest )
        {
            m_nMakeCallRequest = 0;

            if( nResult == 0  )
            {
                LogStatus("Call placed.\r\n");
            }
            else
            {
                VERIFY(::lineClose(m_hLine) == 0);
                m_hLine = 0;

                LogStatus("Call cannot be placed.\r\n");
            }
        }
        else if( nRequestID == m_nDropCallRequest )
        {
            m_nDropCallRequest = 0;

            LogStatus("Call dropped.\r\n");
        }

        UpdateStatus();
    }
```

An application that desires more control over the dialing process can use line-
MakeCall with an empty szDestAddress parameter. Once the call has been
established (usually when a dial tone is detected), the application can dial digits
using the lineDial function:

```
LONG
lineDial(
        HCALL  hCall,             // Established call handle.
        LPCSTR lpszDestAddress,   // Dial string.
        DWORD  dwCountryCode)     // Called country code.
```

The lineDial is typically used only to transfer a call or to add another party to a
conference call. This kind of functionality is beyond the capabilities of many TSPs.

Monitoring Call Progress

Once `lineMakeCall` has returned its asynchronous result, the application has a valid call object. This is a logical connection between an address on a line under the application's control and an address on a line somewhere else in the world that is out of the application's control. Any physical event will be signaled to your end of the call via some in-band mechanism (such as voltage changes on an analog line) or out-of-band mechanism (such as LAP-D frames on the D-Channel of an ISDN line). These signals indicate that the state of the call has changed. TAPI will notify your application of these call state changes via the line callback function and the `LINE_CALLSTATE` event. The possible states of a call are enumerated in the `LINECALLSTATE_*` constants and given in Table 3.6.

Any given TSP does not have to generate any more call state messages than actually make sense for the device. The `LINEADDRESSCAPS` structure, available via the `lineGetAddressCaps` function, exposes the call states an application should expect in the `dwCallStates` field. Even if some of the states are skipped, call progress of an outgoing call will look like the diagram in Figure 3.5. It is the application's job to give feedback to the user about the current state of the call. The sample does this by appending a string to an edit box to indicate the state changes of the call. This information is received via the line callback function in the `LINE_CALLSTATE` event like this:

```
void CtDialDlg::OnCallState(
    HCALL     hCall,
    DWORD     nCallState,
    DWORD     dwParam2,
    DWORD     nCallPrivilege)
{
    struct FlagMap { DWORD nFlag; LPCSTR szFlag; };
    static FlagMap aFlags[] =
    {
        {LINECALLSTATE_IDLE,         "idle"},
        {LINECALLSTATE_ACCEPTED,     "accepted"},
        {LINECALLSTATE_DIALTONE,     "dial tone detected"},
        {LINECALLSTATE_DIALING,      "dialing"},
        {LINECALLSTATE_RINGBACK,     "ring-back detected"},
        {LINECALLSTATE_BUSY,         "busy detected"},
        {LINECALLSTATE_SPECIALINFO,  "error detected"},
        {LINECALLSTATE_CONNECTED,    "connected"},
        {LINECALLSTATE_PROCEEDING,   "proceeding"},
```

Hex

Table 3.6: `LINECALLSTATE_*` constants.	
Call State	Meaning
1 `LINECALLSTATE_IDLE`	The call no longer exists.
2 `LINECALLSTATE_OFFERING`	A new call has arrived.
4 `LINECALLSTATE_ACCEPTED`	The call has been claimed by an application.
8 `LINECALLSTATE_DIALTONE`	The switch is ready to receive a number.
10 `LINECALLSTATE_DIALING`	The switch is receiving dialing information.
20 `LINECALLSTATE_RINGBACK`	A ring was heard on the call.
40 `LINECALLSTATE_BUSY`	A busy signal was heard on the call.
80 `LINECALLSTATE_SPECIALINFO`	An error tone was heard on the call.
100 `LINECALLSTATE_CONNECTED`	The call has been connected to the other end.
200 `LINECALLSTATE_PROCEEDING`	Dialing has completed but the call has not yet been connected.
400 `LINECALLSTATE_ONHOLD`	The call is on hold.
800 `LINECALLSTATE_CONFERENCED`	The call is conferenced.
1000 `LINECALLSTATE_ONHOLDPENDCONF`	The call is on hold before being conferenced.
2000 `LINECALLSTATE_ONHOLDPENDTRANSFER`	The call is on hold before being transferred.
4000 `LINECALLSTATE_DISCONNECTED`	The other end has dropped the call.
8000 `LINECALLSTATE_UNKNOWN`	The TSP cannot determine the current state of the call.

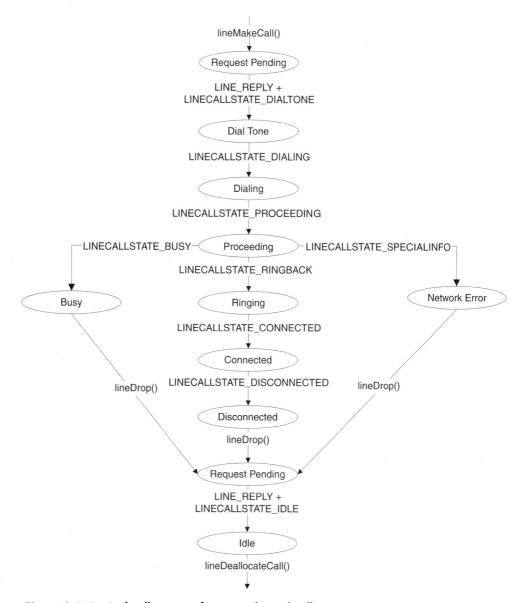

Figure 3.5: Typical call process for an outbound call.

```
        {LINECALLSTATE_DISCONNECTED,"disconnected"},
    };

    for( int i = 0; i < DIM(aFlags); i++ )
    {
        if( aFlags[i].nFlag == nCallState )
        {
            LogStatus("Call %s.\r\n", aFlags[i].szFlag);
            break;
        }
    }

    switch( nCallState )
    {
    case LINECALLSTATE_DISCONNECTED:
        OnHangUp();
    break;

    case LINECALLSTATE_IDLE:
        VERIFY(::lineDeallocateCall(m_hCall) == 0);
        m_hCall = 0;

        VERIFY(::lineClose(m_hLine) == 0);
        m_hLine = 0;
    break;
    }

    UpdateStatus();
}
```

Ending a Call

Notice that when the call is disconnected on the other end, the sample code calls another function: OnHangUp. This function also is called if the user clicks the Hang Up button in the main window. To hang up a call, TAPI provides the line-Drop function:

```
LONG
lineDrop(
```

```
HCALL   hCall,             // Call to drop
LPCSTR lpsUserUserInfo, // ISDN-specific
DWORD   dwSize)           // lpsUserUserInfo size
```

The `lineDrop` function is used to terminate our end of a call. This does not destroy the call, but it does cause the logical connection between the two ends of the call to be severed. Here's how the asynchronous `lineDrop` function is used in the `OnHangUp` function:

```
void CtDialDlg::OnHangUp()
{
    // Can't hang up a call w/o a handle 'cuz
    // there's no way to cancel a pending TAPI request.
    ASSERT(m_hCall);

    LONG    tr = ::lineDrop(m_hCall, 0, 0);
    if( tr > 0 )
    {
        m_nDropCallRequest = tr;
        LogStatus("Call dropping...\r\n");
        UpdateStatus();
    }
    else
    {
        LogStatus("Can't drop call.\r\n");
    }

    UpdateStatus();
}
```

After a call has been dropped (as indicated by a `LINE_REPLY` event with the `lineDrop` request identifier), the call will transition to the idle state. Once the call has gone to its idle state and the application no longer needs it, it should deallocate the resources associated with the call by using the `lineDeallocate-Call` function (as shown in the previous `OnCallState` example):

```
LONG
lineDeallocateCall(
    HCALL hCall) // Call handle
```

Closing the Line

Once the call has been deallocated and the line is no longer needed, the application should close the line using the `lineClose` function (as shown in the previous `OnCallState` example):

```
LONG
lineClose(
    HLINE hLine) // Open line handle
```

Once the line has been closed, the line handle is no longer valid and the line callback function will receive no more events for that line.

Shutdown

When the application has no more use for the line part of TAPI (for example, application shutdown), the application must call the `lineShutdown` function:

```
LONG
lineShutdown(
    HLINEAPP hLineApp) // Line usage handle
```

At this point, the line usage handle is no longer valid and the application may not use TAPI functions beginning with the "line" prefix.

Summary

There are many details to be concerned about even when simply placing a call using TAPI. The good news is that the developer no longer has to develop for a single telephony device, understand AT command strings, or coach the user through complicated configurations. TAPI provides a layer of abstraction between the application and the telephony device. Instead of programming for a specific device, a developer decides on a specific set of capabilities required to perform the desired telephony tasks. Thus a TAPI application must be flexible in dealing with many possible telephony devices, canonical and dialable phone number formats, variable-sized data structures, multiple phone lines, flexible configurations, asynchronous requests, and spontaneous telephony events.

The amount of code to deal with even the simplest TAPI application is sometimes overwhelming and cries out for an additional layer of abstraction. My approach to such an abstraction is the Telephony Framework, the subject of the next chapter.

The Telephony Framework

Initialization and Shutdown

Capabilities Discovery

Telephony Objects

Event Routing

Miscellany

Using the TFX

*Everyone's got their own
wrapper for TAPI.*
David Chouinard
Intel Corporation

The Windows Telephony API is fairly large, but the sample from the previous chapter used only a small part of it to make a call. Even so, there was still a great deal of telephony-related code. Some of the code was application-specific—filtering lines based on capabilities, determining when and how to dial, and handling the call status messages. Most, however, was fairly boilerplate and will be present in every TAPI application—filling variable-length structures, routing messages, negotiating versions, and so on.

The application-generic code is a ripe candidate for inclusion in a library of routines. In fact, every TAPI application I've ever seen uses some form of wrapper around TAPI; it is just too grungy to be used in the raw. In the previous chapter, the sample used some wrapper functions to help with TAPI, for example:

- `CtDialDlg::InitializeLines` initialized TAPI, negotiated the line versions, and cached the results.
- `MyGetLineDevCaps` filled the `LINEDEVCAPS` structure.
- `MyGetLineName` pulled the line name string out of the `LINEDEVCAPS` structure.
- `MyLineCallback` routed telephony events.

Together, these functions added a layer of abstraction on top of TAPI to make programming easier. However, the average C++ programmer prefers a set of objects to another set of global functions.

The Telephony Framework (TFX) is my version of a class library for TAPI. It's modeled on the Microsoft Foundation Classes (MFC). The TFX is like MFC in many ways:

- It is a set of explicit classes that model implicit objects in the underlying API.
- It is a thin wrapper that does not provide a large learning curve or hinder direct access to the underlying API.
- Its functions and classes are based on the naming conventions of TAPI to make it easy to find desired functionality.
- It provides application-generic services for debugging, wrapping difficult to use structures, providing meaningful defaults for long parameter lists, routing events, and even fixing bugs in the underlying API implementation.

This chapter describes the TFX architecture and shows how the services are provided and how they are used. The sample application from the previous chapter has been rewritten using the TFX to illustrate how much simpler it is to use than raw TAPI.

Initialization and Shutdown

As you might expect, the TFX provides explicit classes for each kind of telephony object that TAPI models implicitly, that is, line, call, and phone. However, before any telephony objects can be used, the TFX must be properly initialized. And just like TAPI, the TFX is initialized in two parts, depending on the functionality required, that is, line functionality is separate from phone functionality. The parts of the TFX are initialized using the global helper functions `TfxLineInitialize` and `TfxPhoneInitialize`:[1]

```
TRESULT[2]
TfxLineInitialize(
    CtAppSink* pAppSink = 0,  // Default: No sink
    LPCSTR     szAppName = 0, // Default: AfxGetAppName
    HINSTANCE hInst = 0)// Default: AfxGetInstanceHandle


TRESULT
TfxPhoneInitialize(
    CtAppSink* pAppSink = 0,  // Default: No sink
    LPCSTR     szAppName = 0, // Default: AfxGetAppName
    HINSTANCE hInst = 0)// Default: AfxGetInstanceHandle
```

The `TfxLineInitialize` function calls `lineInitialize`, caching the number of devices available. The number of devices can be obtained by calling the `TfxGetNumLines` global helper function. The `TfxLineInitialize` function also negotiates all of the API versions using `lineNegotiateAPIVersion`, caching the results for use by the TAPI wrapper member functions of the telephony objects. The current implementation of the TFX assumes a low

---

[1] Because the phone part of the TFX mirrors the line part, as in TAPI, and because the line part of the TFX is used far more often than the phone part, the rest of this chapter concentrates on the line part of the TFX.

[2] `TRESULT` is a type definition for a `long`, the return type of TAPI functions.

TAPI version number of 1.3 and a high version number of whatever is the definition of the `TAPI_CURRENT_VERSION` symbol.

The `TAPI_CURRENT_VERSION` symbol was added to the TAPI headers for TAPI 2.0 and, if undefined, is assumed to be 0x00020000, that is, TAPI 2.0. A developer interested in narrowing an application's functionality to TAPI 1.4 should define the `TAPI_CURRENT_VERSION` symbol to 0x00010004 before including `tapi.h` (and therefore also before including any of the TFX header files).

On successful initialization, the negotiated API version numbers are available via the `CtLine` static member function `GetApiVersion`:

```
static DWORD
GetApiVersion(DWORD nLineID);
```

This function is mostly used internally to provide the proper version numbers based on the line ID and the kind of version number required by the function, that is, application version or negotiated version as discussed in Chapter 3.

Once the initialized part of the TFX is no longer needed, the proper shutdown is performed via the `TfxLineShutdown` and `TfxPhoneShutdown` functions:

```
void TfxLineShutdown();
void TfxPhoneShutdown();
```

The complete telephony initialization, version negotiation, and shutdown process that the sample uses is shown next:

```
BOOL CtDialApp::InitInstance
{
    // Initialize the line
    if( ::TfxLineInitialize() != 0 )
    {
        ::AfxMessageBox(IDS_CANT_INIT_TAPI);
        return FALSE;
    }

    CtDialDlg   dlgDial;
    m_pMainWnd = &dlgDial;
    dlgDial.DoModal;

    return FALSE;
}
```

```
int CtDialApp::ExitInstance
{
    ::TfxLineShutdown();
    return CWinApp::ExitInstance;
}
```

The Windows 95 Telephony Shutdown Bug

Windows 95 TAPI programs have a particular problem. If your application is stopped before properly shutting down TAPI 1.4 under Windows 95, you may have to restart Windows before you can run another telephony application. This tends to be a drawback when you're developing.

To avoid the wear and tear on my hard drive, I've implemented the Microsoft-recommended work-around in the Debug versions of the TFX libraries. In essence, the TFX caches the HLINEAPP returned by lineInitialize until lineShutdown is called. If lineShutdown is never called—for example, the application crashes or is stopped by the debugger—then the next time the Initialize member function is called, the cached HLINEAPP is passed to lineShutdown before a new session is started. You'll know the TFX is working for you when you see the following message in the Debug output:

```
The Win95 TAPI Recovery just saved you a restart.
```

Capabilities Discovery

Recall from Chapter 3 that the lineGetDevCaps function was used to fill the LINEDEVCAPS structure. Because the LINEDEVSTRUCTURE was a variable-length structure (VLS), it was difficult to fill it completely and even more difficult to pull out the data from it. To avoid this, the TFX provides the CtVariable-Data class. This class knows how to fill in any VLS and provides helper functions for pulling out the data.

```
class CtVariableData
{
public:
    CtVariableData();
    virtual ~CtVariableData();

protected:
    struct VARDATA
```

```
    {
        DWORD    dwTotalSize;
        DWORD    dwNeededSize;
        DWORD    dwUsedSize;
    };


    VARDATA*    m_pd;

    TRESULT UpdateData();
    LPCSTR  GetStringPtr(DWORD nOffset,
                         DWORD nSize,
                         DWORD dwStringFormat =
                             STRINGFORMAT_ASCII) const;
    void*   GetDataPtr(DWORD nOffset) const;

    // Must be implemented by derived class!
    virtual TRESULT FillBuffer =0;
};
```

The algorithm for filling in a VLS is kept in the `UpdateData` member function and is just a more robust version of the algorithm from Chapter 3:

```
TRESULT CtVariableData::UpdateData()
{
  // Empirically, 512 often works the first time.
  // Note: This number must be at least as big as the
  // largest variable-sized structure in TAPI
  // TAPI will complain about being too small and not
  // fill in m_pd->dwNeededSize.
  DWORD   dwNeededSize = 512;
  TRESULT tr = 0;

  do
  {
    // Get some more memory if we don't have enough.
    if( !m_pd || m_pd->dwTotalSize < dwNeededSize )
    {
      if( m_pd = (VARDATA*)::realloc(m_pd, dwNeededSize) )
      {
        m_pd->dwTotalSize = dwNeededSize;
      }
```

```
      else
      {
        return LINEERR_NOMEM;
      }
    }

    // Call the derived call to fill in the buffer.
    tr = FillBuffer();

    // Check how much memory we need.
    if( tr == LINEERR_STRUCTURETOOSMALL ||
        // Some TSPs succeed even if the data
        // size is too small.
        (TSUCCEEDED(tr) && m_pd->dwTotalSize <
                        m_pd->dwNeededSize) )
    {
      dwNeededSize = m_pd->dwNeededSize;
      tr = LINEERR_STRUCTURETOOSMALL;
    }
  }
  while( tr == LINEERR_STRUCTURETOOSMALL );

  // Trim excess memory use.
  if( TSUCCEEDED(tr) &&
      m_pd->dwUsedSize < m_pd->dwTotalSize )
  {
    m_pd = (VARDATA*)::realloc(m_pd, m_pd->dwUsedSize);
    ASSERT(m_pd);
    m_pd->dwTotalSize = m_pd->dwUsedSize;
  }
  // Release unset memory
  else if( TFAILED(tr) && m_pd )
  {
    ::free(m_pd);
    m_pd = 0;
  }

  return tr;
}
```

Notice that the variable-length data is kept in the **m_pd** data member of type
VARDATA. The CtVariableData class doesn't know about every possible

TAPI VLS, but it does know that all of them have those three DWORD fields in the same order: dwTotalSize, dwNeededSize, and dwUsedSize. This allows the UpdateData member function to do all of the size negotiation without knowledge of any specific VLS. The VARDATA structure has only these data members, but they are all that is needed for the algorithm.

The UpdateData member function can do everything except actually fill the allocated memory of the VLS. For that, it relies on the pure virtual member function FillBuffer, which must be implemented by a derived class of CtVariable-Data. The derived class uses the memory allocated by the base class to call the proper TAPI function to retrieve the data. The derived class must also provide a member function to initiate the data retrieval process. The data provided to this member function is cached as member data in the derived class for use in implementing the FillBuffer member function.

For example, the CtTranslateOutput class derives from CtVariable-Data to wrap the LINETRANSLATEOUTPUT structure filled by the line-TranslateAddress function:

```
class CtTranslateOutput : public CtVariableData
{
public:
  TRESULT TranslateAddress(DWORD nLineID,
                           LPCSTR pszAddressIn,
                           DWORD nCardID = 0,
                           DWORD dwTranslateOptions = 0);

  // Field accessors
  LPCSTR  GetDialableString() const;
  LPCSTR  GetDisplayableString() const;
  DWORD   GetCurrentCountry() const;
  DWORD   GetDestCountry() const;
  DWORD   GetTranslateResults() const;

protected:
  virtual TRESULT FillBuffer();

private:
  DWORD   m_nLineID;
  LPCSTR  m_pszAddressIn;
  DWORD   m_nAddressID;
  DWORD   m_nCardID;
  DWORD   m_dwTranslateOptions;
```

```
      const LPLINETRANSLATEOUTPUT GetData const;
};
```

The `TranslateAddress` member function caches the parameters as member data and calls `UpdateData` to start the VLS retrieval process:

```
inline
TRESULT CtTranslateOutput::TranslateAddress(
    DWORD    nLineID,
    LPCSTR   pszAddressIn,
    DWORD    nCardID,            // = 0
    DWORD    dwTranslateOptions) // = 0
{
    m_nLineID = nLineID;
    m_pszAddressIn = pszAddressIn;
    m_nCardID = nCardID;
    m_dwTranslateOptions = dwTranslateOptions;

    return UpdateData();
}
```

The `UpdateData` member function implemented in the `CtVariableData` base class allocates memory as needed and calls the `FillBuffer` member function implemented in the derived class `CtTranslateOutput`. The `FillBuffer` function uses the cached member data, the base class m_pd data buffer, and the appropriate class data to retrieve the data via the `lineTranslateAddress` function:

```
inline
TRESULT CtTranslateOutput::FillBuffer()
{
  return ::lineTranslateAddress(CtLine::GetAppHandle,
                      m_nLineID,
                      CtLine::GetApiVersion(m_nLineID),
                      m_pszAddressIn,
                      m_nCardID,
                      m_dwTranslateOptions,
                      LPLINETRANSLATEOUTPUT(m_pd));
}
```

Once the data has been retrieved, the derived class may use two helper functions to access the data held in the VLS: `GetStringPtr` and `GetDataPtr`. These are provided in the `CtVariableData` base class and perform the offset calculations from the base of the **m_pd** data.

```
inline
void* CtVariableData::GetDataPtr(
    DWORD    nOffset) const
{
    ASSERT(m_pd);
    return LPVOID((BYTE*)m_pd + nOffset);
}

inline
LPCSTR CtVariableData::GetStringPtr(
    DWORD    nOffset,
    DWORD    nSize,
    DWORD    dwStringFormat) const // = STRINGFORMAT_ASCII
{
    if( dwStringFormat == STRINGFORMAT_ASCII )
    {
        if( nSize )
        {
            return LPCSTR(GetDataPtr(nOffset));
        }
        else
        {
            return "";
        }
    }
    else
    {
        // Only supporting ASCII strings
        return 0;
    }
}
```

In addition, the `CtTranslateOuput` class provides the `GetData` member function to perform the cast from VARDATA* to LINETRANSLATEOUTPUT*. Using these three helpers, the `CtTranslateOutput` class provides member functions to access the retrieved data:

```
inline
LPCSTR CtTranslateOutput::GetDialableString const
{
    return GetStringPtr(GetData()->dwDialableStringOffset,
                    GetData()->dwDialableStringSize);
}


inline
LPCSTR CtTranslateOutput::GetDisplayableString const
{
    return GetStringPtr(
            GetData()->dwDisplayableStringOffset,
            GetData()->dwDisplayableStringSize);
}


inline
DWORD CtTranslateOutput::GetCurrentCountry const
{
    return GetData()->dwCurrentCountry;
}


inline
DWORD CtTranslateOutput::GetDestCountry const
{
    return GetData()->dwDestCountry;
}


inline
DWORD CtTranslateOutput::GetTranslateResults const
{
    return GetData()->dwTranslateResults;
}
```

With the `CtTranslateOutput` class, retrieving and accessing data is now much easier than using the raw `lineTranslateAddress` function and the `LINETRANSLATEOUTPUT` variable-length structure:

```
CString             sDisplayable;
CtTranslateOutput   to;
if( to.TranslateAddress(m_nLineID, pszPhoneNo)) == 0 )
```

```
    {
        sDisplayable = to.GetDisplayableString();
    }
```

The TFX doesn't provide wrappers around all of the variable-length structures in TAPI, but it does support the more common ones, including `LINECOUNTRY-LIST`, `LINECALLINFO`, and `LINEDEVCAPS`. The `tDial` sample uses the `CtLineDevCaps` wrapper to find the lines on which placing a call is suitable:

```
void CtDialDlg::CacheValidLines()
{
  ASSERT(m_rgbValidLines == 0);

  // Get valid lines.
  DWORD   nLines = ::TfxGetNumLines();
  ASSERT(nLines);

  DWORD   nValidLines = 0;
  m_rgbValidLines = new BOOL[nLines];
  if( m_rgbValidLines )
  {
    CtLineDevCaps   ldc;
    for( DWORD nLineID = 0; nLineID < nLines; nLineID++ )
    {
      if( TSUCCEEDED(ldc.GetDevCaps(nLineID)) &&
(ldc.GetBearerModes() & LINEBEARERMODE_VOICE) &&
(ldc.GetMediaModes() & LINEMEDIAMODE_INTERACTIVEVOICE) &&
(ldc.GetLineFeatures() & LINEFEATURE_MAKECALL) )
      {
        m_rgbValidLines[nLineID] = TRUE;
        nValidLines++;
      }
      else
      {
        m_rgbValidLines[nLineID] = FALSE;
        LogStatus("Line %d doesn't support "
                  "voice calls.\r\n", nLineID);
      }
    }
  }
```

```
  if( !nValidLines )
  {
    delete[] m_rgbValidLines;
    m_rgbValidLines = 0;
    LogStatus("No lines support voice calls.\r\n");
  }
}
```

Telephony Objects

After the initialization of that part of the TFX your application is interested in and the devices that match its requirements have been discovered, it can create and use the TFX telephony objects. The TFX class hierarchy is shown in Figure 4.1. The most important classes in the TFX are the classes that represent the underlying telephony objects:[3] `CtLine`, `CtCall`, and `CtPhone`. Each of these classes provides the following services:

- Static member functions for class-level operations that don't require an object (like initializing the line portion of the API)
- Member functions that wrap one or more TAPI calls
- Member functions for managing the object's resources (like getting the `HCALL` from a `CtCall` object)
- Two-stage construction to ensure proper initialization

Several of the often-used static member functions are further wrapped with global functions for convenience. For example, the `TfxLineInitialize` function calls the `CtLine` static member function `Initialize`.

The member functions that wrap TAPI calls are handy for several reasons. Instead of an application's managing an `HLINE` or an `HCALL` that is passed to global functions, it can create an object that maintains its own state as well as access the state maintained in the rest of the TFX, for example, version information and pending asynchronous requests. This makes function calls much simpler. Information that the object has access to does not have to be passed as arguments

---

[3] Earlier versions had a class representing an address as well, but for simplicity's sake, this functionality was merged with the `CtLine` class.

to a member function. For example, when raw TAPI is used, opening the line looks like this:

```
void CtDialDlg::Dial(LPCSTR pszPhoneNo)
{
    // Code removed for clarity...

    if( dlg.DoModal == IDOK )
    {
        // Open the line for an outgoing call
        if( ::lineOpen(m_hLineApp,
                    dlg.m_nLineID,
                    &m_hLine,
                    m_aApiVersions[dlg.m_nLineID],
                    0,
                    (DWORD)this,
                    LINECALLPRIVILEGE_NONE,
                    LINEMEDIAMODE_INTERACTIVEVOICE,
                    0) == 0 )
        {
            // et cetera.
        }
    }
}
```

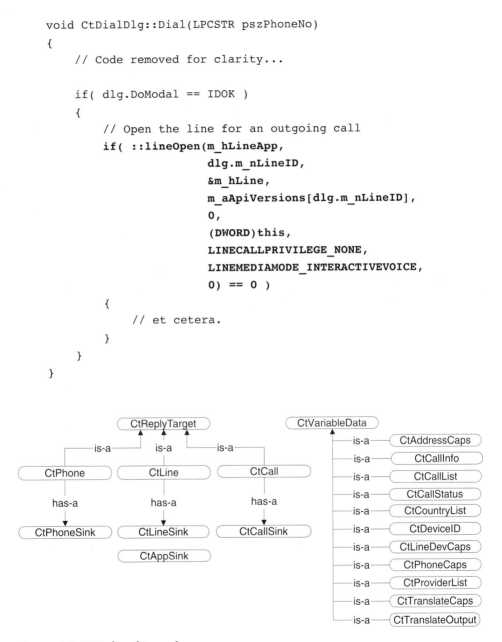

Figure 4.1: TFX class hierarchy.

On the other hand, when a `CtLine` object is used, opening a line looks like this:

```
void CtDialDlg::Dial(LPCSTR pszPhoneNo)
{
    // Code removed for clarity...

    if( dlg.DoModal == IDOK )
    {
        // Open the line for an outgoing call
        if( m_line.Open(dlg.m_nLineID, this) == 0 )
        {
            // et cetera.
        }
    }
}
```

When the `Open` member function of `CtLine` is called, only information the object doesn't already have is needed: the line identifier on which to place the call and a pointer to an object that will receive telephony event notifications. All of the other parameters are maintained as class or object state or are set to reasonable defaults.

Each of the telephony objects is constructed in two stages to ensure proper initialization. The first stage is performed by the C++ constructor and initializes the object as empty. The second stage uses TAPI to create a handle for communication with an actual telephony device. For example, the `Open` member function of the `CtLine` is used to perform the same service as the `lineOpen` function, that is, to open a line for use.

CtLine

In the TFX, the `CtLine` object represents a TAPI `HLINE`. A line object really has only two uses. One, when a line is open, telephony events on that line can be handled by the application. Two, an open line is used to place and receive calls. Opening and closing the line is accomplished with the `Open` and `Close` member functions:

```
TRESULT
CtLine::Open(
    DWORD nLineID,
    CtLineSink* pSink = 0,
    DWORD dwPrivileges = LINECALLPRIVILEGE_OWNER,
```

Two-stage Construction

Two-stage construction is handy when an object's resources may not be available during the execution of its constructor. In MFC, for example, a CDialog-derived object may have many CWnd-derived objects that act as wrappers of the dialog's controls. These control objects will be constructed as part of the construction process of the CDialog container. However, until the dialog has received the WM_INITDIALOG message and passed it to the default message handler, the control objects can't properly initialize their own member data, that is, the HWND.

To solve this problem, MFC makes heavy use of two-stage construction. The control objects are created in the first stage during the CDialog container's construction. However, after the dialog has received the WM_INITDIALOG message, the second stage of the construction can happen via the Create or the Attach member function of the contained control objects. Breaking up construction into two stages enables an object to exist before all of its resources are available.

Two-stage construction is used in the TFX for the same reason that it's used in MFC, for example, a CtLine object can exist before the user has selected the line identifier. Once the line identifier is known and communication with the line device needs to be established, the Open member function of the CtLine is called to complete the construction process.

```
            DWORD dwMediaModes = LINEMEDIAMODE_INTERACTIVEVOICE);


   TRESULT
   CtLine::Close( )
```

Predictably, the Open member function uses the TAPI function lineOpen to open the line and to acquire the HLINE. If the call to lineOpen succeeds, the Open member function also calls the TAPI function lineSetStatus-Messages to request all device state change events.

CtCall

Calls are represented in the TFX with the CtCall class. A CtCall object is created on a specific line, that is, the CtCall constructor must be called with a pointer to a CtLine object. A CtCall can be constructed in two ways. In the first, the constructor without an HCALL parameter is used, in anticipation of making a new call via the MakeCall member function. In the second, when TAPI has detected a new call and has presented it to the application, the CtCall constructor that takes an HCALL is used. These two constructors look like this:

```
CtCall(CtLine* pLine);

CtCall(
    CtLine* pLine,
    HCALL hCall,
    CtCallSink* pInitialSink = 0);
```

Once the `CtCall` object has established its `HCALL`, the TAPI wrapper functions that `CtCall` provides can be used to manipulate the call. Following is a list of commonly used `CtCall` wrapper functions and the TAPI functions they wrap:

```
// lineAnswer
tfxasync⁴ TRESULT
CtCall::Answer(
    LPCSTR psUserUserInfo = 0,
    DWORD nSize = 0);

// lineDial
tfxasync TRESULT
CtCall::Dial(
    LPCSTR szDestAddress,
    DWORD dwCountryCode = 0);

// lineDrop (destructor calls as necessary)
tfxasync TRESULT
CtCall::Drop(
    LPCSTR psUserUserInfo = 0,
    DWORD nSize = 0);

// lineGenerateDigits
tfxasync TRESULT
CtCall::GenerateDigits(
    LPCSTR szDigits,
    DWORD nDuration = 0,
    DWORD nDigitMode = LINEDIGITMODE_DTMF);

// lineDeallocate (destructor calls as necessary)
```

---

[4] `tfxasync` is a precompiler symbol that expands to nothing. It is meant as documentation only.

```
TRESULT
CtCall::Deallocate();

// lineMakeCall
tfxasync TRESULT
CtCall::MakeCall(
    LPCSTR szDestAddress = 0,
    DWORD nCountryCode = 0,
    CtCallSink* pSink = 0);
```

Event Routing

Once TAPI is initialized and objects are constructed, telephony events can be processed. Each TAPI event is routed by a TFX callback function to the TFX object that is responsible for handling that message. The TFX callback function turns the event identifier—for example, `LINE_LINEDEVSTATE` or `LINE_CALLSTATE`—into a member function on the appropriate object, such as `CtLine::OnDevState` or `CtCall::OnCallState`. The telephony objects preprocess these events to update their internal states and pass them on to the application.

There needs to be a place to send telephony object events. So part of the second stage of construction is the setting of a target object for receiving telephony event notifications for the object being constructed. For example, by passing the `CtDialDlg` object's *this* pointer to the `CtLine` member function `Open`, the dialog is designated as the receiver of all of the line and address telephony events that happen on that line. Such an object is called an *event sink*. Every telephony object will handle the events it receives by calling the proper member function of the corresponding sink object.

Each telephony class has a corresponding sink class: `CtLineSink`, `CtPhoneSink`, and `CtCallSink`. The event sink classes are base classes that contain nothing but virtual member functions. By deriving from an event sink class, the object interested in an event must only override the implementation of the specific function it's interested in so as to receive the event. If the event sink doesn't want a specific event notification, it simply doesn't override the implementation provided by the event sink base class (which, by default, does nothing). Here's an example telephony event sink base class, `CtCallSink`:

```
class CtCallSink
{
public:
```

```
CtCallSink() {}
virtual ~CtCallSink() {}

// Sink events (placeholders for overriding only)
virtual void
OnCallInfo(CtCall* pCall, DWORD nCallInfo) {}

virtual void
OnCallState(CtCall* pCall, DWORD nCallState,
            DWORD dwParam2, DWORD nCallPrivilege) {}

virtual void
OnCallGatherDigits(CtCall* pCall, DWORD nGatherTerm) {}

virtual void
OnCallGenerate(CtCall* pCall, DWORD nGenerateTerm) {}

virtual void
OnCallMonitorDigits(CtCall* pCall, char cDigit,
                    DWORD nDigitMode) {}

virtual void
OnCallMonitorMedia(CtCall* pCall, DWORD nMediaMode) {}

virtual void
OnCallMonitorTone(CtCall* pCall, DWORD dwAppSpecific) {}

virtual void
OnCallReply(CtCall* pCall, TREQUEST nRequestID,
            TRESULT tr, DWORD nRequestType) {}
};
```

A sink object can receive notifications for a specific class of telephony object by deriving from the sink base class and passing a reference to itself to the second-stage constructor of the telephony object. Figure 4.2 shows how events are routed in the TFX. For example, following is the routing of the LINE_LINEDEVSTATE event from the TFX callback function to the CtLine object and finally to the sink:

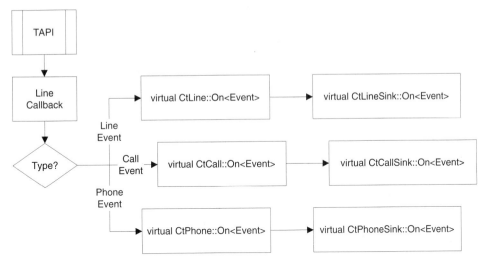

Figure 4.2: TFX event routing.

```
void CALLBACK
TfxLineCallback(
   DWORD     dwDevice,
   DWORD     nMsg,
   DWORD     dwInstance,
   DWORD     dwParam1,
   DWORD     dwParam2,
   DWORD     dwParam3)
{
   ... // code removed for clarity

   // Pull the CtLine* out of the dwInstance set
   // in CtLine::Open when calling lineOpen.
   CtLine*   pLine = (CtLine*)dwInstance;
   if( pLine )
   {
     // Send the event to the CtLine object.
     pLine->OnEvent(dwDevice, nMsg,
                    dwParam1, dwParam2, dwParam3);
   }
}

void CtLine::OnEvent(
```

```
   DWORD    dwDevice,
   DWORD    nMsg,
   DWORD    dwParam1,
   DWORD    dwParam2,
   DWORD    dwParam3)
{
  switch( nMsg )
  {
  ... // other event cases

  case LINE_LINEDEVSTATE:
    // Pass the parameters on to the specific
    // CtLine member function.
    OnDevState(dwParam1, dwParam2, dwParam3);
  break;
  }
}


void CtLine::OnDevState(
   DWORD    nDevState,
   DWORD    dwParam2,
   DWORD    dwParam3)
{
  for( int i = 0; i <= m_rgSinks.GetUpperBound(); i++ )
  {
    CtLineSink* pSink = (CtLineSink*)m_rgSinks[i];
    if( pSink )
    {
      // Route the event to each part of the
      // application interested in this event.
      pSink->OnLineDevState(this, nDevState,
                            dwParam2, dwParam3);
    }
  }
}
```

In the tDial sample, the CtDialDlg is interested in line and call telephony events. Therefore it must derive from the CtLineSink and CtCallSink sink object base classes, in addition to its primary base class CDialog. It also must handle the events in which it's interested:

```
class CtDialDlg : public CDialog,
                  public CtLineSink,
                  public CtCallSink
{
    ... // code removed for clarity

    // Handle CtLineSink event
    virtual void OnLineClose(CtLine* pLine);

    // Handle CtCallSink events
    virtual void OnCallState(CtCall* pCall,
                             DWORD nCallState,
                             DWORD dwParam2,
                             DWORD nCallPrivilege);
    virtual void OnCallReply(CtCall* pCall,
                             TRESULT nRequestID,
                             TREQUEST nResult,
                             DWORD nRequestType);
};
```

The call to the `CtLine` member function `Open` shown previously causes the line to be opened and the line events to be routed to the `CtDialDlg` object. The `Open` member function is the `CtLine` object's second-stage constructor and looks like this:

```
TRESULT
CtLine::Open(
    DWORD nLineID,
    CtLineSink* pInitialSink = 0,
    DWORD dwPrivileges = LINECALLPRIVILEGE_NONE,
    DWORD dwMediaModes = LINEMEDIAMODE_INTERACTIVEVOICE)
```

When placing a call, the `CtCall` object's `MakeCall` member function takes a pointer to a sink object that derives from `CtCallSink`. The `CtCall`'s second-stage constructor looks like this:

```
tfxasync TRESULT
CtCall::MakeCall(
    LPCSTR szDestAddress = 0,
```

Multiple Inheritance versus Message Maps

The TFX uses a different message-routing scheme than does MFC. MFC uses a table data structure called a Message Map that associates Windows messages with member functions to call. To support more than four billion (2^{32}) possible Windows messages, of which only a small fraction need to be handled by any one window, a Message Map is a wonderful invention. Using inheritance to handle these messages in a derived window class would exact a high toll[5] even though most of the messages would end up in DefWindowProc.

However, Message Maps are difficult to set up. This is why Microsoft provides the Class Wizard. It knows how to set up the Message Maps and makes them nearly effortless to use and maintain.

The TFX, however, has no Class Wizard. It doesn't need one because it uses inheritance instead of Message Maps. As a developer, it's your job to decide what class of message you'd like to handle, to derive from the appropriate sink object base, and to override the event member functions as needed. The multiple inheritance mechanism is used for type safety and convenience. And since there are a maximum of 23 total notifications, the TFX does not have the overhead concerns that MFC has.

If you think C++ multiple inheritance is scary and should be avoided, well, you're mostly right. When you're deriving from multiple base classes, each of which has its own data, there may be strangeness as to how many copies of the data there are. You may want to avoid this kind of multiple inheritance. On the other hand, since none of the TFX sink classes have member data, there is no ambiguity and no strangeness. TFX avoids the problems of multiple inheritance by using *inheritance of interface,* a technique made popular by both Microsoft's Component Object Model and Sun's Java.

```
        DWORD nCountryCode = 0,
        CtCallSink* pInitialSink = 0)
```

The function creates a new call, which it caches in an `HCALL` private member variable, and routes all events to the provided sink object.

Asynchronous Function Calls

In TAPI, the results of an asynchronous function call are provided in a `LINE_REPLY` event provided to the line callback function. To distinguish the type of each request, the TFX has defined a set of constants, one for each of the asynchro-

---

[5] A C++ virtual function table of four billion entries would take up 16MB of memory.

nous function wrappers it supports. When the wrapper function successfully starts an asynchronous operation, it puts the request identifier, the request type, and the object's *this* pointer into a TFX-managed map. For example, the implementation of the `CtCall` member function `Drop` uses the TFX-defined constant `CALL-REQUEST_DROP`:

```
TRESULT CtCall::Drop(
  LPCSTR  psUserUserInfo, // = 0
  DWORD   nSize)          // = 0
{
  ASSERT(m_hCall);
  TREQUEST    tr;
  tr = ::lineDrop(m_hCall, psUserUserInfo, nSize);
  if( TPENDING(tr) )
  {
    // Put new request on list of pending requests.
    m_pLine->AddRequest(tr, this, CALLREQUEST_DROP);
  }

  return tr;
}
```

When the request is completed, the `LINE_REPLY` event includes the request ID originally returned when the call was made. This request ID is used to look up the object that made the request and the type of request it was. The reply event is routed to an object of type `CtReplyTarget`. All telephony objects that make asynchronous requests derive from `CtReplyTarget` and implement the `On-Reply` member function to handle asynchronous replies. Following is the event-handling code that uses the `dwRequestID` to look up the appropriate request and route it to the appropriate `CtReplyTarget`:

```
void CtLine::OnEvent(
  DWORD   dwDevice,
  DWORD   nMsg,
  DWORD   dwParam1,
  DWORD   dwParam2,
  DWORD   dwParam3)
{
  switch( nMsg )
  {
  ... // other events
```

```
case LINE_REPLY:
{
  // If a reply target can be found for this request,
  // let the target handle the reply.
  CtReplyTarget*  pTarget = 0;
  DWORD           dwRequest;
  if( m_listRequests.RemoveRequest(dwParam1, &pTarget,
                                   &dwRequest) )
  {
    pTarget->OnReply(dwParam1, dwParam2, dwRequest);
  }
  // If a reply target can't be found for this request,
  // let the line handle it as an unhandled reply.
  // This allows app-specific reply handling for calls
  // made directly to TAPI via the handle.
  else
  {
    OnReply(dwParam1, dwParam2, LINEREQUEST_UNKNOWN);
  }
}
break;
}
```

Both the `CtLine` and the `CtCall` implementation of `OnReply` route the event to the interested event sinks. For example, the tDial sample uses two asynchronous functions, `CtCall::MakeCall` and `CtCall::Drop`, and handles the replies from both:

```
void
CtDialDlg::OnCallReply(
    CtCall* pCall,
    TREQUEST nRequestID,
    TRESULT nResult,
    DWORD nRequestType)
{
  switch( nRequestType )
  {
  case CALLREQUEST_MAKECALL:
    if( TSUCCEEDED(nResult) )
    {
      LogStatus("Call placed.\r\n");
    }
```

```
    else
    {
      VERIFY(TSUCCEEDED(m_line.Close()));
      LogStatus("Call cannot be placed.\r\n");
    }
  break;

  case CALLREQUEST_DROP:
    if( TSUCCEEDED(nResult) )
    {
      LogStatus("Call dropped.\r\n");
    }
    else
    {
      LogStatus("Call cannot be dropped.\r\n");
    }
  break;
  }

  UpdateStatus();
}
```

The list of pending requests is useful for providing user feedback as well as for routing events. To make it easier for an application to provide a user interface that accurately reflects currently available telephony operations, all telephony objects have two member functions to allow tracking of pending requests:

```
BOOL
IsRequestPending(
    TREQUEST nRequestID,
    DWORD* pnRequestType = 0) const;

BOOL
IsRequestTypePending(DWORD nRequestType) const;
```

The sample uses these functions to disable the Dial and Hang Up buttons in the event that a request is pending which makes these operations unavailable:

```
void CtDialDlg::UpdateStatus
{
    if( m_call.GetHandle )
    {
```

```
        m_btnDial.EnableWindow(FALSE);
        m_btnHangUp.EnableWindow(TRUE);
    }
    else if(
     m_call.IsRequestTypePending(CALLREQUEST_MAKECALL) ||
     m_call.IsRequestTypePending(CALLREQUEST_DROP) )
    {
        m_btnDial.EnableWindow(FALSE);
        m_btnHangUp.EnableWindow(FALSE);
    }
    else
    {
        m_btnDial.EnableWindow(TRUE);
        m_btnHangUp.EnableWindow(FALSE);
    }
}
```

Miscellany

The TFX has several other features that make it helpful. For example, the TFX provides the following macros to allow developers to think about success, failure, or pending results instead of zero, negative, or positive result codes:

```
#define TSUCCEEDED(tr)   (tr == 0)
#define TFAILED(tr)      (tr < 0)
#define TPENDING(tr)     (tr > 0)
```

For those cases in which the application is simply interested in success or failure, these macros allow the following usage:

```
// Open the line for an outgoing call.
if( TSUCCEEDED(m_line.Open(dlg.m_nLineID, this)) )
{
    // et cetera.
}
```

In addition, to distinguish telephony result codes and asynchronous request identifiers from a plain vanilla long, the TFX provides the following typedefs:

```
typedef LONG TRESULT;
typedef LONG TREQUEST;
```

The TFX uses these types in its prototypes to designate what kind of number is being passed. For example, the prototype of the `OnCallReply` event in the `CtCallSink` passes both a request identifier and the result of the request:

```
virtual void
CtCallSink::OnCallReply(
    CtCall* pCall,
    TREQUEST nRequestID,
    TRESULT tr,
    DWORD nRequestType);
```

The TAPI documentation is fairly subtle about which functions are synchronous and which are asynchronous. The TFX header files make this more clear by using the empty symbol `tfxasync`. This symbol has no meaning to the compiler, but it is handy when you need to know when a function is going to return. For example, the prototype for the `CtCall` member function `Drop` looks like this:

```
tfxasync TRESULT
CtCall::Drop(LPCSTR psUserUserInfo = 0, DWORD nSize = 0);
```

One other feature that the TFX provides is debugging output. When an error is returned from a TAPI function, the debug version of the TFX prints a string describing the error into the debug output window of the debugger. Also, when a spontaneous event or asynchronous reply is received, a string is output. The event codes and error messages are kept in a table of strings, but the description of a TAPI error is actually available with the `tapi32.dll` itself by using the `FormatMessage` function:

```
DWORD
FormatMessage(
    DWORD dwFlags,
    LPCVOID lpSource,
    DWORD dwMessageId,
    DWORD dwLanguageId,
    LPTSTR lpBuffer,
    DWORD nSize,
    va_list *Arguments)
```

The `FormatMessage` function can be used to translate any system error number into a description string. It also allows custom error messages to be kept in a DLL. The `tapi32.dll` keeps error messages for all of the line and phone errors, but the negative error numbers are not directly suitable for use with the `Format-Message` function. To convert a TAPI error code into a number for use with `FormatMessage`, `tapi.h` defines the `TAPIERROR_FORMATMESSAGE` macro:

```
#define TAPIERROR_FORMATMESSAGE( __ErrCode__ ) \
  ( ( ( __ErrCode__ ) > 0xFFFF0000 ) ? \
  ( ( __ErrCode__ ) & 0x0000FFFF ) : \
  ( ( ( __ErrCode__ ) & 0x10000000 ) ? \
  ( ( __ErrCode__ ) - 0x90000000 + 0xF000 ) : \
  ( ( __ErrCode__ ) - 0x80000000 + 0xE000 ) ) )
```

The TFX uses this macro with `FormatMessage` to turn any TAPI error code into a descriptive string:

```
// Get error from tapi32.dll
char    szTapiError[256] = "<unknown>";
FormatMessageA(FORMAT_MESSAGE_FROM_HMODULE,
               GetModuleHandle("tapi32.dll"),
               TAPIERROR_FORMATMESSAGE(tr),
               0,
               szTapiError,
               sizeof(szTapiError),
               0);
```

The debug strings make debugging the ebb and flow of your telephony application much easier. These messages can be seen in the debug version of your application when being run under the debugger. The release version of the TFX does not perform this operation.

Using the TFX

Using the TFX is simply a matter of including one or two header files, depending on the part of the TFX in which you're interested. These are given in Table 4.1.

The TFX is packaged as four static libraries—two for TAPI 1.4 (release and debug modes) and two for TAPI 2.0 (release and debug modes). See Table 4.2. The name of the library used by your application is determined for you by the

Table 4.1: Header files.

Functionality Desired	Header File to Include
CtLine, CtCall, and related classes.	TfxLine.h
CtPhone and related classes.	TfxPhone.h

Table 4.2: Library names.

TAPI_CURRENT_VERSION	_DEBUG	Library Name
0x00020000	Not #defined.	tfx20.lib
0x00020000	#defined.	tfx20d.lib
0x00010004	Not #defined.	tfx14.lib
0x00010004	#defined.	tfx14d.lib

combination of the TAPI_CURRENT_VERSION macro and the _DEBUG macro.

The proper library is included for you by either TfxLine.h or Tfx-Phone.h, so no additional libraries are needed on the link line on your project settings. Since I anticipate most users of the TFX to use MFC when building their telephony applications, I built TFX using some of the facilities of MFC.[6] All TFX samples in this book use MFC and include the necessary TFX header files in the stdafx.h file, for example:

```
// stdafx.h : include file for standard system include files,
// or project specific include files that are used frequently,
// but are changed infrequently
//

#define VC_EXTRALEAN // Exclude rarely-used stuff from Windows
                     // headers

#include <afxwin.h>        // MFC core and standard components
#include <afxext.h>        // MFC extensions
```

---

[6] At the time of this writing, MFC was the undisputed champion of application frameworks, so I took the liberty of depending on it. However, nothing that the TFX does is intrinsically tied to MFC and the TFX could easily be rebuilt without MFC.

```
#ifndef _AFX_NO_AFXCMN_SUPPORT
#include <afxcmn.h>          // MFC support for Windows 95
                            // Common Controls
#endif // _AFX_NO_AFXCMN_SUPPORT

#include <tfxline.h>        // TFX support for TAPI lines
#include <tphoneno.h>       // Support for phone numbers
```

If you also want to use the `CtPhoneNo` class, your application should include `tPhoneNo.h` (as shown in the previous code sample) and compile in `tPhone-No.cpp`, as it is not part of the TFX libraries.

Summary

The tDial sample from Chapter 3 was rewritten to make use of the TFX library. All of the low-level TAPI functions were removed in favor of the higher-level TFX functions and classes. In general, however, the application still flows in the same way. `TfxLineInitialize` is used where `lineInitialize` was used before. A `CtCountryList` object is used instead of the `LINECOUNTRYLIST` structure. The `MakeCall` member function replaces the call to the `lineMake-Call` global function. Events and request replies are routed to handlers automatically by using the `CtLineSink` and the `CtCallSink` objects instead of routing them via a `LineCallback` function. The application-generic code has been moved to the TFX, and the sample application is left to do its job with much less code.

You may have noticed that this chapter does not document every TFX function. For example, I didn't mention `CtPhone` and related classes. Instead, I defined the framework that TFX uses to perform its services. The architectural overview and the naming conventions are meant to give you insight into what the TFX is trying to do and how. For a full reference to TFX, see Appendix B.

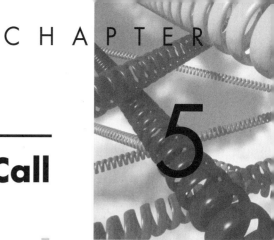

CHAPTER 5

Answering a Call

Valid Lines Opening

Privileges and Media Modes

Application Priority

Incoming Call Detection

Call Answering

Automated Voice Calls

Speakerphones

One ringy-dingy. . . .
Two ringy-dingy . . .
Lily Tomlin

Like making a call, answering a call involves a few TAPI functions and a few events. In this chapter, we'll build on the tDial sample by adding the capability to answer a phone call. The updated sample removes the About button from the main window to make room for the Answer button, as shown in Figure 5.1.

One popular feature of interactive voice applications is simulating a speakerphone. Another popular thing to do after answering a call is to play a greeting and record a message. This chapter discusses both features. It also presents about two-thirds of the tMonitor sample, as shown in Figure 5.2. The other one-third is presented in the next chapter.

Valid Lines Opening

In the sample in Chapter 4, tDial built a list of lines that allowed voice calls and opened the appropriate line only when the call was about to be placed. However, to detect an incoming call, the updated tDial must open all of the valid lines when the application starts. This is done in a helper function of `CtDialDlg`, `Open-ValidLines`, which is called when the dialog is first initialized:

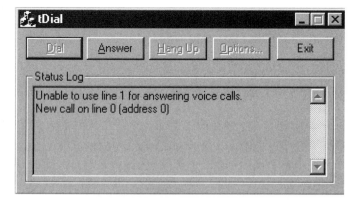

Figure 5.1: Updated tDial sample.

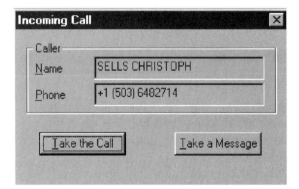

Figure 5.2: Incoming Call dialog of the tMonitor sample.

```
void CtDialDlg::OpenValidLines()
{
    ASSERT(m_rgbValidLines == 0);

    // Get and open valid lines.
    DWORD   nLines = ::TfxGetNumLines();
    DWORD   nOpenedLines = 0;

    if( (m_rgbValidLines = new BOOL[nLines]) &&
        (m_rgpLines = new CtLine*[nLines]) )
    {
        // Assume we can't use any line.
        ZeroMemory(m_rgbValidLines,
                   nLines * sizeof(BOOL));
        ZeroMemory(m_rgpLines,
                   nLines * sizeof(CtLine*));

        for( DWORD nLineID = 0;
             nLineID < nLines;
             nLineID++ )
        {
            CtLineDevCaps    ldc;
            if( TSUCCEEDED(ldc.GetDevCaps(nLineID)) &&
    (ldc.GetBearerModes() & LINEBEARERMODE_VOICE) &&
    (ldc.GetMediaModes() & LINEMEDIAMODE_INTERACTIVEVOICE) &&
    (ldc.GetLineFeatures() & LINEFEATURE_MAKECALL) )
                {
```

```
                if( (m_rgpLines[nLineID] = new CtLine) &&
        TSUCCEEDED(m_rgpLines[nLineID]->Open(nLineID, this,
                    LINECALLPRIVILEGE_OWNER,
                    LINEMEDIAMODE_INTERACTIVEVOICE |
                    LINEMEDIAMODE_UNKNOWN)) )
            {
                m_rgbValidLines[nLineID] = TRUE;
                nOpenedLines++;
            }
            else
            {
                delete m_rgpLines[nLineID];
                m_rgpLines[nLineID] = 0;
                LogStatus("Unable to use line %d "
                        "for answering voice "
                        "calls.\r\n",
                        nLineID);
            }
        }
        else
        {
            LogStatus("Line %d doesn't support "
                    "voice calls.\r\n", nLineID);
        }
    }
}

if( !nOpenedLines )
{
    delete[] m_rgbValidLines; m_rgbValidLines = 0;
    delete[] m_rgpLines; m_rgpLines = 0;

    LogStatus("Unabled to open any lines.\r\n");
}
}
```

[handwritten annotation:] AUTOMATED VOICE

As in the previous sample, tDial needs an array of BOOLs to know which lines are valid for voice calls.[1] The m_rgbValidLines variable is dynamically allo-

---

[1] This code assumes that outgoing calls can be made only on lines that supports incoming voice calls. This is not a necessary restriction, but it does make the code considerably simpler.

cated based on the number of lines available and set based on each line's device capabilities. When the Dial button is clicked to tell it which lines are valid for making a call, this array is used as input for the Dialing Options dialog.

To track lines, tDial keeps a dynamic array of `CtLine` pointers, one for each potentially open line. A non-`NULL` pointer in this array means that the line has been successfully opened for the purpose of answering interactive voice calls and calls of unknown media types. The lines that have been opened are the ones on which incoming call notifications will be received.

Privileges and Media Modes

The call to the `lineOpen` function (via the `Open` member function of `CtLine`) includes two parameters that I haven't talked much about: `dwPrivileges` and `dwMediaModes`. These values are important only when opening a line for incoming call requests. When tDial was only making calls, `LINECALL-PRIVILEGE_NONE` and `LINEMEDIAMODE_INTERACTIVEVOICE` were fine choices. Now that tDial needs to be notified of incoming calls, these values are going to have to change. Before these values make sense, however, I have to talk about call owners and monitors.

Every call must have at least one *owner*. An owner is an application that can affect the state of a call, for example, by dropping the call. Owners receive notifications for all events associated with the call. An application is an owner of a call when it places a call. Optionally, an application can be the owner of an incoming call on a line for which it sets the proper privileges.

In addition, each call can have one or more *monitors*. A monitor cannot affect the state of a call, but it can get information about the call and will receive notifications for all events associated with the call.

An owner or a monitor can request a change of its call ownership via the `lineSetCallPrivilege` function:

```
LONG
lineSetCallPrivilege(
    HCALL hCall,
    DWORD dwCallPrivilege);
```

When a line is opened, the `dwPrivilege` parameter allows an application to determine what kind of ownership it would like for incoming calls on that line. Table 5.1 shows the available call privileges and their meanings. The `dwMedia-Modes` parameter of the `lineOpen` function allows the application to handle

Table 5.1: TAPI Call Privileges.	
dwPrivilege	*Application Privileges*
`LINECALLPRIVILEGE_NONE`	The application will receive notifications only for calls it makes.
`LINECALLPRIVILEGE_MONITOR`	The application will be notified of incoming and outgoing call events but will not be the owner for the calls it doesn't make.
`LINECALLPRIVILEGE_OWNER`	Just like MONITOR, but the application will be given ownership of any incoming call that has a media type matching dwMediaMode.
`LINECALLPRIVILEGE_MONITOR` | `LINECALLPRIVILEGE_OWNER`	Just like OWNER, but the application will still receive notifications for calls it doesn't own, that is, calls make by other applications on the same system.

only incoming calls of a specific type, for example, `LINEMEDIAMODE_INTER-ACTIVEVOICE`. For digital telephony networks like ISDN, this is a wonderful option. The caller can determine the media type of the call and when it reaches the callee, the Data channel will contain the media type of the call. The TSP handling the ISDN line will detect this media mode and notify TAPI of a new call with a specific media mode, and TAPI will provide notifications only to applications interested in that media mode. In this way, calls can be routed automatically by TAPI.

Unfortunately, most of us use POTS, a telephony network that doesn't know the media mode of the call before it has been answered. When an incoming call is detected by the TSP and it doesn't know the media mode, it notifies TAPI using the `LINEMEDIAMODE_UNKNOWN` bit. In this case, TAPI will route the call to the running application that is interested in accepting calls of unknown media mode. The media modes that an application can handle are listed in Chapter 1.

Application Priority

If there is more than one running application interested in taking ownership of an incoming call of either a specific known media mode or the unknown media mode, TAPI hands the call to the application that has the highest priority. This priority is set using the `lineSetAppPriority` function:

```
LONG
lineSetAppPriority(
     LPCSTR              lpszAppFilename,
     DWORD               dwMediaMode,        // A single bit
     LPLINEEXTENSIONID   lpExtensionID,
     DWORD               dwRequestMode,
     LPCSTR              lpszExtensionName,
     DWORD               dwPriority)         // 0 or 1
```

For example, to set an application as the highest priority to accept calls of unknown media mode, you would write code like this:

```
Void SetTopUnknownPriority()
{
     char szAppPath[MAX_PATH+1];
     GetModuleFileName(0, szAppPath, MAX_PATH);

#if (TAPI_CURRENT_VERSION < 0x00020000)
     // Get the application's short filename.
     // (TAPI 1.4 only understands short filenames.)
     GetShortPathName(szAppPath, szAppPath, MAX_PATH);
#endif

     lineSetAppPriority(szAppPath,
                        LINEMEDIAMODE_UNKNOWN,
                        0, 0, 0,
                        1); // Set as the highest priority.
}
```

If an application is interested in its current priority mode for a given media mode, it can call lineGetAppPriority:

```
LONG
lineGetAppPriority(
     LPCSTR              lpszAppFilename,
     DWORD               dwMediaMode,
     LPLINEEXTENSIONID   lpExtensionID,
     DWORD               dwRequestMode,
     LPVARSTRING         lpExtensionName,
     LPDWORD             lpdwPriority)
```

The TFX has a pair of global helper functions to make these calls easier:

```
TRESULT
TfxGetAppPriority(
    DWORD nMediaMode,
    LPDWORD pnPriority,
    LPLINEEXTENSIONID const pExtID = 0,
    DWORD nRequestMode = LINEREQUESTMODE_MAKECALL,
    LPVARSTRING pvsExtName = 0);

TRESULT
TfxSetAppPriority(
    DWORD nMediaMode,
    DWORD nPriority,
    LPLINEEXTENSIONID const pExtID = 0,
    DWORD nRequestMode = LINEREQUESTMODE_MAKECALL,
    LPCSTR pszExtName = 0);
```

Using the TFX and setting an application at the highest priority to accept calls of unknown media mode, you would have a call like this:

```
Void SetTopUnknownPriority()
{
    TfxSetAppPriority(LINEMEDIAMODE_UNKNOWN, 1);
}
```

Setting an application's priority is also used to notify TAPI that the application will be handling Assisted Telephony requests. This is discussed in Chapter 6.

Incoming Call Detection

Once a line has been opened, new calls will be presented to the application via the LINE_APPNEWCALL message:

```
LINE_APPNEWCALL
dwDevice = (DWORD) hLine;
dwCallbackInstance = (DWORD) dwInstanceData;
dwParam1 = (DWORD) dwAddressID;
```

```
dwParam2 = (DWORD) hCall;
dwParam3 = (DWORD) dwPrivilege;
```

This message allows the monitor to add another entry to the list of calls it is monitoring. Unfortunately, the `LINE_APPNEWCALL` message does not exist under TAPI 1.*x*. Instead, an application is notified via a `LINE_CALLSTATE` event that has a call handle that the application hasn't seen before. To detect a new call, a TAPI 1.*x* application must check the call handle on each `LINE_CALLSTATE` event against a list of calls it already knows about. Applications that expect to run under both TAPI 2.0 and TAPI 1.*x* may want to detect a new call and simulate a `LINE_APPNEWCALL` event. This makes the code path consistent for both platforms.

The TFX unifies the notification of new calls for both TAPI 1.*x* and TAPI 2.0 applications. When a `LINE_APPNEWCALL` event is sent *or* a `LINE_CALL` state event is sent with a new call handle, the TFX provides notification to the application via the `CtLineSink` member function `OnLineNewCall`:

```
void
CtLineSink::OnLineNewCall(
    CtLine* pLine,
    HCALL   hCall,
    DWORD   nAddressID,
    DWORD   nCallPrivilege)
```

The tDial sample handles this notification by creating a `CtCall` object to hold the `HCALL` and updates the UI so that the Answer button is enabled:

```
void CtDialDlg::OnLineNewCall(
    CtLine* pLine,
    HCALL   hCall,
    DWORD   nAddressID,
    DWORD   nCallPrivilege)
{
    LogStatus("New call on line %d (address %d)\r\n",
            pLine->GetDeviceID(), nAddressID);

    // If we're not already handling a call,
    if( !m_pCall )
    {
        // we've got a new call
        m_pCall = new CtCall(pLine, hCall, this);
```

```
        // Check to see if call needs to be answered.
        m_bCallUnanswered = FALSE;
        if( m_pCall )
        {
            CtCallStatus    cs;
            if( TSUCCEEDED(cs.GetCallStatus(m_pCall)) )
            {
                if( cs.GetCallFeatures() &
                        LINECALLFEATURE_ANSWER )
                {
                    m_bCallUnanswered = TRUE;
                }
            }
        }

        UpdateStatus();
    }
}
```

It's not safe for an application to just assume that every new call it gets is an inbound call. For example, a call made from another application on the same machine will also register as a new call in every application that is also monitoring calls. So, to make sure that the call is answered only if it needs to be, the tDial sample maintains the m_bCallUnanswered flag. This flag is set by using the lineGetCallStatus function to fill in a LINECALLSTATUS structure:

```
LONG
lineGetCallStatus(
    HCALL               hCall,
    LPLINECALLSTATUS    lpCallStatus);

typedef struct linecallstatus_tag
{
    DWORD       dwTotalSize;
    DWORD       dwNeededSize;
    DWORD       dwUsedSize;
    DWORD       dwCallState;
    DWORD       dwCallStateMode;
    DWORD       dwCallPrivilege;
    DWORD       dwCallFeatures;
    DWORD       dwDevSpecificSize;
```

```
    DWORD          dwDevSpecificOffset;

#if (TAPI_CURRENT_VERSION >= 0x00020000)
    DWORD          dwCallFeatures2; // TAPI v2.0
#if WIN32
    SYSTEMTIME  tStateEntryTime; // TAPI v2.0
#else
    WORD           tStateEntryTime[8]; // TAPI v2.0
#endif
#endif
} LINECALLSTATUS, FAR *LPLINECALLSTATUS;
```

The LINECALLSTATUS structure is another TAPI VLS meant for reporting the current status of the call. Specifically, the tDial sample uses the dwCall-Features flags to determine if the LINECALLFEATURE_ANSWER bit is currently set. If it's not, this call cannot be answered, so we shouldn't light up the Answer button. As a convenience, the TFX wraps the LINECALLSTATUS structure in the CtCallStatus class, which is what the tDial sample uses.

The message that notifies the application of a new call (either LINE_APP-NEWCALL or the first LINE_CALLSTATE) will inform the application if it is the owner of the call. The dwParam3 parameter will be LINECALLPRIVI-LEGE_OWNER or LINECALLPRIVILEGE_MONITOR, depending on whether the application is the owner. The owner of the new call should check the LINE-ADDRCAPFLAGS_ACCEPTTOALERT bit and call lineAccept if it is set; otherwise, the call will not ring. This is important for certain ISDN lines.

```
LONG
lineAccept(
    HCALL   hCall,
    LPCSTR  lpsUserUserInfo,
    DWORD   dwSize)
```

The user-user information is also for ISDN lines and allows the callee to send data back to the caller at call acceptance time or call answer time.

The CtCall object wraps the lineAccept function in the Accept member function:

```
tfxasync TRESULT
CtCall::Accept(
    LPCSTR  psUserUserInfo = 0,
    DWORD   nSize = 0)
```

Because the `lineAccept` call is asynchronous, success or failure will be indicated via the `LINE_REPLY` event. The TFX will map this to the `OnCall-Reply` member function of `CtCallSink` and pass in an nRequestType of `CALLREQUEST_ACCEPT`.

Call Answering

Once a new call is offered to the application, and the application is the owner of the call, it can be answered at any time (assuming the call needs to be answered at all). To answer the call, the owner uses the `lineAnswer` function:

```
LONG
lineAnswer(
    HCALL  hCall,
    LPCSTR lpsUserUserInfo,
    DWORD  dwSize)
```

The `CtCall` object wraps this call with the `Answer` member function:

```
tfxasync TRESULT
CtCall::Answer(
    LPCSTR  psUserUserInfo = 0,
    DWORD   nSize = 0)
```

Because the `lineAnswer` call is asynchronous, success or failure will be indicated via the `LINE_REPLY` event. The TFX will map this to the `OnCall-Reply` member function of `CtCallSink` and pass in an nRequestType of `CALLREQUEST_ANSWER`. Answering the call establishes a physical connection between the caller and the callee over which data can be sent and telephony events can happen. The tDial sample answers a call when the user presses the Answer button.

```
void CtDialDlg::OnAnswer()
{
    ASSERT(m_pCall);

    // Can't answer a call we've already answered.
    ASSERT(m_bCallUnanswered);
```

```
    m_bCallUnanswered = FALSE;
    if( TPENDING(m_pCall->Answer()) )
    {
        LogStatus("Answering call...\r\n");
    }
    else
    {
        LogStatus("Can't answer call.\r\n");
    }

    UpdateStatus();
}
```

If an application does not wish to answer the call, it must deallocate the call handle allocated for it by TAPI by using the `lineDeallocateCall` function (described in Chapter 3). If the application is not the sole owner of the call, that is, the call privilege is not `LINECALLPRIVILEGE_OWNER` when the call is offered to the application, it can deallocate the call immediately. However, if the application is the sole owner of the call (and running under TAPI 1.4 or less), it must wait for the call to go idle—as indicated via the `LINECALLSTATE_IDLE` event—before it can deallocate the call. In the event that the user of the tDial sample never clicks the Answer button, the call will eventually go idle and the `CtCall` object will be destroyed. The `CtCall` destructor in turn calls `lineDeallocateCall`.

```
void CtDialDlg::OnCallState(
    CtCall*   pCall,
    DWORD     nCallState,
    DWORD     dwParam2,
    DWORD     nCallPrivilege)
{
    // (some code removed for clarity)

    switch( nCallState )
    {
    case LINECALLSTATE_DISCONNECTED:
        OnHangUp();
    break;

    case LINECALLSTATE_IDLE:
        delete m_pCall; m_pCall = 0;
    break;
```

```
    }

    UpdateStatus();
}
```

The TFX provides support for an application that ignores a call completely. This is done via its handling of the LINECALLSTATE_OFFERING event. If the application fails to create a CtCall object to wrap the new HCALL, the TFX will build its own CtCall and put it into a list of ignored calls. When the call finally goes idle, the CtCall object will be removed from the list and destroyed.

Automated Voice Calls

One benefit of computer-telephony integration is that a computer can answer the phone in the event that a human is unavailable or unwilling to do so. TAPI supports this with the LINEMEDIAMODE_AUTOMATEDVOICE media mode. This is the media mode that indicates that the application is willing to answer the phone unless the human gets to it first. Once an automated voice application answers the phone, the application is likely to conduct a conversation with the caller (albeit a one-sided conversation) and record any responses, transferred either as audio or touch-tones. Once the conversation is complete, the call is disconnected and both the human and the computer go about their normal lives.

Toll-saver Support

The automated voice application should wait for a minimum number of rings before answering the call. This allows the caller to detect that a person is not likely to be answering the call and hang up before the computer answers, thereby saving long distance changes. If the automated application waits in this manner, it can claim to support the *toll-saver* feature, a must for the marketing department.[2]

To determine the minimum number of rings, TAPI maintains a machine global variable of all applications interested in supporting the toll-saver feature. This is done via the functions lineGetNumRings and lineSetNumRings:

---

[2] Marketers don't tend to have a problem with the moral implications of using the phone company's expensive telephony equipment to convey information, that is, no one is home, without actually paying for it. Unless, of course, they're marketing the expensive phone equipment.

```
LONG
lineGetNumRings(
     HLINE   hLine,
     DWORD   dwAddressID,
     LPDWORD lpdwNumRings)

LONG
lineSetNumRings(
     HLINE hLine,
     DWORD dwAddressID,
     DWORD dwNumRings)
```

The `CtLine` object wraps these calls with the `GetNumRings` and `SetNum-Rings` member functions:

```
TRESULT
GetNumRings(
     DWORD nAddressID,
     DWORD* pnRings);

TRESULT
SetNumRings(
     DWORD nAddressID,
     DWORD nRings);
```

Every automated application, when it starts, will use `lineSetNumRings` to set the minimum number of rings to occur before it will answer (based on user settings). Then, when a new call is offered, the automated application will call `lineGet-NumRings` to obtain that number. An application can detect a ring on an incoming call via the `LINE_LINEDEVSTATELINEDEVSTATE_RINGING` event.

Playing and Recording Audio

After the call is answered, the computer usually commences a simulation of human conversation. For the computer to simulate a human, it must be able to speak and to be spoken to. This is accomplished by playing and recording audio data.[3]

---

[3] The Microsoft Speech API is useful for generating audio data from text data (text-to-speech) and for generating text data from audio data (speech recognition). See the Microsoft SDK documentation for more information.

TAPI provides no direct support for data management of any kind, including audio data. Instead of including functions for sending and retrieving data of all kinds— for example, data, fax, and voice—TAPI supports only call management. Once a call has been established, the application must use another API to manage data transfer. To expose the services of a telephony object—a line, call, or phone—for use with another Win32 API, TAPI defines the concept of a *device class*. Recall from Chapter 1 that a device class is a description of a device that provides access to a specific type of media. The device class name is used to identify the desired device class. A device class name allows an application to obtain a service that is associated with a telephony object but is outside the scope of TAPI itself. The TSP provides the mapping between the telephony object and a handle for use with another API. A client can discover this mapping with the `lineGetID` function:

```
LONG
lineGetID(
    HLINE           hLine,
    DWORD           dwAddressID,
    HCALL           hCall,
    DWORD           dwSelect,
    LPVARSTRING     lpDeviceID,
    LPCSTR          lpszDeviceClass);
```

The `lineGetID` function is one of a number of polymorphic functions in TAPI. It takes an `HLINE`, an `HLINE` and a `dwAddressID`, *or* an `HCALL` based on the value of `dwSelect`. The `dwSelect` parameter can be `LINECALL-SELECT_LINE`, `LINECALLSELECT_ADDRESS`, or `LINECALLSELECT_CALL`, depending on whether you'd like the device ID for the line, address, or call, respectively. This allows a TSP to provide different handles for different devices. Based on the `lpszDeviceClass` string (as described in Chapter 1), the TSP will fill in the `VARSTRING` pointed to by the `lpDeviceID` parameter:

```
typedef struct varstring_tag
{
    DWORD       dwTotalSize;
    DWORD       dwNeededSize;
    DWORD       dwUsedSize;
    DWORD       dwStringFormat;
    DWORD       dwStringSize;
    DWORD       dwStringOffset;

} VARSTRING, FAR *LPVARSTRING;
```

Notice that the `VARSTRING` is another TAPI variable-length structure. Because of this, you should allocate enough memory for the structure required by the device class you're using. The data return from `lineGetID` will be the unique identifier for use with the data management API. Each device class has its own requirements, which are listed in Appendix A.

CtWave

The API needed to send and receive audio data under Windows is the Win32 Multimedia API. This API provides all kinds of fancy functions for manipulating audio data in the Windows wave file format.[4] To hide the messy details, the sample uses the `CtWave` class, a class I built for the simple handling of wave data. The `CtWave` class knows how to load wave data from files and resources, play loaded wave data, record wave data, and save recorded wave data to files. It can do all this using any low-level wave device ID. Here is the declaration of the `CtWave` class:

```
class CtWave : private InvisibleWindowSink
{
public:
    CtWave(CtWaveSink* pSink = 0);
    ~CtWave();

    // Load from a resource
    bool    Load(HINSTANCE hinst, UINT nID);
    bool    Load(HINSTANCE hinst, LPCTSTR pszID);

    // Load and save to/from a file
    bool    Load(LPCSTR pszFileName);
    bool    Save(LPCSTR pszFileName);

    // Sends OnWaveOutXxx() to sink as progress
    bool    Play(UINT nWaveOut, bool bLoop = false);

    // Sends OnWaveInXxx() to sink as progress
    bool    Record(UINT nWaveIn, UINT nSecs);

    bool    Stop();
```

---

[4] A description of the API itself is beyond the scope of this book, but it is thoroughly described in Tim Kientzle's *A Programmer's Guide to Sound* from Addison-Wesley.

```
bool    Close();

...  // implementation removed for clarity
};
```

Both the `Play` and the `Record` member functions are asynchronous, meaning they start the process but return immediately. Progress is sent to an optional sink object, that is, the holder of a `CtWave` object, that implements the `CtWave-Sink` interface:

```
class CtWaveSink
{
public:
    // WaveOut events (playing)
    virtual void OnWaveOutOpen() {}
    virtual void OnWaveOutDone() {}
    virtual void OnWaveOutClose() {}

    // WaveIn events (recording)
    virtual void OnWaveInOpen() {}
    virtual void OnWaveInData() {}
    virtual void OnWaveInClose() {}
};
```

When using `CtWave` with TAPI, the `CtWave` object needs a wave device ID obtained using `lineGetID`. The device classes exposed by the TSP are different, based on the direction in which the wave data is being transferred. The `wave/out` device class is for playing wave data, and the `wave/in` device class is for recording wave data. A successful return from `lineGetID` indicates that the wave device ID is held in a `DWORD` located at `dwStringOffset` in the `VARSTRING` structure. Once the wave device ID is obtained, the application is free to play or record the audio data on the call at any time.

However, not all (or even most) current telephony equipment can play or record audio data. On the low end, modems with the word "voice" in their name typically can, if the right drivers are present on the system. Having the right drivers means either having a TSP provided by the manufacturer or having the proper configuration files for the Unimodem/V TSP from Microsoft. Unimodem/V is supported only under either Windows 9x or Windows NT 5.0 or better. If the drivers are not available or the configuration file has not been installed or the planets are not all properly aligned, `lineGetID` for the wave device classes will fail. This means there will be no wave input or output on the call. The best course of action for the automated voice application in this case is to hang up and pretend the whole thing never happened.

Gathering Digits

Another mode of data input when a human is conversing with a computer is touch-tones. Touch-tones[5] are the noises generated when you press one of the 10 digit keys or the star or pound key on your phone. These tones have been designed by Bell Laboratory engineers to be easy for computers to detect, even across poor-quality lines. Your telephony equipment, too, can detect these tones, if it is up to the task (even most modems can do it). TAPI provides two functions for starting the digit-gathering process on a call—`lineMonitorDigits` and `lineGatherDigits`:

```
LONG
lineMonitorDigits(
    HCALL               hCall,
    DWORD               dwDigitModes);

LONG
lineGatherDigits(
    HCALL               hCall,
    DWORD               dwDigitModes,
    LPSTR               lpsDigits,
    DWORD               dwNumDigits,
    LPCSTR              lpszTerminationDigits,
    DWORD               dwFirstDigitTimeout,
    DWORD               dwInterDigitTimeout);
```

The `lineMonitorDigits` function is the simpler of the two. Calling this function tells the TSP to notify the application when a touch-tone is detected.[6] This notification happens via the `LINE_MONITORDIGITS` event:

---

[5] Dual-Tone Multi-Frequency (DTMF) is the technical term for touch-tones.
[6] Actually, `lineMonitorDigits` and `lineGatherDigits` both allow a `dwDigitMode` value of `LINEDIGITMODE_PULSE` as well as `LINEDIGITMODE_DTMF`. However, recognizing pulse tones requires much more complicated, more expensive, and therefore rarer equipment than does recognizing DTMF tones. Isn't it ironic that the FCC still allows phone companies to charge customers extra for touch-tone support on their phones when it would actually cost the companies more to detect pulse phones?

```
LINE_MONITORDIGITS
dwDevice = (DWORD) hCall;
dwCallbackInstance = (DWORD) hCallback;
dwParam1 = (DWORD) Digit; // LOBYTE(Digit) is touch tone
dwParam2 = (DWORD) DigitMode;
dwParam3 = (DWORD) 0;
```

If only one digit is required, this is a straightforward technique to use. However, using `lineMonitorDigits` quickly becomes complicated when gathering a variable number of digits that is terminated with a specific touch-tone and when handling initial digit and interdigit timeouts. For this kind of functionality, the telephony application would be implementing a state machine, whereby each digit has to be timed and checked.

On the other hand, the `lineGatherDigits` function was designed to perform just this kind of digit-gathering operation. To handle more complicated requirements, the function takes a string of digits to terminate the gathering process as well as millisecond delays for the initial digit timeout and interdigit timeouts. Calling `lineGatherDigits` tells the TSP to gather `dwNumDigits` touch-tones and store them in the `lpsDigits` string. Since `lineGather-Digits` is asynchronous, the buffer referenced by the `lpsDigits` string must stay around until after the digit-gathering process has terminated, as indicated by the `LINE_GATHERDIGITS` event:

```
LINE_GATHERDIGITS
dwDevice = (DWORD) hCall;
dwCallbackInstance = (DWORD) hCallback;
dwParam1 = (DWORD) GatherTermination;
dwParam2 = (DWORD) 0;dwParam3 = (DWORD) 0;
```

The `LINE_GATHERDIGITS` event has several subevents, based on the condition under which the digit-gathering process has terminated. These are given in Table 5.2. The number of termination conditions is what makes `lineGather-Digits` so flexible. With a single call, an application can indicate the many parameters necessary to perform touch-tone input. For example, to obtain a variable-length login ID of up to four digits for a voicemail application, the `lineGatherDigits` function could be used like this:

```
TRESULT GetLoginID(HCALL hcall, LPSTR pszLoginID)
{
  return lineGatherDigits(
```

Table 5.2: `LINE_GATHERDIGITS` subevents.

`LINE_GATHERDIGITS dwParam1`	Termination Condition
LINEGATHERTERM_BUFFERFULL	dwNumDigits have been gathered and are available in the lpsDigit buffer.
LINEGATHERTERM_TERMDIGIT	One of the digits in the termination string has been encountered.
LINEGATHERTERM_FIRSTTIMEOUT	The number of milliseconds indicated in dwFirstDigitTimeout has elapsed with no user input.
LINEGATHERTERM_INTERTIMEOUT	The number of milliseconds indicated in dwInterDigitTimeout has elapsed between digit entries with no user input.
LINEGATHERTERM_CANCEL	The digit-gathering process was canceled by a call to lineGatherDigits with an lpsDigit value of NULL.

```
            hcall, // Currently open call handle
            LINEDIGITMODE_DTMF, // DTMF tones
            pszLoginID, // Login ID buffer
            5, // Login ID + '#'
            "#", // Terminate on '#'
            5000, // Wait 5 seconds for initial digit.
            3000); // Wait 3 seconds between digits.
    }
```

Unfortunately, because of its complexity, few TSPs support `lineGather-Digits`, although many support `lineMonitorDigits`. To provide the widest support of TSPs, it currently is best to use only `lineMonitorDigits`. The sample uses `lineMonitorDigits` to allow the user to enter a touch-tone to terminate the recording of a message. This is a much simpler job and is representative of what `lineMonitorDigits` was designed to do.

The TFX wraps both `lineMonitorDigits` and `lineGatherDigits` in `CtCall` member functions:

```
    TRESULT
    MonitorDigits(
       DWORD dwDigitModes = LINEDIGITMODE_DTMF)

    TRESULT
```

```
GatherDigits(
  LPSTR pszDigits,
  DWORD nDigits,
  LPCSTR pszTerminationDigits = 0,
  DWORD nFirstDigitTimeout = 5000,
  DWORD nInterDigitTimeout = 5000,
  DWORD nDigitMode = LINEDIGITMODE_DTMF);
```

The tMonitor Sample

The tMonitor sample is actually three samples in one. It's an answering machine, a call monitoring application, and a speakerphone. Its call monitoring is discussed in Chapter 6. The tMonitor application is shown in Figure 5.3. Because tMonitor acts as an answering machine, it opens each line in both automated voice and unknown media modes. It sets the privilege to owner to be allowed to own incoming calls. (tMonitor also sets the privilege to LINECALLPRIVILEGE_MONITOR to be notified of events that happen on calls it does not own. This is discussed in Chapter 6.)

To handle toll-saver settings, tMonitor provides the Call Screen Settings dialog box, shown in Figure 5.4. This dialog manages the user settings for the number of rings to wait before answering an incoming call. This number is used to call the SetNumRings member function of CtMonitorView that sets the number of rings on every line:

```
void CtMonitorView::SetNumRings(DWORD nRings)
{
  if( m_rgLines )
  {
```

Figure 5.3: The tMonitor sample.

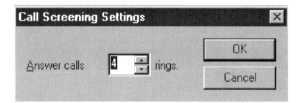

Figure 5.4: Call Screening Settings dialog.

```
for( DWORD nLineID = 0;
     nLineID < ::TfxGetNumLines();
     nLineID++ )
{
  if( m_rgLines[nLineID].GetHandle() )
  {
    CtLineDevCaps    ldc;
    if( TSUCCEEDED(ldc.GetDevCaps(nLineID)) )
    {
      for( DWORD nAddressID = 0;
           nAddressID < ldc.GetNumAddresses();
           nAddressID++ )
      {
        m_rgLines[nLineID].SetNumRings(nAddressID,
                                       nRings);
      }
    }
  }
}
```

Once an incoming call is detected, a new call record is created. This call record keeps track of things like the `CtCall` object that represents the call, how many rings have been detected, the state the call is in, and the maximum number of rings to wait before answering. The maximum number of rings is obtained from TAPI when the call is detected using `lineGetNumRings` (via the `CtLine` member function `GetNumRings`).

After the call record has been created, a dialog is presented to the user, as shown in Figure 5.5. This dialog shows who is calling if Caller ID information is available. At this point, the user can decide to take the call, let the application

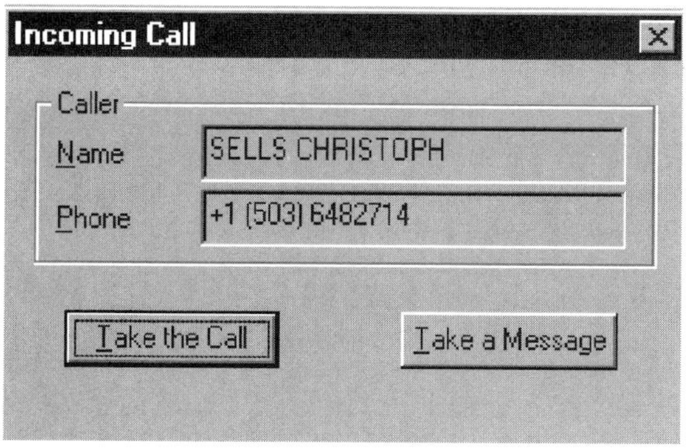

Figure 5.5: Incoming Call dialog.

take a message immediately, or ignore the call and let the application take a message after the number of rings indicated by `lineGetNumRings` occurs. If the application is to take a message, this is where the answering machine capabilities take over. The call is answered using the `CtCall` member function Answer:

```
// User has pressed the Take a Message button
// or the maximum number of rings has happened.
void CIncomingCallDlg::OnTakeMessage()
{
    m_todo = todoTakeMessage;
    GetDlgItem(IDC_TAKE_CALL)->ShowWindow(SW_HIDE);
    GetDlgItem(IDC_TAKE_MESSAGE)->ShowWindow(SW_HIDE);
    GetDlgItem(IDC_TAKING_MESSAGE)->ShowWindow(SW_SHOW);

    // Answer the call and wait for
    // OnCallState(LINECALLSTATE_CONNECTED).
    Answer();
}

void CIncomingCallDlg::Answer()
{
    if( TFAILED(m_pCall->Answer()) )
    {
        AfxMessageBox(IDS_CANT_ANSWER_CALL);
    }
}
```

When the call has been connected, the device is checked for a wave/out device class by using the `CtDeviceID` member function `GetID`. If the call supports the `wave/out` device class, you'll be able to play the greeting. The greeting is a wave file bundled with the application as a resource. The resource is loaded using the `CtWave` member function `Load`. If the greeting is successfully loaded, it is then played on the wave device returned from the call to `GetID` using the `CtWave` member function Play. The greeting lets the caller know to leave a message and press 1.

```cpp
void CIncomingCallDlg::OnCallState(
    CtCall* pCall,
    DWORD    nCallState,
    DWORD    dwParam2,
    DWORD    nCallPrivilege)
{
  switch( m_todo )
  {
  case todoTakeMessage:
    switch( nCallState )
    {
    case LINECALLSTATE_CONNECTED:
    {
      // Get the output wave device ID for the call
      CtDeviceID  did;
      if( TSUCCEEDED(did.GetID("wave/out",
                               m_pCall->GetHandle())) )
      {
        // Load and play the greeting
        // (and wait for OnWaitOutDone event from CtWave)
        if( !m_wave.Load(AfxGetResourceHandle(),
                    IDR_GREETING) ||
            !m_wave.Play(did.GetDeviceID()) )
        {
          // If load fails, fake it
          TRACE0("Failed to load or play wav file —"
                 "faking it.\n");
          OnWaveOutDone();
        }
      }
    }
```

```
      break;

    case LINECALLSTATE_DISCONNECTED:
      TRACE0("Recording complete\n");
      m_wave.Stop();
    break;
    }
  break;

  case todoTakeCall:
  ... // code removed for clarity
  break;

  case todoNothing:
    switch( nCallState )
    {
    case LINECALLSTATE_CONNECTED:
      // Someone else is dealing with it.
      ShowWindow(SW_HIDE);
    break;
    }
  break;
  }
}
```

Once the greeting has been played, the `CtWave` object sends the `OnWave-OutDone` event via the `CIncomingCallDlg`'s implementation of `CtWave-Sink`. Then the recording can begin using the `CtWave` member function `Record`. The low-level wave device ID is obtained using the device class string "`wave/in`."

In addition to recording audio data after the greeting is played, we also want to listen for a touch-tone to terminate the recording. This is necessary because many telephony devices aren't very good at detecting a hang-up on the other end of a call. If the user is not allowed to signal the end of the recording, it's very possible that a lot of silence will trail each recording. To alert the TSP that the application is interested in touch-tone notifications, it calls the `CtCall` member function `MonitorDigits`:

```
// Greeting finished playing — record the message.
void CIncomingCallDlg::OnWaveOutDone()
{
```

```
// Get the input wave device ID for the call
CtDeviceID  did;
if( TSUCCEEDED(did.GetID("wave/in",
                         m_pCall->GetHandle())) )
{
  // Record a 2-minute message (max).
  const UINT  nSecs = 120;
  TRACE1("Recording for %d seconds\n", nSecs);

  // Record the greeting and wait for OnWaveInData.
  if( !m_wave.Record(did.GetDeviceID(), nSecs) )
  {
    TRACE0("Can't record message — dropping call\n");
    m_pCall->Drop();
    return;
  }

  // Also allow a DTMF to complete recording
  if( TFAILED(m_pCall->MonitorDigits()) )
  {
    TRACE0("Unable to terminate message with DTMF\n");
  }
}
}
```

If a digit is detected, the monitoring of digits is stopped, the recording is stopped, and the call is dropped:

```
// Got a DTMF — stop the recording
void CIncomingCallDlg::OnCallMonitorDigits(
    CtCall* pCall,
    char    cDigit,
    DWORD   nDigitMode)
{
    // If we've gotten a digit, stop recording
    m_pCall->MonitorDigits(0);
    m_wave.Stop();
    m_pCall->Drop();
}
```

Likewise, if the call is disconnected, the recording is stopped, as shown previously in the `OnCallState` member function of `CIncomingDlg`. When the wave device has stopped recording, the `CtWave` object will send an `OnWaveInData` event. The `CtWave` object supports saving data to a file using the `Save` member function. It also allows the data it is holding to be cleared using the `Close` member function. The `CIncomingDlg` handles the `OnWaveInData` event by saving the data in the `CtWave` object to a file and closing the `CtWave` object:

```
// Message finished recording — save it to a file.
void CIncomingCallDlg::OnWaveInData()
{
  // Construct message file path name.
  const CString   sMessages = "Messages";

  CString sPathName;
  GetModuleFileName(0, sPathName.GetBuffer(MAX_PATH+1),
                    MAX_PATH);
  sPathName.ReleaseBuffer();
  sPathName = sPathName.Left(sPathName.ReverseFind('\\'));
  sPathName += '\\';
  sPathName += sMessages;
  sPathName += '\\';

  if( !SetCurrentDirectory(sPathName) &&
      !CreateDirectory(sPathName, 0) )
  {
      TRACE1("Failed to create messages directory: %s\n",
             (LPCSTR)sPathName);
      return;
  }

  if( !m_sName.IsEmpty() && m_sName[0] != '<' )
  {
      sPathName += m_sName;
      sPathName += ' ';
  }

  if( !m_sPhoneNo.IsEmpty() && m_sPhoneNo[0] != '<' )
  {
      sPathName += ", ";
```

```
        sPathName += m_sPhoneNo;
        sPathName += ' ';
    }

    const int    nBufLen = 64;
    CString      sDateTime;
    time_t       nTime = time(0);
    const char* pszFormat = "%a, %b %d, %H%M hours";

    strftime(sDateTime.GetBuffer(nBufLen+1), nBufLen,
            pszFormat, localtime(&nTime));
    sDateTime.ReleaseBuffer();

    sPathName += sDateTime;
    sPathName += ".wav";

    TRACE1("Saving wave file to %s\n", sPathName);

    // Save the message and clean out the buffer
    m_wave.Save(sPathName);
    m_wave.Close();
}
```

Speakerphones

When the user decides to take a call, tMonitor provides the Take the Call button.
tMonitor then answers the call and allows the user to have control until the call is
disconnected. When the call is answered, the tMonitor application attempts to set
the call into speakerphone mode by logically attaching the computer speaker and
microphone to the line.

Recall from Chapter 1 the idea of a *terminal*. A terminal is a device attached to
the end of a line, either physically or logically. Each terminal can be matched with
a set of events that will be routed to it. For example, the phone can be the terminal
on the line that receives ringing events and the voice information could be routed
to a speaker and microphone attached to the computer. The routing of events to
terminals can be achieved using the lineSetTerminal function:

```
LONG
lineSetTerminal(
```

```
HLINE              hLine,
DWORD              dwAddressID,
HCALL              hCall,
DWORD              dwSelect,
DWORD              dwTerminalModes,
DWORD              dwTerminalID,
DWORD              bEnable)
```

The `lineSetTerminal` function is another of the polymorphic functions in TAPI. This allows a TSP to route events in a hierarchical fashion. For example, all events on a line can be routed to the phone except when a call is answered, in which case `lineSetTerminal` can be used to route the events for the call to the speaker and the microphone.

The `dwTerminalModes` parameter is one of a number of flags. See Table 5.3. The `dwTerminalID` is one of the terminal identifiers available in the `LINEDEVCAPS` structure (shown in Chapter 3), that is, between 0 and `dwNum-Terminals` −1. The `LINEDEVCAPS` structure also contains an array of `LINE-TERMCAPS` structures, thus indicating the kind of terminals that are available for the line:

```
typedef struct linetermcaps_tag
{
     DWORD          dwTermDev;
     DWORD          dwTermModes;
```

Table 5.3: Terminal mode flags and events.	
Terminal Mode Flag	*Events*
LINETERMMODE_BUTTONS	Button presses.
LINETERMMODE_DISPLAY	Display changes.
LINETERMMODE_LAMPS	Lamp lighting changes.
LINETERMMODE_RINGER	Rings.
LINETERMMODE_HOOKSWITCH	Hook switches, that is, hang-ups.
LINETERMMODE_MEDIATOLINE	Audio meant for the line.
LINETERMMODE_MEDIAFROMLINE	Audio originating from the line.
LINETERMMODE_MEDIABIDIRECT	Both audio meant for the line and audio originating from the line.

Table 5.4: Types of `dwTermDev` flags.	
Terminal Device Flag	Device Type
`LINETERMDEV_PHONE`	Phone.
`LINETERMDEV_HEADSET`	Head set, that is, headphones and a microphone.
`LINETERMDEV_SPEAKER`	External speaker *and* microphone.

```
        DWORD          dwTermSharing;

} LINETERMCAPS, FAR *LPLINETERMCAPS;
```

The `dwTermDev` flag is one of those given in Table 5.4. The `dwTermModes` are the terminal events that the device is allowed to receive; the dwTermSharing determines how many lines can share the device. So, assuming that the zeroeth terminal is a phone and the first terminal is a speaker/microphone combination, a call could be turned into speakerphone mode with the following use of `line-SetTerminal`:

```
TRESULT SetSpeakerPhoneMode(
   HCALL hcall,
   bool  bSpeakerPhoneMode = true)
{
   // Send audio to the phone or the speaker/microphone
   // based on the bSpeakerPhoneMode flag.
   DWORD  nDeviceID = (bSpeakerPhoneMode ? 1 : 0);
   return lineSetTerminal(0, 0, hcall, LINECALLSELECT_CALL,
                   LINETERMMODE_MEDIABIDIRECT,
                   nDeviceID);
}
```

Unfortunately, the `dwNumTerminals` for some TSPs is 0. These TSPs just don't support terminals; they support phones. Specifically, the Unimodem/V TSP provides a single phone for voice-enabled modems. If the device capabilities of the phone attached to the line supports the `PHONEHOOKSWITCHMODE_MIC-SPEAKER` hook switch mode, that phone can be set into speakerphone mode using the `phoneSetHookSwitch` function:

```
LONG
phoneSetHookSwitch(
    HPHONE               hPhone,
```

```
DWORD                dwHookSwitchDevs,
DWORD                dwHookSwitchMode)
```

When taking a call, the tMonitor sample uses this technique to turn on speakerphone mode:

```
void CIncomingCallDlg::OnCallState(
  CtCall* pCall,
  DWORD   nCallState,
  DWORD   dwParam2,
  DWORD   nCallPrivilege)
{
  switch( m_todo )
  {
  case todoTakeMessage:
    ... // Code removed for clarity.
  break;

  case todoTakeCall:
  // Set up speakerphone mode if available.
  if( nCallState == LINECALLSTATE_CONNECTED )
  {
    // Get the phone from the line
    CtDeviceID  did;
    HLINE       hline = m_pCall->GetLine()->GetHandle();
    if( TSUCCEEDED(did.GetID("tapi/phone",
                           hline)) )
    {
      DWORD      nPhoneID = did.GetDeviceID();
      CtPhoneCaps pc;

      // Check for speakerphone mode and
      // set it if available.
      if( TSUCCEEDED(pc.GetDevCaps(nPhoneID)) &&
         (pc.GetSpeakerHookSwitchModes() &
            PHONEHOOKSWITCHMODE_MICSPEAKER) &&
          TSUCCEEDED(m_phone.Open(nPhoneID)) &&
          TPENDING(m_phone.SetHookSwitch(
                     PHONEHOOKSWITCHDEV_SPEAKER,
                     PHONEHOOKSWITCHMODE_MICSPEAKER)) )
      {
        TRACE0("Speakerphone mode set\n");
```

```
      }
      else
      {
        TRACE0("Speakerphone mode unavailable\n");

        if( m_phone.GetHandle() )
        {
          m_phone.Close();
        }
      }
    }
  }
  break;

  case todoNothing:
    switch( nCallState )
    {
    case LINECALLSTATE_CONNECTED:
      // Someone else is dealing with it.
      ShowWindow(SW_HIDE);
      break;
    }
  break;
  }
}
```

Summary

Once an application has accomplished the basics of initialization, line management, event handling, and variable-length data structures, adding support for detecting and answering incoming calls is relatively straight-forward. For applications that automatically answer an incoming call, TAPI provides support for a toll-saver feature to save the caller long distance charges. Applications that answer the call can "talk" to the caller by playing wave files and record callers' responses by recording wave files.

CHAPTER

Call Management

6

Assisted Telephony Request Recipients

Unhandled Media Modes

Data Calls

Call Monitoring

Did you ever dial someone on the
phone and forget who you're calling?
George Carlin

Think of TAPI as a backbone for managing information about telephony objects currently active on the system. Under Win32, all incoming and outgoing calls happen through TAPI. Because TAPI allows shared access to all telephony objects, any number of applications can monitor telephony events, not just the owner. In this chapter, I discuss how to use the shared access to telephony objects to create a call monitor application.

In addition, TAPI provides an interprocess communications channel between telephony applications. Recall that in Chapter 2 an Assisted Telephony application used TAPI to send a make call request to a willing request recipient. In this chapter, I talk about how to make an application a request recipient.

Another IPC mechanism that TAPI supports is that of handing off calls that an application isn't equipped to handle, for example, an automated voice application getting a fax call. For these situations, TAPI supports handing off the call to another application that is more capable of dealing with the call's current media mode. In this chapter, I discuss detecting changes in a call's media mode as well as handing off the call to another application.

This system-wide information sharing about telephony objects is the single biggest benefit of TAPI. Telephony applications can work together not because of some proprietary IPC mechanism that only some applications support, but because there is an operating system standard backbone. Each TSP provides access to a device or set of devices, and TAPI allows shared access to all of the devices among all of the telephony applications. In the case of a modem, the TSP provides access to the call management features of the modem via TAPI. For data management, however, the TSP must support the Win32 Communications API. In this chapter, I also talk about how to access the handle for the modem for use with the Communications API.

Assisted Telephony Request Recipients

Recall the discussion of Assisted Telephony in Chapter 2. The idea was to allow an application to make a call without having to manage it during the call's lifetime. An application can take advantage of the services of Assisted Telephony by using the `tapiRequestMakeCall` function:

```
LONG
tapiRequestMakeCall(
    LPCSTR              lpszDestAddress,
    LPCSTR              lpszAppName,
    LPCSTR              lpszCalledParty,
    LPCSTR              lpszComment);
```

When TAPI receives a make call request, it looks for a running Assisted Telephony request recipient. An application can notify TAPI that it is interested in handling call requests. It does this by calling the `lineRegisterRequest-Recipient` function:

```
LONG
lineRegisterRequestRecipient(
    HLINEAPP            hLineApp,
    DWORD               dwRegistrationInstance,
    DWORD               dwRequestMode,
    DWORD               bEnable);
```

The `hLineApp` parameter comes from a successful call to `lineInitialize`. The `dwRegistrationInstance` is an application-supplied `DWORD`. This data will be sent back as the `dwCallbackInstance` parameter to the application with every make call request in the `LINE_REQUEST` message. Since 32-bit TAPI supports only make call requests (and not media call requests), the `dwRequestMode` parameter can only be `LINEREQUESTMODE_MAKECALL`. Finally, the `bEnable` parameter is `TRUE` if the application wants to register itself as a request recipient (typically at start-up) and `FALSE` if it wants to remove itself as a request recipient (typically at shutdown).

In the event that no running application has registered itself as a request recipient when an Assisted Telephony application makes a request, TAPI will attempt to start such an application. It will do this by consulting a prioritized list of applications willing to handle Assisted Telephony requests. At installation, Windows assumes that the Phone Dialer application will be the system's request recipient. Under TAPI 2.x, this information is kept in the Registry:

```
[HKEY_CURRENT_USER\Software\Microsoft\Windows\
CurrentVersion\Telephony\HandoffPriorities]
RequestMakeCall=DIALER.EXE
```

Under TAPI 1.x, this list is maintained in the `telephon.ini` file under the `[HandoffPriorities]` section:

```
[HandoffPriorities]
RequestMakeCall=DIALER.EXE
```

To manage this information without dealing directly with either the Registry or `telephon.ini`, TAPI provides the `lineSetAppPriority` and `line-GetAppPriority` functions (discussed in Chapter 5):

```
LONG
lineSetAppPriority(
     LPCSTR               lpszAppFilename,
     DWORD                dwMediaMode,
     LPLINEEXTENSIONID    lpExtensionID,
     DWORD                dwRequestMode,
     LPCSTR               lpszExtensionName,
     DWORD                dwPriority);

LONG
lineGetAppPriority(
     LPCSTR               lpszAppFilename,
     DWORD                dwMediaMode,
     LPLINEEXTENSIONID    lpExtensionID,
     DWORD                dwRequestMode,
     LPVARSTRING          lpExtensionName,
     LPDWORD              lpdwPriority);
```

For dealing with request recipient priorities, the `dwMediaMode` parameter is 0 and the `dwRequestMode` parameter is `LINEREQUESTMODE_MAKECALL`. The `lpExtensionID` and `lpExtensionName` parameters are typically `NULL`. The `dwPriority` can be either 1 or 0. The value 1 indicates that the application should be put at the beginning of the list, that is, given the highest priority. The value 0 indicates that the application should be removed from the list.

If there is contention—more than one application that wants to handle a request (or a specific media mode)—the application with the highest priority wins, that is, the last one to call `lineSetAppPriority`. This can be checked with `lineGetAppPriority`.

If an application registers itself with TAPI as the highest priority request recipient application, it must be prepared to be started by TAPI and to handle Assisted Telephony requests with all due speed. This means calling `line-Initialize` and `lineRegisterRequestRecipient` immediately at application start-up. Otherwise, Assisted Telephony requests will fail.

Once an application has registered itself as a request recipient, it can expect to receive `LINE_REQUEST` messages whenever another application makes a call to `lineRequestMakeCall`. To retrieve the four pieces of information an Assisted Telephony application has supplied with its make call request, the request recipient uses the `lineGetRequest` function:

```
LONG
lineGetRequest(
    HLINEAPP            hLineApp,
    DWORD               dwRequestMode,
    LPVOID              lpRequestBuffer);
```

Again, the `hLineApp` comes from a successful `lineInitialize` and the `dwRequestMode` must be `LINEREQUESTMODE_MAKECALL`. The `lpRequestBuffer` is a pointer to a `LINEREQMAKECALL` structure:

```
typedef struct linereqmakecall_tag
{
    char        szDestAddress[TAPIMAXDESTADDRESSSIZE];
    char        szAppName[TAPIMAXAPPNAMESIZE];
    char        szCalledParty[TAPIMAXCALLEDPARTYSIZE];
    char        szComment[TAPIMAXCOMMENTSIZE];

} LINEREQMAKECALL, FAR *LPLINEREQMAKECALL;
```

A successful return from `lineGetRequest` means that the four arguments from `tapiRequestMakeCall` have been copied into the `LINEREQMAKE-CALL` structure. It is now the application's responsibility to make a call using this information and manage it during the call's lifetime. When the request recipient receives the `LINE_REQUEST` message, this indicates that there are zero or more requests queued. A request recipient capable of handling multiple calls should keep calling `lineGetRequest` and making calls until `lineGetRequest` fails. TAPI will return `LINEERR_NOREQUEST` when the request queue is empty.

LINECALLPARAMS

The information in the `LINEREQMAKECALL` structure isn't just for the application servicing the request. Rather, this information should be shared with any other application that happens to be monitoring the line being used to make the outbound call. For example, a call logging application discussed later in this chapter can provide a better log if it knows the phone number that was dialed, the person the call was placed to, and whatever comment the user cared to make while placing the phone call. All of this information is available in the `LINEREQMAKECALL` structure and should be passed to `lineMakeCall` via the `LINECALLPARAMS` structure.

Recall the `lineMakeCall` function and the `CtCall` member function wrapper, `MakeCall`:

```
LONG
lineMakeCall(
    HLINE               hLine,
    LPHCALL             lphCall,
    LPCSTR              lpszDestAddress,
    DWORD               dwCountryCode,
    LPLINECALLPARAMS    const lpCallParams);

tfxasync TRESULT
MakeCall(
    LPCSTR szDestAddress = 0,
    DWORD nCountryCode = 0,
    CtCallSink* pInitialSink = 0,
    LINECALLPARAMS* pCallParams = 0);
```

The `LINECALLPARAMS` structure is the last parameter to both of these functions. This structure has the following fields (and defaults):

```
typedef struct linecallparams_tag           // Defaults:
{
    DWORD       dwTotalSize;                 // ——
    DWORD       dwBearerMode;                // voice
    DWORD       dwMinRate;                   // (3.1kHz)
    DWORD       dwMaxRate;                   // (3.1kHz)
    DWORD       dwMediaMode;                 // interactiveVoice
    DWORD       dwCallParamFlags;            // 0
    DWORD       dwAddressMode;               // addressID
    DWORD       dwAddressID;                 // (any available)
    ...
} LINECALLPARAMS, FAR *LPLINECALLPARAMS;
```

The `LINECALLPARAMS` structure is an optional argument to `lineMake-Call`, that is, a NULL pointer can be passed. In that event, the default parameters assume an interactive voice call on any available address. However, the default does not fill in the phone number dialed, so any monitoring applications will know that a call was made, but not the phone number. Also, in the event that a call of another media mode, for example, `LINEMEDIAMODE_DATA`, is made, a `LINECALLPARAMS` structure is required so that the `dwMediaMode` element can be set (see the tDaemon sample later in this chapter).

The `LINECALLPARAMS` structure is another TAPI VLS. Recall that TAPI requires a VLS to be allocated in a contiguous array of bytes and to have its size in the `dwTotalSize` field. Each variable-length portion of memory is indicated with a `dwXxxOffset` and `dwXxxSize` pair to indicate the offset from the base address of the data as well as the size of the data. Since we want to pass along the variable-length `szDestAddress`, `szCalledParty`, and `szComment` fields from the `LINEREQMAKECALL` structure, it's our job to set up the `LINECALL-PARAMS` structure properly before calling `lineMakeCall` (or the `CtCall` method `MakeCall`).[1] To encapsulate the code to fill a `LINECALLPARAMS`, the tDial sample has a function called `AllocateCallParams`:

```
LINECALLPARAMS* AllocateCallParams(
    LPCSTR pszAddress = 0,
    LPCSTR pszCalledParty = 0,
    LPCSTR pszComment = 0);
```

The `AllocateCallParams` function takes three of the four parameters from the `LINEREQMAKECALL` structure (the application name can't be passed in the `LINE-CALLPARAMS` structure) and packs them into a `LINECALLPARAMS` structure.

The first step in populating any VLS is calculating the size and allocating the memory in a contiguous block. The size of the required memory will be the size of the fixed portion of the structure plus the size of each of the variable-sized portions. In `AllocateCallParams`, the total size is the size of `LINECALL-PARAMS` plus the size of each of the variable-length strings (including the trailing NULLs). If any of the string pointers are NULL or the strings that they point to are empty, no space should be allocated for them. While it's legal in TAPI to indicate an empty string with an offset/size pair that points to a single NULL, this is a waste and should be avoided. `AllocateCallParams` calculates the total amount of memory like this:

```
// Caller responsible for setting flags
// (if they are other than zero)
// and calling delete[] on result when
// buffer is no longer needed.
```

---

[1] Chapter 3 shows a picture of another variable-sized structure, `LINEDEVCAPS`.

```
LINECALLPARAMS* AllocateCallParams(
    LPCSTR pszAddress = 0,
    LPCSTR pszCalledParty = 0,
    LPCSTR pszComment = 0)
{
    // Calculate LINECALLPARAMS sizes
    size_t  cbAddress     = (pszAddress && *pszAddress
                               ? strlen(pszAddress) + 1
                               : 0);
    size_t  cbCalledParty = (pszCalledParty &&
                               *pszCalledParty
                               ? strlen(pszCalledParty) + 1
                               : 0);
    size_t  cbComment     = (pszComment && *pszComment
                               ? strlen(pszComment) + 1
                               : 0);
    size_t  cbCallParams  = sizeof(LINECALLPARAMS) +
                               cbAddress + cbCalledParty +
                               cbComment;

    // Allocate LINECALLPARAMS structure
    LINECALLPARAMS* pCallParams =
        (LINECALLPARAMS*)(new BYTE[cbCallParams]);
    if( pCallParams )
    {
        ZeroMemory(pCallParams, cbCallParams);
        pCallParams->dwTotalSize = cbCallParams;

        // Fill LINECALLPARAMS...
    }
    return pCallParams;
}
```

Once the size is calculated, an array of bytes is allocated and cast to a LINE-
CALLPARAMS*. At this point, it's important to remember to set the dwTotal-
Size parameter so that TAPI knows how much data is present in the structure.
Once the data is allocated, each chunk of variable-length data is copied to the right
spot in the block and memory and each offset/size pair must be set to point to the
data. The offset is calculated by adding the size of the fixed-length portion of the
structure to the sizes of all of the variable-length portions that have been copied in
so far. The copying is most easily accomplished by using a cast to get a pointer at

the correct offset and using the pointer to perform the copy. `AllocCall-Params` does it this way:

```
LINECALLPARAMS* AllocateCallParams(
    LPCSTR pszAddress = 0,
    LPCSTR pszCalledParty = 0,
    LPCSTR pszComment = 0)
{
    // Allocate LINECALLPARAMS structure...

    if( pCallParams )
    {
        ZeroMemory(pCallParams, cbCallParams);
        pCallParams->dwTotalSize = cbCallParams;

        // Fill in a LINECALLPARAMS structure.

        // pszAddress
        pCallParams->dwDisplayableAddressSize = cbAddress;
        if( cbAddress )
        {
            pCallParams->dwDisplayableAddressOffset =
                sizeof(LINECALLPARAMS);
            char*  psz = (char*)((BYTE*)pCallParams +
                pCallParams->dwDisplayableAddressOffset);
            strcpy(psz, pszAddress);
        }
        else
        {
            pCallParams->dwDisplayableAddressOffset = 0;
        }

        // pszCalledParty
        pCallParams->dwCalledPartySize = cbCalledParty;
        if( cbCalledParty )
        {
            pCallParams->dwCalledPartyOffset =
                sizeof(LINECALLPARAMS) + cbAddress;
            char*  psz = (char*)((BYTE*)pCallParams +
                pCallParams->dwCalledPartyOffset);
            strcpy(psz, pszCalledParty);
```

```
    }
    else
    {
        pCallParams->dwCalledPartyOffset = 0;
    }

    // pszComment
    pCallParams->dwCommentSize = cbComment;
    if( cbComment )
    {
        pCallParams->dwCommentOffset =
            sizeof(LINECALLPARAMS) + cbAddress +
            cbCalledParty;
        char*    psz = (char*)((BYTE*)pCallParams +
            pCallParams->dwCommentOffset);
        strcpy(psz, pszComment);
    }
    else
    {
        pCallParams->dwCommentOffset = 0;
    }
}

return pCallParams;
}
```

The `AllocateCallParams` does not set any of the flags, for example, `dw-BearerMode` and `dwMediaMode`. This is up to the caller of the `Allocate-CallParams` function. In the event of a voice call, these two values are set at `LINEBEARMODE_VOICE` and `LINEMEDIAMODE_INTERACTIVEVOICE`, respectively. Once these values have been set, the `LINECALLPARAMS` structure can be sent to the `lineMakeCall` function. All monitoring applications will now have access to this additional information about outbound calls.

TFX Support for Request Recipients

Although the TFX provides no help in setting up TAPI VLSs, it does provide wrappers around the functions used to handle make call requests. Most of the parameters for both `lineGetPriority` and `lineSetPriority` can be determined based on TFX-managed data after a successful `TfxLineInitialize` call. So the TFX wrappers for getting and setting media mode and make call request priority require little additional information:

```
TRESULT
TfxGetAppPriority(
    LPDWORD pnPriority,
    LPCSTR pszAppName = 0,
    DWORD nMediaMode = 0, // Assisted Telephony requests
    LPLINEEXTENSIONID const pExtID = 0,
    DWORD nRequestMode = LINEREQUESTMODE_MAKECALL,
    LPVARSTRING pvsExtName = 0);

TRESULT
TfxSetAppPriority(
    DWORD nPriority,
    LPCSTR pszAppName = 0,
    DWORD nMediaMode = 0, // Assisted Telephony requests
    LPLINEEXTENSIONID const pExtID = 0,
    DWORD nRequestMode = LINEREQUESTMODE_MAKECALL,
    LPCSTR pszExtName = 0);
```

The tDial sample uses these two functions to implement the Options dialog, illustrated in Figure 6.1. When the user clicks the Options button on the main window, `TfxGetAppPriority` is used to determine whether tDial is currently being used to service make call requests. When the OK button is clicked, tDial uses the state of the checkbox to determine how it should call `TfxSetApp-Priority`, that is, put tDial at the front of the list or remove it from the list of applications handling make call requests.

In addition to wrapping the application priority functions, the TFX provides two wrappers for calling `lineRegisterRequestRecipient`—one for registration and one for unregistration:

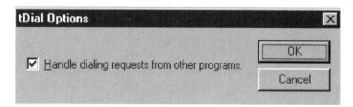

Figure 6.1. tDial Options dialog.

```
TRESULT
TfxRegisterRequestRecipient(
    DWORD dwRequestMode = LINEREQUESTMODE_MAKECALL);

void
TfxUnregisterRequestRecipient(
    DWORD dwRequestMode = LINEREQUESTMODE_MAKECALL);
```

The tDial sample uses these two functions at start-up or when the user has changed the option to handle make call requests in the Options dialog. The following code shows how tDial uses the TFX wrappers for registering as an Assisted Telephony request recipient:

```
// Let TAPI know whether we'd like to handle
// make call requests or not.
void CtDialDlg::UpdateRequestRecipientStatus()
{
    DWORD    nPriority;

    // A media mode of 0 indicates make call requests.
    if( TSUCCEEDED(::TfxGetAppPriority(0, &nPriority)) &&
        nPriority > 0 )
    {
        ::TfxRegisterRequestRecipient();
    }
    else
    {
        ::TfxUnregisterRequestRecipient();
    }
}

// Main window initialization
BOOL CtDialDlg::OnInitDialog()
{
    ... // Code removed for clarity

    // Update request recipient status
    UpdateRequestRecipientStatus();

    return TRUE;
```

```
    }

    // User presses Options button.
    void CtDialDlg::OnOptions()
    {
        COptionsDlg dlg;
        DWORD       nPriority = 0;

        ::TfxGetAppPriority(0, &nPriority);
        dlg.m_bRequestRecipient =
            (nPriority == 1 ? TRUE : FALSE);

        if( dlg.DoModal() == IDOK )
        {
            nPriority = (dlg.m_bRequestRecipient ? 1 : 0);
            ::TfxSetAppPriority(0, nPriority);
            UpdateRequestRecipientStatus();
        }
    }
```

Once TAPI knows that the application wants to handle make call requests, all calls to `lineRequestMakeCall` will result in a `LINE_REQUEST` message to the application. Since `LINE_REQUEST` messages aren't for a specific line, call, or phone, the TFX needs another place to send these messages. For this reason, the TFX provides another message sink, `CtAppSink`:

```
class CtAppSink
{
  // Sink events (placeholders for overriding only)
  virtual void OnLineCreate(DWORD nLineID) {}
  virtual void OnPhoneCreate(DWORD nPhoneID) {}
  virtual void OnLineRequest(DWORD nRequestMode,
                             HWND hRequestWnd,
                             TREQUEST nRequestID) {}
};
```

The TFX receives a pointer to an implementation of `CtAppSink` in the call to `TfxLineInitialize`:

```
TRESULT
TfxLineInitialize(
```

```
CtAppSink* pAppSink = 0,
LPCSTR szAppName = 0,
HINSTANCE hInst = 0);
```

If the caller of `TfxLineInitialize` provides a non-NULL `CtAppSink*`, then a `LINE_REQUEST` message that is detected will result in a call to the `CtAppSink` method `OnLineRequest`. Under Win32, the first argument of `OnLineRequest`, `dwRequestMode`, will always be `LINEREQUEST-MODE_MAKECALL`. The other two parameters can be safely ignored (they are provided for `LINEREQUESTMODE_MEDIACALL` only).

> ## The Need for `CtAppSink`
>
> A separate event sink was needed for `LINE_REQUEST` messages because TAPI does not associate a make call request with a specific line. In fact, the application doesn't even have to open a line to receive a make call request. This allows the application to open the line only when necessary, thereby helping to minimize application resource usage.
>
> In addition to `OnLineRequest`, `CtAppSink` has two other methods: `On-LineCreate` and `OnPhoneCreate`. These are called when the TFX receives a `LINE_CREATE` message or a `PHONE_CREATE` message, respectively. These messages allow dynamic configuration of telephony devices while telephony applications are running. An application interested in handling all lines and/or all phones may add these new devices to its list as they become available.
>
> Note that TAPI will not send line or phone creation messages unless the appropriate part of the API has been initialized. For example, if your application is interested in `LINE_CREATE` messages, it must call `lineInitialize` (for example, via `TfxLineInitialize`) to give TAPI a function to call.

In the tDial sample, `CtDialDlg` derives from `CtAppSink` and implements the `OnLineRequest` method:

```
class CtDialDlg : public CDialog,
                  public CtAppSink,
                  public CtLineSink,
                  public CtCallSink
{
    ... // Code removed for clarity.

    // Handle CtAppSink event
    virtual void OnLineRequest(DWORD, HWND, nRequestID);
};
```

The `CtAppSink` is provided to the TFX in the `CtDialApp` method, `Init-Instance`:

```
BOOL CtDialApp::InitInstance()
{
    CtDialDlg   dlgDial; // Implements CtAppSink

    // Initialize the line
    if( TFAILED(::TfxLineInitialize(&dlgDial)) )
    {
        ::AfxMessageBox(IDS_CANT_INIT_TAPI);
        return FALSE;
    }

    m_pMainWnd = &dlgDial;
    dlgDial.DoModal();
    return FALSE;
}
```

To retrieve make call request information, the TFX provides a wrapper around `lineGetRequest`:

```
TRESULT
TfxGetMakeCallRequest(
    LPLINEREQMAKECALL plmc);
```

In the implementation of `OnLineRequest`, tDial uses `TfxGetMakeCallRequest` to retrieve the information it needs to fill in a LINECALLPARAMS structure and to make the call:

```
void CtDialDlg::OnLineRequest(DWORD, HWND, TREQUEST)
{
    LINEREQMAKECALL lmc;
    if( TSUCCEEDED(::TfxGetMakeCallRequest(&lmc)) )
    {
        // Show user we've received an AT request....

        // TAPI starts as minimized.
        ShowWindow(SW_RESTORE);
        SetForegroundWindow();

        // Fill in a LINECALLPARAMS structure.
```

```
LINECALLPARAMS* pCallParams =
    AllocateCallParams(lmc.szDestAddress,
                       lmc.szCalledParty,
                       lmc.szComment);
if( pCallParams )
{
    pCallParams->dwBearerMode =
        LINEBEARERMODE_VOICE;
    pCallParams->dwMediaMode =
        LINEMEDIAMODE_INTERACTIVEVOICE;
}

Dial(lmc.szDestAddress, pCallParams);
delete[] pCallParams;
    }
}
```

Unhandled Media Modes

Because of the ability to have shared access to a call, TAPI encourages separate applications for separate jobs. Interactive voice applications allow your computer to act like a phone. Automated voice applications allow your computer to act like an answering machine. Fax applications allow your computer to act like a fax machine. All of these applications can be running simultaneously. However, a call can have only one owner. In the event of a new incoming call, how does the call get to the right application?

Since the vast majority of incoming calls are of an unknown media mode, it's the job of every application to participate in routing a call after it has been answered and the media mode has been detected. How this is handled depends on the type of application that first answers the call. For example, an answering machine application will expect to answer the phone and talk to a human. If a fax machine is calling, it will be sending a periodic fax tone announcing a desire to send a fax. If the TSP detects the fax announcement tone (most do, especially the Unimodem TSP), the application will be notified of a media mode change, that is, the media mode has changed from Unknown to Fax. This notification comes via the `LINE_CALLINFO` event with `dwParam1` set to `LINECALLINFOSTATE_MEDIAMODE`:

```
LINE_CALLINFO
dwDevice = (DWORD) hCall;
dwCallbackInstance = (DWORD) hCallback;
```

```
dwParam1 = (DWORD) CallInfoState;
dwParam2 = (DWORD) 0;
dwParam3 = (DWORD) 0;
```

When the application detects a media mode change, it should find out to what the media mode has changed so that it can determine how to handle it. The current media mode is in the dwMediaMode of the LINECALLINFO structure, which is filled with the lineGetCallInfo function:

```
LONG
lineGetCallInfo(
    HCALL           hCall,
    LPLINECALLINFO lpCallInfo)
```

For convenience, the TFX wraps the variable-length LINECALLINFO structure with the CtCallInfo class.

Once the media mode is known, the application is responsible for whatever behavior is appropriate for the new media mode. For example, if the answering machine application can handle faxes, it should begin the communications handshake necessary for receiving a fax. If the answering machine application is not equipped to handle faxes, it should hand it off to an application that can. It can do this using the lineHandoff function:

```
LONG
lineHandoff(
    HCALL   hCall,
    LPCSTR lpszFileName,
    DWORD   dwMediaMode)
```

Using lineHandoff, an application can attempt a *direct handoff* or an *indirect handoff*. A direct handoff is appropriate if the application handing off the call has a specific executable in mind to receive the call, for example, takefax.exe.

Alternatively, the application can handoff the call to another application that has registered itself (via lineSetAppPriority) to accept calls of the call's new media mode. This is known as an indirect handoff because the application handing off the call has no direct knowledge of the application receiving the call. An indirect handoff is performed by calling lineHandoff with a NULL lpszFileName and the call's new media mode. If TAPI determines that the application attempting the indirect handoff is the appropriate application to accept the handoff, it will short-circuit the handoff process by immediately returning LINEERR_TARGETSELF.

When an application attempts a direct or an indirect handoff, TAPI checks that the application has the line open and is willing to accept ownership of calls that have the specified media mode. If so, the call is handed to the application via the `LINE_CALLSTATE` message. If not, `lineHandoff` will fail with a `LINEERR_TARGETNOTFOUND` error.

The `CtCall` class wraps the direct and indirect handoff strategies with these two member functions:

```
TRESULT
CtCall::Handoff(LPCSTR szFileName)

TRESULT
CtCall::Handoff(DWORD nMediaMode)
```

When `lineHandoff` is used, the routing of calls that have an unknown media mode can continue even after the call has been answered.

Data Calls

So far I've talked about how to build voice applications. While voice applications are wonderful for call management applications, there is another, potentially even more popular, use of telephony equipment—to handle data modem and fax calls. Luckily, the call management techniques discussed so far are completely consistent with the making and receiving of data modem and fax calls (which I call "data calls" from now on). The differences are as follows.

- When finding lines valid for placing and/or answering data calls, look for the appropriate `dwMediaMode` in the `LINEDEVCAPS` structure, for example, `LINEMEDIAMODE_DATAMODEM` and `LINEMEDIAMODE_G3FAX`.
- If your application is interested in receiving data calls, then specify when opening the line one or more of the data call media modes, as well as `LINEMEDIAMODE_UNKNOWN`.
- If your application is interested in placing data calls, specify one of the data call media modes in the `dwMediaMode` field of the `LINECALLPARAMS` structure passed to `lineMakeCall`. This will cause the modem to begin rate negotiation when connecting to another modem. If you want to limit the range of available data transfer rates, set the `LINECALLPARAMS` members `dwMinRate` and/or the `dwMaxRate`. The default setting for `dwMaxRate` is available in the `LINEDEVCAPS` structure for the line.

Once the connection has been made, TAPI cannot help with the actual data transfer part of a data application. Instead, as discussed in Chapter 5, you need to obtain a handle from the call for use with another Win32 API, in this case, the Win32 Communications API.[2] The name of the device class needed to obtain this kind of handle is `comm/datamodem`. A successful return from `lineGetID` with this string will set `dwStringFormat` to `STRINGFORMAT_BINARY`. It also will fill in a data structure past the end of the fixed-size `VARSTRING` data that looks like this:

```
struct HandleAndString
{
    HANDLE hComm;
    LPCSTR szCommPortName[];
};
```

The `szCommPortName` is the friendly name of the Windows Communications port (COMM port) that the TSP is using to communicate with the modem. The `hComm` is an open handle to the communications port for use with the Comm API and the Win32 `ReadFile` and `WriteFile` functions. This handle is opened in overlapped mode (via the `FILE_FLAG_OVERLAPPED` bit documented with the Win32 `CreateFile` function). I/O will happen asynchronously.

Asynchronous I/O allows a single-threaded application to begin a read or a write operation, continue processing Windows messages, and handle the I/O request when it has completed. Because this asynchronous I/O is more flexible, it is also more complicated. To simplify things, the tDaemon sample uses some tricks of the Comm API to turn the asynchronous I/O into polling. You may or may not want to use this technique in you own applications.[3]

The tDaemon Sample

The tDaemon sample is an example of a simple data modem application. Like the daemon dialer from the movie *War Games,* the tDaemon application dials a sequence of phone numbers, looking for a modem. When it finds one, it logs the phone number and captures the first four seconds of output, for example, the remote computer's login screen. The tDaemon sample is shown in Figure 6.2.

---

[2] Neither Windows nor TAPI has any built-in support for sending or receiving faxes.

[3] If you believe, as I do, that polling is not a good general-purpose technique, you should see John Hart's *Win32 System Programming* from Addison-Wesley for a thorough description of asynchronous I/O under Win32.

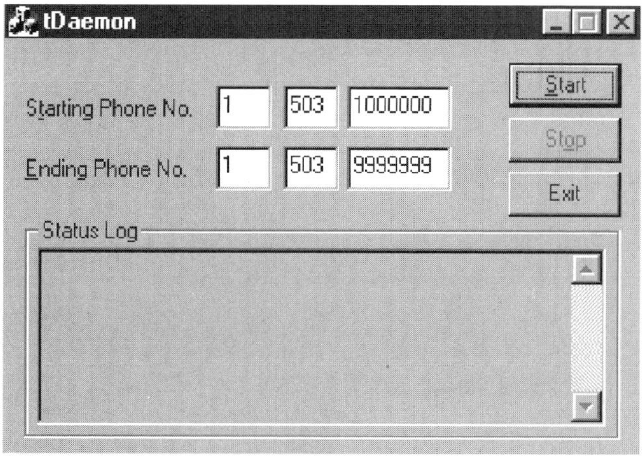

Figure 6.2: tDaemon sample.

Don't Use tDaemon!

I should mention that the tDaemon sample is meant only as an interesting example of how to send and receive data via a call established using TAPI. Do I have to say, "Don't hack into other people's computers!"? Actually, using tDaemon as a means of dialing unknown numbers is a violation of United States federal law, as stated in Title 47, Section 227 of the United States Code:

(b) Restrictions on use of automated telephone equipment

(1) Prohibitions

It shall be unlawful for any person within the United States—

(A) to make any call (other than a call made for emergency purposes or made with the prior express consent of the called party) using any automatic telephone dialing system or an artificial or prerecorded voice—

(i) to any emergency telephone line (including any "911" line and any emergency line of a hospital, medical physician or service office, health care facility, poison control center, or fire protection or law enforcement agency);

(ii) to the telephone line of any guest room or patient room of a hospital, health care facility, elderly home, or similar establishment; or

(iii) to any telephone number assigned to a paging service, cellular telephone service, specialized mobile radio service, or other radio common carrier service, or any service for which the called party is charged for the call.

The reason I felt comfortable publishing this sample at all is that most modern hackers use the Internet. Please don't prove me wrong.

The bulk of the tDaemon sample is contained in the `CtDaemonDlg` class. Notice how the `OpenValidLine` function opens the first line it finds that can make calls by using the `LINEMEDIAMODE_DATAMODEM` media mode:

```
bool CtDaemonDlg::OpenValidLine()
{
  DWORD    nLines = ::TfxGetNumLines();
  for( DWORD nLineID = 0; nLineID < nLines; nLineID++ )
  {
      CtLineDevCaps    ldc;
      if( TSUCCEEDED(ldc.GetDevCaps(nLineID)) &&
        (ldc.GetBearerModes() & LINEBEARERMODE_VOICE) &&
        (ldc.GetMediaModes() & LINEMEDIAMODE_DATAMODEM) &&
        (ldc.GetLineFeatures() & LINEFEATURE_MAKECALL) &&
        TSUCCEEDED(m_line.Open(nLineID, this)) )
        {
            return true;
        }
    }

    return false;
}
```

When making a call in the Dial method of `CtDaemonDlg`, the tDaemon application uses the `dwMediaMode` member of the `LINECALLPARAMS` structure to indicate that it is interested in making a call that has the `LINEMEDIA-MODE_DATAMODEM` media mode:

```
void CtDaemonDlg::Dial()
{
    CString sCountry; sCountry.Format("%d", m_nCountry);
    CString sArea;    sArea.Format("%d", m_nArea);
    CString sPhoneNo; sPhoneNo.Format("%d", m_nPhoneNo);
    CtPhoneNo pno(sCountry, sArea, sPhoneNo);

    CtTranslateOutput    to;
    TRESULT              tr;
    tr = to.TranslateAddress(
                    m_line.GetDeviceID(),
                    pno.GetTranslatable(0),
```

```
                            0,
                    LINETRANSLATEOPTION_CANCELCALLWAITING);

        if( TSUCCEEDED(tr) )
        {
            CString sDisplayable = to.GetDisplayableString();
            CString sDialable = to.GetDialableString();

            // Allocate a LINECALLPARAMS structure.
            LINECALLPARAMS* pCallParams =
                        AllocateCallParams(sDisplayable);
            if( pCallParams )
            {
                pCallParams->dwBearerMode =
                            LINEBEARERMODE_VOICE;
                pCallParams->dwMediaMode =
                            LINEMEDIAMODE_DATAMODEM;

                tr = m_call.MakeCall(sDialable,
                                pno.GetCountryCodeNum(),
                                this,
                                pCallParams));
                if( TPENDING(tr) )
                {
                    const UINT  nTimeOut = 30000;
                    m_nTimer = SetTimer(1, nTimeOut, 0);
                    LogStatus("Placing a call to '%s'...\r\n",
                            (LPCSTR)sDisplayable);
                }

                delete[] pCallParams;
            }
        }
    }
```

When the call has been connected, TAPI has done its job. Since TAPI provides no functions for data transfer, the underlying TSP must provide a handle for use with another Windows API. For example, the Unimodem TSP—the TSP that drives modems—can provide a handle for use with the Comm API. Once the call has been established, this handle can be obtained using the `lineGetID` function.

To automate the filling and access of a VARSTRING structure, the TFX provides the CtDeviceID class. This class wraps the variable-length VAR-STRING structure filled by the lineGetID function. To fill the structure, tDaemon passes the comm/datamodem device class name to the CtDeviceID method GetID. To retrieve the port name and communications port handle, tDaemon uses the CtDeviceID method GetHandleAndString. If this succeeds, the handle can be used to transfer data during the lifetime of the call.

```
void CtDaemonDlg::OnConnected()
{
    LogStatus("Got one! Output follows:\r\n");

    // Kill the timer
    KillTimer(m_nTimer); m_nTimer = 0;

    // Read data
    CtDeviceID   did;
    if( TSUCCEEDED(did.GetID("comm/datamodem",
                             m_call.GetHandle())) )
    {
        HANDLE   hComm;
        LPCSTR   pszPortName;
        pszPortName = did.GetHandleAndString(&hComm);

        if( hComm )
        {
            ReadData(hComm);
            CloseHandle(hComm);
        }
    }

    // Drop the call (and dial the next one)
    m_call.Drop();
}
```

For the purposes of the tDaemon sample, the flexibility provided by asynchronous I/O is a bit more than we need. To simplify things, when calling ReadFile we use the Comm API function SetCommTimeouts to turn off blocking or queuing of asynchronous I/O requests. Instead, the ReadData function in the tDaemon sample polls the COMM port for four seconds, dumping any data sent during that time to the status log. After four seconds, we use `PurgeComm` so that any pending data is discarded.[4]

```
void CtDaemonDlg::ReadData(HANDLE hComm)
{
  // Temporarily boost thread priority
  SetThreadPriority(GetCurrentThread(),
                    THREAD_PRIORITY_HIGHEST);

  // Cause read operation to return immediately with
  // the characters that have already been received,
  // even if no characters have been received.
  COMMTIMEOUTS     cto = { 0 };
  cto.ReadIntervalTimeout = MAXDWORD;
  SetCommTimeouts(hComm, &cto);

  const DWORD nTicks = 4000;  // 4 seconds
  const DWORD nTickStart = GetTickCount();

  // Needed with devices opened asynchronously.
  OVERLAPPED  ol = { 0 };

  while( GetTickCount() - nTickStart < nTicks )
  {
    char      sz[1024];
    DWORD     nBytes;
    if( ReadFile(hComm, sz, sizeof(sz)-1, &nBytes, &ol) &&
        nBytes )
    {
      sz[nBytes] = 0;
      LogStatus(sz);
    }
  }

  // Clear pending bytes and reset thread priority.
  PurgeComm(hComm, PURGE_RXCLEAR);
```

---

[4]This call to `PurgeComm` turns out to be extremely important under less-robust implementations of Win32. Don't forget it in your own data call applications.

```
SetThreadPriority(GetCurrentThread(),
                     THREAD_PRIORITY_NORMAL);
   LogStatus("\r\n");
}
```

Configuration Settings

If you're interested in building more-robust modem applications, you need to set more than just the transfer rate before making the call, for example, the flow control, speaker settings, and parity. The CPhoneNoDlg in the tDial sample shows the use of the function lineConfigDialog. This function allows the user to set system-wide device settings, for example, modem-specific settings for a modem device. However, many data call applications wish to keep device configuration on a per-call basis—the Windows HyperTerminal accessory does this. To allow the user to set device configuration settings, but not to change the system-side settings for the device, TAPI provides the lineConfigDialogEdit function:

```
LONG
lineConfigDialogEdit(
     DWORD             dwDeviceID,
     HWND              hwndOwner,
     LPCSTR            lpszDeviceClass,
     LPVOID            const lpDeviceConfigIn,
     DWORD             dwSize,
     LPVARSTRING       lpDeviceConfigOut);
```

The result of lineConfigDialogEdit is a VARSTRING structure filled with device-specific configuration settings. This data can be set before a call is placed using the TAPI function lineSetDevConfig:

```
LONG
lineSetDevConfig(
     DWORD             dwDeviceID,
     LPVOID            const lpDeviceConfig,
     DWORD             dwSize,
     LPCSTR            lpszDeviceClass);
```

If the current device configuration is needed, TAPI provides the lineGet-DevConfig function:

```
LONG
lineGetDevConfig(
     DWORD                   dwDeviceID,
     LPVARSTRING             lpDeviceConfig,
     LPCSTR                  lpszDeviceClass);
```

Using this technique, your data call application can allow the user to configure a device using `lineConfigDialogEdit` and store the results in an application-defined configuration file. When the user is prepared to place a call using a previously defined configuration, the device configuration is passed in as a parameter to `lineSetDevConfig` before the call is made.

Call Monitoring

A call monitoring application (or monitor, for short) is an application that watches calls without necessarily acting on them. This is useful for tracking incoming calls and logging caller ID information or displaying call notifications. This is also handy for logging outgoing calls and maintaining call duration information. To monitor active calls, a monitor must be able to discover active calls and to log the events of those calls. The monitor will typically use this information to show the user the calls that have happened (and are happening) on the system, the state of each call, the duration of each call, and, optionally, the name and phone number associated with each call.

Discovering Active Calls

A call monitor's job is to keep track of calls and log their activity. Therefore a monitor application must be able to determine what calls are active and in what state they are. When a monitor application starts, it will open all lines maintained by TAPI by using the `LINECALLPRIVILEGE_MONITOR` call privilege. This tells TAPI that the monitor wants information about calls it doesn't own. When a new call, either inbound or outbound, is detected, the monitor will be notified via the `LINE_APPNEWCALL` event.[5] The TFX routes the `LINE_APPNEWCALL`

---

[5] See Chapter 5 for a description of how the TFX simulates a `LINE_APPNEWCALL` event under TAPI 1.*x*.

event to the `OnLineNewCall` method in the `CtLineSink` (as discussed in Chapter 5).

To determine if a new call is inbound or outbound, the monitor needs to fill in a `LINECALLINFO` structure using the `lineGetCallInfo` function:

```
LONG
lineGetCallInfo(
    HCALL               hCall,
    LPLINECALLINFO      lpCallInfo);

typedef struct linecallinfo_tag
{
    DWORD       dwTotalSize;
    DWORD       dwNeededSize;
    DWORD       dwUsedSize;
    HLINE       hLine;
    DWORD       dwLineDeviceID;
    DWORD       dwAddressID;
    DWORD       dwBearerMode;
    DWORD       dwRate;
    DWORD       dwMediaMode;
    ...
    DWORD       dwCallStates;
    DWORD       dwOrigin;
    DWORD       dwCallerIDFlags;
    DWORD       dwCallerIDSize;
    DWORD       dwCallerIDOffset;
    DWORD       dwCallerIDNameSize;
    DWORD       dwCallerIDNameOffset;
    DWORD       dwAppNameSize;
    DWORD       dwAppNameOffset;
    DWORD       dwDisplayableAddressSize;
    DWORD       dwDisplayableAddressOffset;
    DWORD       dwCalledPartySize;
    DWORD       dwCalledPartyOffset;
    DWORD       dwCommentSize;
    DWORD       dwCommentOffset;
    ...
} LINECALLINFO, FAR *LPLINECALLINFO;
```

The `dwOrigin` member has the following values to decide whether the call is inbound or outbound:

```
#define LINECALLORIGIN_OUTBOUND          0x00000001
#define LINECALLORIGIN_INTERNAL          0x00000002
#define LINECALLORIGIN_EXTERNAL          0x00000004
#define LINECALLORIGIN_UNKNOWN           0x00000010
#define LINECALLORIGIN_UNAVAIL           0x00000020
#define LINECALLORIGIN_CONFERENCE        0x00000040
#define LINECALLORIGIN_INBOUND           0x00000080
```

`LINECALLORIGIN_OUTBOUND` means an outbound call. Everything else means an inbound call.

For most calls a monitor log will be created after the monitor application has been started. However, it's also possible that there are calls active before the monitor was started. A monitor will not receive any `LINE_APPNEWCALL` events for calls that have been placed before the monitor starts. `LINE_CALLSTATE` events will be sent with call handles that the application has not yet seen, but this will happen only during the transition of a call from one state to another. For a monitor to determine the calls that are active when it started, it must use the function `lineGetNewCalls`:

```
LONG
lineGetNewCalls(
    HLINE               hLine,
    DWORD               dwAddressID,
    DWORD               dwSelect,
    LPLINECALLLIST      lpCallList);
```

The `lineGetNewCalls` function is another polymorphic TAPI function. It takes an `HLINE` and possibly an address ID, depending on whether the `dwSelect` is `LINECALLSELECT_LINE` or `LINECALLSELECT_ADDRESS`. The result is a `LINECALLLIST` structure with a list of the calls the application doesn't know about:

```
typedef struct linecalllist_tag
{
    DWORD           dwTotalSize;
    DWORD           dwNeededSize;
    DWORD           dwUsedSize;
    DWORD           dwCallsNumEntries;
```

```
        DWORD          dwCallsSize;
        DWORD          dwCallsOffset;

} LINECALLLIST, FAR *LPLINECALLLIST;
```

A successful result from `lineGetNewCalls` will return call handles to all of the new calls on the line (or just for the address). Each of the calls will have been opened in monitor mode. These calls can be used to start the list of calls to monitor. Of course, like any call handle, the call handles returned from `lineGetNew-Calls` must be deallocated when the monitor is done with them, that is, after the call transitions to `LINECALLSTATE_IDLE`.

Caller ID

One piece of information a monitor is typically interested in is the name and phone number associated with the call. In the case of an outbound call made with a `LINECALLPARAMS` structure, the *callee information* is available in the `DisplayableAddress` and `CalledParty` size/offset pairs in the `LINECALLINFO` structure. In the case of an inbound call, the *caller information* is available in the `CallerID` and `CallerIDName` size/offset pairs.

Caller ID is a national standard data format for sending the phone number and the name of the caller when a call is made. Over a POTS line, Caller ID, if available, is sent as a burst of data between the first and second rings. Whether Caller ID is available depends on many factors. These include the capabilities of your local phone company, the capabilities of the company from where the call is originating, and the options you have on your telephone line (specifically, the caller ID option). Also a factor is the options the caller has on his or her telephone line, that is, whether they're blocking Caller ID or not. However, there are many varying shades of not having Caller ID information (as well as what Caller ID information is available) as defined by the `LINECALLPARTYID` flags:

```
#define LINECALLPARTYID_BLOCKED          0x00000001
#define LINECALLPARTYID_OUTOFAREA        0x00000002
#define LINECALLPARTYID_NAME             0x00000004
#define LINECALLPARTYID_ADDRESS          0x00000008
#define LINECALLPARTYID_PARTIAL          0x00000010
#define LINECALLPARTYID_UNKNOWN          0x00000020
#define LINECALLPARTYID_UNAVAIL          0x00000040
```

Although Caller ID may be available when a call is first presented to a monitor application (ISDN has this information immediately), it's more likely to be made available later in the call's life. When Caller ID information is available, the call's `LINECALLINFO` structure will change. This, in turn, will trigger a `LINE_CALLINFO` event from TAPI, with the `LINECALLINFO_CALLERID` subevent:

```
LINE_CALLINFO
dwDevice = (DWORD) hCall;
dwCallbackInstance = (DWORD) hCallback;
dwParam1 = (DWORD) CallInfoState;
dwParam2 = (DWORD) 0;
dwParam3 = (DWORD) 0;
```

When the monitor receives the `LINECALLINFO_CALLERID` event, it can use `lineGetCallInfo` to fill a `LINECALLINFO` structure and retrieve the Caller ID information, if it is available, or the reason for its unavailability, and add it to the information it's keeping about the call.

The tMonitor Sample

The call monitoring capabilities of tMonitor are supported by its use of the TFX. To handle `LINE_CALLINFO` messages, the `CtMonitorView` class implements the `OnCallInfo` method of `CtCallSink`. To fill the `LINECALLINFO`, the sample uses the `CtCallInfo` wrapper class.

```
void CtMonitorView::OnCallInfo(
    CtCall* pCall,
    DWORD    nCallInfo)
{
    // Possible to get several callinfo
    // notifications in one message.
    if( nCallInfo & LINECALLINFOSTATE_CALLERID )
    {
        CALLRECORD* pcr;
        int         nItem;
        if( FindCallRecord(pCall, &pcr, &nItem) )
        {
            ASSERT(pcr);

            CtCallInfo  ci;
            if( TSUCCEEDED(ci.GetCallInfo(pCall)) )
            {
                GetBestCallerID(ci, &(pcr->sName),
```

```
                                         &(pcr->sPhoneNo));
                    pcr->UpdateDialog();
                    GetListCtrl().Update(nItem);
                }
            }
        }
    }


static
void GetBestCallerID(
    const CtCallInfo&    ci,
    CString*             psName,
    CString*             psPhoneNo)
{
    LPCSTR      pszName = 0;
    LPCSTR      pszPhoneNo = 0;
    CtPhoneNo   pno;

    if( ci.GetCallerIDFlags() &
            LINECALLPARTYID_BLOCKED )
    {
        pszName = "<blocked>";
        pszPhoneNo = "<blocked>";
    }
    else if( ci.GetCallerIDFlags() &
                LINECALLPARTYID_OUTOFAREA )
    {
        pszName = "<out of area>";
        pszPhoneNo = "<out of area>";
    }
    else if( ci.GetCallerIDFlags() &
                LINECALLPARTYID_UNKNOWN )
    {
        pszName = "<unknown>";
        pszPhoneNo = "<unknown>";
    }
    else if( ci.GetCallerIDFlags() &
                LINECALLPARTYID_UNAVAIL )
    {
        pszName = "<unavailable>";
```

```
        pszPhoneNo = "<unavailable>";
    }
    else
    {
        pszName = ci.GetCallerIDName();

        pno.SetWholePhoneNo(ci.GetCallerID());
        pszPhoneNo = pno.GetTranslatable(0);
    }

    *psName = (pszName ? pszName : "<unknown>");
    *psPhoneNo = (pszPhoneNo ? pszPhoneNo : "<unknown>");
}
```

tMonitor also monitors the number of rings on a call before it was answered or abandoned and monitors the call duration. To monitor the number of rings, the tMonitor must adopt a separate strategy for outbound and inbound calls. For outbound calls, one of the call states is LINECALLSTATE_RINGBACK. When this state is detected (in the implementation of the CtCallSink method OnCall-State), the monitor uses this information to manually increment the number of rings from zero to one. Unfortunately, LINECALLSTATE_RINGBACK is only a notification that the far end of the call is being alerted. It is sent to the application only once and can't be used to keep an actual ring count.

In contrast, in the case of an inbound call, the call doesn't ring, the line does. This means a ring will be indicated as a LINEDEVSTATE_RINGING subevent (of the LINE_DEVSTATE event) and the dwParam3 parameter will hold the number of rings that have occurred so far. The TFX routes the LINE_DEVSTATE event to the OnLineDevState methods of CtLineSink.

Since call state changes rarely happen after a call has been connected, that is, when people are talking or data is being transferred, a monitor can't rely on messages from TAPI to notify it of changes in call duration. Instead, it must update the call's duration manually. The tMonitor sample uses a shared Windows timer for this purpose. If there is at least one active call, a timer will be used to update call durations every five seconds. In the handling of the WM_TIMER message, the tMonitor walks the list of all calls, updating the duration of active calls. This allows the user to see a periodically updated display of the duration of the active calls on the system.

Summary

TAPI is the logical switchboard of the 90s, routing calls to the proper applications based on the capabilities of the applications. Assisted Telephony requests are routed to willing request recipients. Calls with a specific media mode are routed to applications built to handle that media mode. If the media mode is unknown when the call is presented to the system, an application that has designated itself willing to answer that kind of call is also willing to continue to route the call in the event the media mode changes.

TAPI applications are often used to write data applications as well as interactive voice and automated voice applications. Although TAPI provides no support for transferring data, it does allow access to TSP-provided handles for use with data transfer APIs. And while all of the telephony information is flowing in the system, a monitor application can detect and log all interesting activity.

7

Telephony Service Providers

Watson, come here. I need you.
Alexander Graham Bell

While TAPI is wonderful, it would be fairly useless without the Telephony Service Providers (TSPs) talking to the telephony hardware. For example, the Unimodem TSP is handy for talking to modems. For more full-featured telephony devices, however, you'll need additional Service Providers. If you're a manufacturer of such devices, you're going to be responsible for building these Service Providers, which is the subject of this chapter.

Overview

Recall from Chapter 1, the overall architecture of TAPI, shown again here in Figure 7.1. Whenever an application makes a function call to TAPI requesting some service on a telephony device, TAPI forwards the request to the appropriate TSP. API's benefit is that applications always use the same functions to request the services of the TSP without being tied to any specific hardware. It's

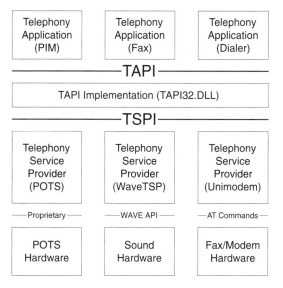

Figure 7.1: TAPI architecture.

the TSP's job to map requests to the hardware it's managing. For example, the Unimodem TSP provided with Windows maps its requests to Hayes AT commands that are sent to the modem via the serial port.

To access a TSP's functionality, TAPI requires that each TSP be packaged as a DLL with a set of well-known entry points. These entry points are explained in the TAPI Service Provider Interface (TSPI) Specification and declared in the `tspi.h` header file. The entry points are broken up into several logical categories, mirroring the TAPI categories of functionality. The TSPI defines over one hundred entry points, of which about twenty-five are needed to implement a basic TSP. In this chapter, I explore basic TSP functionality, including installation, initialization and shutdown, capabilities negotiation, exposure of telephony objects, event notification, and how to provide a user interface from a TSP.

Each area of TSP functionality consists of one or more functions exposed from the DLL. A TSP exposes a function by implementing it and putting it into the `.def` file, for example,

```cpp
// MyTSP.cpp
LONG TSPIAPI TSPI_providerInit(
    DWORD               dwTSPIVersion,
    DWORD               dwPermanentProviderID,
    DWORD               dwLineDeviceIDBase,
    DWORD               dwPhoneDeviceIDBase,
    DWORD               dwNumLines,
    DWORD               dwNumPhones,
    ASYNC_COMPLETION    pfnCompletionProc,
    LPDWORD             pdwTSPIOptions)
{
    ...
}

LONG TSPIAPI TSPI_providerShutdown(
    DWORD   dwTSPIVersion,
    DWORD   dwPermanentProviderID)
{
    ...
}

// MyTSP.def
LIBRARAY MYTSP
EXPORTS
```

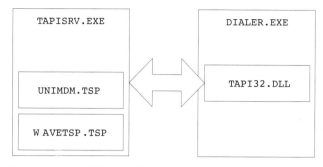

Figure 7.2: TAPISRV address space.

```
TSPI_providerInit
TSPI_providerShutdown
...
```

Under TAPI 2.0, when the first TAPI application calls `lineInitialize` or `phoneInitialize`, all of the installed TSPs are loaded into a single process separate from all of the TAPI applications. Each TSP is given a unique identifier. When a TAPI function is called, TAPI uses the arguments it's given, for example, the `HLINE` or the `HCALL`,[1] to map the call to the proper TSP's entry point. If the corresponding entry point isn't exposed from the TSP, TAPI returns the `LINEERR_OPERATIONUNAVAIL` error code.

The TAPISRV is the background process that loads and calls the TSPs. The `tapi32.dll` acts is the communications channel between the TAPI applications and the TAPISRV process. This separation is really for the convenience of the TSP implementer. Most TSPs access hardware, and it's much easier to write hardware access code if you can be guaranteed that only one address space is accessing that hardware. Figure 7.2 shows TAPISRV and the TSPs in relation to TAPI applications.

The Sample

The WaveTSP is a sample TSP using the simplest possible telephony device: your computer's speakers. How can your computer's speakers be considered a telephony device? When you punch numbers on your telephone keypad, the

---

[1] Of course, for the phone portion of the API, TAPI uses `HPHONE` arguments as well. Because phone functionality is so rarely provided, it won't be discussed in this chapter. However, it works in the same way that the line portion works.

Table 7.1: Bitness requirements for TSPs.			
	TAPI 1.3	*TAPI 1.4*	*TAPI 2.0*
Windows 3.x	16-bit TSPs.	N/A.	N/A.
Windows 95/OSR2 and Windows 98	16-bit TSPs.	16-bit TSPs.	16-bit and 32-bit TSPs.[2]
Windows NT 4.0 and Windows NT 5.0	N/A.	N/A.	32-bit TSPs.

[2] Windows 95 supports 32-bit TSPs only if TAPI 2.x has been installed.

telephone generates touchtones and sends them as audio to the Central Office (CO). The CO interprets these signals as digits to be dialed and uses them to establish a connection. However, there's no reason for the telephone itself to generate these tones. All that's required is that the CO hears the tones in enough fidelity to interpret them as digits. Your computer speakers work wonderfully for this task. Using the Windows Multiple Media API to play WAVE data, you can easily play DTMF tones and, if you hold the phone up to your speakers, the CO will hear the DTMF tones just as if the phone had generated them. This works with POTS as well as with many proprietary PBX and Key systems. In this chapter, I use the WaveTSP sample to explore a minimal TSP implementation.

One other interesting note about the sample TSP: It is 32-bit and works only for TAPI 2.0 or greater. Under TAPI 1.3 and 1.4, TSPs may only be 16-bit. Even when 32-bit applications are using 32-bit TAPI 1.4, TAPI will access only 16-bit TSPs.

Under TAPI 2.0, TSPs may be 32-bit. In fact, under NT4.0 or better, TAPI 2.0 TSPs are *required* to be 32-bit. Table 7.1 summarizes the bitness requirements for TSPs under the various versions of TAPI and Windows. I'm concentrating on 32-bit TSPs because they're required for NT4.0 and supported under the Windows 9x variants. For future development, 32-bit TAPI is clearly the way to go.

Initialization and Shutdown

A TAPI application begins its communications with the TSP in its first call: `line-Initialize`. The first application to do this causes TAPISRV to load all of the available TSPs and to call three functions on each one of them—`TSPI_line-NegotiateTSPIVersion`, `TSPI_providerInit`, and `TSPI_provider-EnumDevices`:

```
LONG
TSPI_lineNegotiateTSPIVersion(
    DWORD    dwDeviceID,
    DWORD    dwLowVersion,
    DWORD    dwHighVersion,
    LPDWORD  pdwTSPIVersion)


LONG
TSPI_providerInit(
    DWORD               dwTSPIVersion,
    DWORD               dwPermanentProviderID,
    DWORD               dwLineDeviceIDBase,
    DWORD               dwPhoneDeviceIDBase,
    DWORD               dwNumLines,
    DWORD               dwNumPhones,
    ASYNC_COMPLETION    pfnCompletionProc,
    LPDWORD             pdwTSPIOptions)


LONG
TSPI_providerEnumDevices(
    DWORD        dwPermanentProviderID,
    LPDWORD      pdwNumLines,
    LPDWORD      pdwNumPhones,
    HPROVIDER    hProvider,
    LINEEVENT    pfnLineCreateProc,
    PHONEEVENT   pfnPhoneCreateProc)
```

TSPI_lineNegotiateTSPIVersion is actually called once by TAPI
before any line is open to let TAPI know the maximum version number your TSP
can support, regardless of the line device ID. To indicate this, it passes in the
special value INITIALIZE_NEGOTIATION in the dwDeviceID parameter.
Using the dwLowVersion and the dwHighVersion, it's the job of the TSP
to calculate the highest version number it's willing to support, which is returned
in *pdwTSPIVersion. A TSP that uses the same maximum version number for
every line device and wants to be compatible with older applications would implement TSPI_lineNegotiateTSPIVersion like this:

```
LONG TSPIAPI TSPI_lineNegotiateTSPIVersion(
    DWORD    dwDeviceID,
    DWORD    dwLowVersion,
    DWORD    dwHighVersion,
    LPDWORD  pdwTSPIVersion)
```

```
{
    LONG     tr = 0;

    if( dwLowVersion <= TAPI_CURRENT_VERSION )
    {
        *pdwTSPIVersion = MIN(TAPI_CURRENT_VERSION,
                                dwHighVersion);
    }
    else
    {
        tr = LINEERR_INCOMPATIBLEAPIVERSION;
    }

    return tr;
}
```

After the call to `lineInitialize` has returned, and the client calls `lineNegotiateAPIVersion`, TAPI will forward these calls to `TSPI_lineNegotiateTSPIVersion` with a specific device ID in case the TSP wants to provide device-specific versioning.

The second call a TSP receives is during the initial call to `lineInitialize`: `TSPI_providerEnumDevices`. TAPI needs to know how many devices there are in the system. Each TSP can provide zero or more line devices and zero or more phone devices. The number of devices that the TSP is providing is returned to TAPI via the `pdwNumLines` and `pdwNumPhones` parameters, respectively. TAPI uses the total number of lines and phones to fill the `dwNumLines` and `dwNumPhones` parameters in `lineInitialize[Ex]` and `phoneInitialize[Ex]`.

The `dwPermanentProviderID` and `hProvider` parameters to `TSPI_providerEnumDevices` are unique identifiers. The first is a unique ID assigned by TAPI when the TSP is installed. The `dwPermanentProviderID` parameter is useful for generating other permanent IDs required by TAPI. The second is a unique ID for as long as the TSP is loaded. The `hProvider` parameter is used to send a special kind of user interface (UI) generating event, as discussed later in the chapter.

The last two parameters, `pfnLineCreateProc` and `pfnPhoneCreateProc`, are callbacks into TAPI for use when devices are created during the lifetime of the TSP. For example, when a user installs a new modem via the Modems Control Panel, the Unimodem TSP uses these two function pointers to notify TAPI that a new line and a new phone have been created. These calls are reflected to TAPI applications via the `LINE_CREATE` and `PHONE_CREATE` events.

A minimal implementation of `TSPI_providerEnumDevices` to expose a single line device would be implemented like this:

```
LONG TSPIAPI TSPI_providerEnumDevices(
    DWORD       dwPermanentProviderID,
    LPDWORD     pdwNumLines,
    LPDWORD     pdwNumPhones,
    HPROVIDER   hProvider,
    LINEEVENT   pfnLineCreateProc,
    PHONEEVENT  pfnPhoneCreateProc)
{
    g_hProvider = hProvider;
    *pdwNumLines = 1;
    *pdwNumPhones = 0;
    return 0;
}
```

TAPI uses the results of `TSPI_providerEnumDevices` to build a table mapping line and phone device identifiers to specific TSPs. Each entry in the table maps a device ID to a TSP and a device ID base. The device ID base can be used by the TSP to calculate a zero-based TSP-relative device ID. For example, on a system with the WaveTSP (which provides a single line device), three modems, and a BRI-ISDN connection, the device IDs for line devices are given in Table 7.2.

Whenever TAPI provides a line ID or a phone ID to a TSP, it is always the system-wide device ID. Each TSP's device ID base is provided in the call to `TSPI_providerInit` as the `dwLineDeviceIDBase` and `dwPhone-DeviceIDBase` parameters. A TSP can calculate a zero-based device ID by subtracting the appropriate ID base from the system-wide device ID.

Table 7.2: Example line device ID table.			
System-wide Device ID	TSP	Device ID Base	TSP-relative Device ID
0	WaveTSP	0	0 − 0 = 0
1	Unimodem	1	1 − 1 = 0
2	Unimodem	1	2 − 1 = 1
3	Unimodem	1	3 − 1 = 2
4	ISDN TSP	4	4 − 4 = 0
5	ISDN TSP	4	5 − 4 = 1

`TSPI_providerInit` is the final function triggered by the first client calling `lineInitialize`. `TSPI_providerInit` is the TSPs chance to get things started by initializing hardware, reading initialization data from the Registry, and so on. The first parameter, `dwTSPIVersion`, should be the result of the initialization call to `TSPI_lineNegotiateAPIVersion`. The second parameter, `dwPermanentProviderID`, is usually cached so that it can be used to compose permanent line identifiers in implementations of `TSPI_lineGetDevCaps` (as shown later in the chapter).

To notify TAPI that an asynchronous operation has been completed, a TSP uses another callback function. This one is provided in the `pfnCompletionProc` parameter of `TSPI_providerInit` and is discussed in full shortly.

The final parameter to `TSPI_providerInit`, `pdwTSPIOptions`, is used to configure how your TSP runs in the TAPISRV process. The only option supported in the current version of TAPI is `LINETSPIOPTION_NONREENTRANT`, which serializes calls to your TSP. This option is handy during development when you're adding functionality to your TSP. It keeps you from having to do multithreaded data synchronization at the same time you're just trying to get stuff to work. However, serializing function calls may significantly degrade performance, so if at all possible, make your TSP thread-safe and do not use the nonreentrant option.

A typical implementation of the `TSPI_providerInit` function will cache, in addition to any TSP-specific initialization, the input permanently and may also set some options, for example:

```
LONG TSPIAPI TSPI_providerInit(
    DWORD                   dwTSPIVersion,
    DWORD                   dwPermanentProviderID,
    DWORD                   dwLineDeviceIDBase,
    DWORD                   dwPhoneDeviceIDBase,
    DWORD                   dwNumLines,
    DWORD                   dwNumPhones,
    ASYNC_COMPLETION        pfnCompletionProc,
    LPDWORD                 pdwTSPIOptions)
    {
    g_dwPermanentProviderID = dwPermanentProviderID;
    g_dwLineDeviceIDBase = dwLineDeviceIDBase;
    g_pfnCompletionProc  = pfnCompletionProc;
    *pdwTSPIOptions = LINETSPIOPTION_NONREENTRANT;
    return 0;
    }
```

After the last TAPI application has called `lineShutdown` and before TAPISRV unloads your TSP, TAPI will let your TSP know to shut down its services. It does this by calling `TSPI_providerShutdown`:

```
LONG
TSPI_providerShutdown(
    DWORD    dwTSPIVersion,
    DWORD    dwPermanentProviderID)
```

Capabilities Negotiation

Before an application opens a line, it typically checks the line capabilities and often also the address capabilities. It does this via the `lineGetDevCaps` and `lineGetAddressCaps` functions. These two functions are forwarded directly to the TSP functions `TSPI_lineGetDevCaps` and `TSPI_lineGetAddressCaps`:

```
LONG
TSPI_lineGetDevCaps(
    DWORD           dwDeviceID,
    DWORD           dwTSPIVersion,
    DWORD           dwExtVersion,
    LPLINEDEVCAPS   pldc)

LONG
TSPI_lineGetAddressCaps(
    DWORD               dwDeviceID,
    DWORD               dwAddressID,
    DWORD               dwTSPIVersion,
    DWORD               dwExtVersion,
    LPLINEADDRESSCAPS   pac)
```

Remember that the capability structures that these functions fill are TAPI VLSs. This time, however, we're on the other side. It's your job to calculate the needed and the used sizes, set the `dwNeededSize` and `dwUsedSize` members in the structure, and compare the needed size against the total size to determine how much of the structure to fill in. If the total size is enough to fit all of the fixed sized and the variable-sized data, then we do so and return successfully. If not, we simply fill in the fixed size portion and still return successfully. Because the size and elements of the structure change with the version of TAPI, only TAPISRV really knows if the structure is too small. It will indicate that to the application with the LINEERR_STRUCTURETOOSMALL.

The WaveTSP implementations of the line and address capability functions look like this:

```
LONG TSPIAPI TSPI_lineGetDevCaps(
    DWORD           dwDeviceID,
    DWORD           dwTSPIVersion,
    DWORD           dwExtVersion,
    LPLINEDEVCAPS   pldc)
{
    LONG            tr = 0;
    const wchar_t   szProviderInfo[] = L"WAVE Service Provider";
    const wchar_t   szLineName[] = L"WaveLine";

    pldc->dwNeededSize = sizeof(LINEDEVCAPS) +
                         sizeof(szProviderInfo) +
                         sizeof(szLineName);

    if( pldc->dwNeededSize <= pldc->dwTotalSize )
    {
        pldc->dwUsedSize = pldc->dwNeededSize;

        pldc->dwProviderInfoSize    = sizeof(szProviderInfo);
        pldc->dwProviderInfoOffset  = sizeof(LINEDEVCAPS) + 0;
        wchar_t* pszProviderInfo = (wchar_t*)((BYTE*)pldc +
                                    pldc->dwProviderInfoOffset);
        wcscpy(pszProviderInfo, szProviderInfo);

        pldc->dwLineNameSize        = sizeof(szLineName);
        pldc->dwLineNameOffset      = sizeof(LINEDEVCAPS) +
                                      sizeof(szProviderInfo);
        wchar_t* pszLineName = (wchar_t*)((BYTE*)pldc +
                                pldc->dwLineNameOffset);
        wcscpy(pszLineName, szLineName);
    }
    else
    {
        pldc->dwUsedSize = sizeof(LINEDEVCAPS);
    }
```

```
    pldc->dwStringFormat        = STRINGFORMAT_ASCII;

#define MAKEPERMLINEID(dwPermProviderID, dwDeviceID) \
    ((LOWORD(dwPermProviderID) << 16) | dwDeviceID)
    pldc->dwPermanentLineID   =
            MAKEPERMLINEID(g_dwPermanentProviderID,
                        dwDeviceID - g_dwLineDeviceIDBase);
    pldc->dwAddressModes        = LINEADDRESSMODE_ADDRESSID;
    pldc->dwNumAddresses        = 1;
    pldc->dwBearerModes         = LINEBEARERMODE_VOICE;
    pldc->dwMediaModes          = LINEMEDIAMODE_INTERACTIVEVOICE;
    pldc->dwGenerateDigitModes= LINEDIGITMODE_DTMF;
    pldc->dwDevCapFlags         = LINEDEVCAPFLAGS_CLOSEDROP;
    pldc->dwMaxNumActiveCalls = 1;
    pldc->dwLineFeatures        = LINEFEATURE_MAKECALL;

    // DialParams
    pldc->MinDialParams = g_dpMin;
    pldc->MaxDialParams = g_dpMax;
    pldc->DefaultDialParams = g_dpDef;

    return tr;
}

LONG TSPIAPI TSPI_lineGetAddressCaps(
    DWORD               dwDeviceID,
    DWORD               dwAddressID,
    DWORD               dwTSPIVersion,
    DWORD               dwExtVersion,
    LPLINEADDRESSCAPS   pac)
{
    if( dwAddressID != 0 )
        return EPILOG(LINEERR_INVALADDRESSID);

    pac->dwNeededSize           = sizeof(LINEADDRESSCAPS);
    pac->dwUsedSize             = sizeof(LINEADDRESSCAPS);

    pac->dwLineDeviceID         = dwDeviceID;
    pac->dwAddressSharing       = LINEADDRESSSHARING_PRIVATE;
    pac->dwCallInfoStates       = LINECALLINFOSTATE_MEDIAMODE |
```

```
                                            LINECALLINFOSTATE_APPSPECIFIC;

      pac->dwCallerIDFlags        = LINECALLPARTYID_UNAVAIL;
      pac->dwCalledIDFlags        = LINECALLPARTYID_UNAVAIL;
      pac->dwRedirectionIDFlags   = LINECALLPARTYID_UNAVAIL;
      pac->dwRedirectingIDFlags   = LINECALLPARTYID_UNAVAIL;

      pac->dwCallStates           = LINECALLSTATE_IDLE |
                                     LINECALLSTATE_DIALING |
                                     LINECALLSTATE_CONNECTED;

      pac->dwDialToneModes        = LINEDIALTONEMODE_UNAVAIL;
      pac->dwBusyModes            = LINEBUSYMODE_UNAVAIL;
      pac->dwSpecialInfo          = LINESPECIALINFO_UNAVAIL;

      pac->dwDisconnectModes      = LINEDISCONNECTMODE_UNAVAIL;

      pac->dwMaxNumActiveCalls    = 1;
      pac->dwAddrCapFlags         = LINEADDRCAPFLAGS_DIALED;

      pac->dwCallFeatures         = LINECALLFEATURE_DIAL |
                                     LINECALLFEATURE_DROP |
                                     LINECALLFEATURE_GENERATEDIGITS;

      pac->dwAddressFeatures      = LINEADDRFEATURE_MAKECALL;

      return 0;
   }
```

Notice that the returned string must be in Unicode. TAPI 2.0 requires that all string handling in the TSP happen in Unicode. Also notice that even though we're returning the string in Unicode format, we are declaring that all strings returned for this line are in ASCII. That is, the implementation of `TSPI_lineGetDevCaps` sets the `dwStringFormat` member of the `LINEDEVCAPS` structure to `STRING-FORMAT_ASCII`. This is an instruction to TAPI to translate the string into ASCII format before handing it to the TAPI client. Returning strings in ASCII is a convenience for the majority of Windows programmers, who have yet to learn to appreciate Unicode.[3]

_____

[3] Not that anyone bothers to check the `dwStringFormat` member anyway.

Just How Permanent Is `dwPermanentLineID`?

Permanent line IDs are used by applications that keep track of a user's "preferred" line. The idea is that if the TSP is uninstalled, an application will be able to tell that the preferred line is no longer available and, instead of using another by mistake, will ask the user to pick another preference. For this functionality to work, the TSP must provide some kind of permanent ID for each of its lines, no matter what the device ID happens to be that day. Microsoft recommends that to calculate a permanent line ID, you combine the zero-based TSP relative device ID with the permanent provider ID, like so:

```
dwPermLineID = (dwPermProviderID << 16 | dwDeviceID -
                dwLineDeviceIDBase);
```

You might question the safety of this algorithm. After all, the permanent provider ID is a 32-bit number, which is certainly larger than the 16 bits it's being shifted by. Put your mind at ease. Since permanent provider IDs are assigned sequentially starting at 1, it seems unlikely that the user will install 65,536 (2^{16}) TSPs on a system and therefore invalidate the algorithm—at least not before having to reformat the hard drive in utter frustration.

Another capability discovery function used by TAPI applications is `line-GetID`. The `lineGetID` function provides the universal backdoor to extending TAPI for any kind of additional API, for example, the Win32 Communications API and the Multimedia API. When TAPI gets a call to `lineGetID`, it forwards it to `TSPI_lineGetID`:

```
LONG TSPIAPI TSPI_lineGetID(
    HDRVLINE    hdLine,
    DWORD       dwAddressID,
    HDRVCALL    hdCall,
    DWORD       dwSelect,
    LPVARSTRING pDeviceID,
    LPCWSTR     pszDeviceClass,
    HANDLE      hTargetProcess);
```

The parameters to `TSPI_lineGetID` are the same as those for `lineGetID` but for two exceptions. One is that the `HLINE` and `HCALL` parameters have been switched to `HDRVLINE` and `HDRVCALL` types. When we are asked to create a new line or a new call (see `TSPI_lineOpen` and `TSPI_lineMakeCall` below), TAPI allows us to set the unique identifiers ourselves. These 32-bit opaque handles make an excellent storage space for an object's *this* pointer, and that's exactly how the WaveTSP uses them.

The second exception between `lineGetID` and `TSPI_lineGetID` is the presence of one additional parameter: `hTargetProcess`. This is the Win32 process handle that identifies the process that wishes to access some additional device provided by the TSP. For example, Unimodem uses the `hTarget-Process` handle to call the Win32 function `DuplicateHandle` on the handle it has open on the communications port.

A TSP is free to implement `TSPI_lineGetID` as it chooses, even going so far as to provide nonstandard device handles. However, this function also has another use. If a TAPI application has an `HLINE` and would like the system-wide device ID, it can call `lineGetID` using the `tapi/line` device class. For example, the following implementation would do the required mapping:

```
LONG TSPIAPI TSPI_lineGetID(
    HDRVLINE    hdLine,
    DWORD       dwAddressID,
    HDRVCALL    hdCall,
    DWORD       dwSelect,
    LPVARSTRING pDeviceID,
    LPCWSTR     pszDeviceClass,
    HANDLE      hTargetProcess)
{
    LONG        tr = 0;
    CtspCall*   pCall = (dwSelect == LINECALLSELECT_CALL
                        ? (CtspCall*)hdCall : 0);
    CtspLine*   pLine = (dwSelect == LINECALLSELECT_LINE
                        ? (CtspLine*)hdLine
                        : (pCall ? pCall->GetLine() : 0));

    if( lstrcmpiW(pszDeviceClass, L"tapi/line") == 0 )
    {
        pDeviceID->dwNeededSize = sizeof(VARSTRING) +
                                    sizeof(DWORD);

        if( pDeviceID->dwNeededSize <=
            pDeviceID->dwTotalSize )
        {
            pDeviceID->dwUsedSize = pDeviceID->dwNeededSize;
            pDeviceID->dwStringFormat = STRINGFORMAT_BINARY;
```

```
          pDeviceID->dwStringSize = sizeof(DWORD);
          pDeviceID->dwStringOffset = sizeof(VARSTRING);

          *((LPDWORD)(pDeviceID + 1)) = pLine->GetDeviceID();
        }
        else
        {
            pDeviceID->dwUsedSize = 3 * sizeof(DWORD);
            tr = LINEERR_STRUCTURETOOSMALL;
        }
      }
      else
      {
        tr = LINEERR_NODEVICE;
      }

      return tr;
    }
```

Because TAPI knows the device ID for every HLINE, it will provide support for the tapi/line device class itself if your TSP simply provides the following implementation:[4]

```
LONG TSPIAPI TSPI_lineGetID(
      HDRVLINE      hdLine,
      DWORD         dwAddressID,
      HDRVCALL      hdCall,
      DWORD         dwSelect,
      LPVARSTRING   pDeviceID,
      LPCWSTR       pszDeviceClass,
      HANDLE        hTargetProcess)
  {
    // Let TAPI handle "tapi/line"
    return LINEERR_NODEVICE;
  }
```

---

[4]This works similarly with TSPI_phoneGetID and tapi/phone.

Lines

After a suitable line has been found, it will be opened with `lineOpen`, which TAPI will forward to `TSPI_lineOpen`:

```
LONG
TSPI_lineOpen(
    DWORD        dwDeviceID,
    HTAPILINE    htLine,
    LPHDRVLINE   phdLine,
    DWORD        dwTSPIVersion,
    LINEEVENT    pfnEventProc)
```

This function is where the TSP will typically reserve some hardware resource for its exclusive use. Once the line is successfully opened, TAPI may hand out many HLINEs representing this device—one to the owner and one to each monitor. However, this single device will have two identifiers. One is assigned by the TSP, and one is assigned by TAPI. As far as TAPI is concerned, you can assign any 32-bit value you like to `*phdLine` and it will be sent back on all function calls for that line. As mentioned earlier in this section, this is an excellent place for an object's *this* pointer. However, when calls are made back into TAPI—to fire a telephony event with the `pfnEventProc` parameter (discussed shortly)—TAPI needs its own ID for the line. This ID is provided in the `htLine` parameter.

The WaveTSP implements the `TSPI_lineOpen` function by creating an instance of a `CtspLine` object and stuffing its address into `phdLine`. The constructor for the `CtspLine` class caches the important values passed into the `TSPI_lineOpen` function:

```
LONG TSPIAPI TSPI_lineOpen(
    DWORD        dwDeviceID,
    HTAPILINE    htLine,
    LPHDRVLINE   phdLine,
    DWORD        dwTSPIVersion,
    LINEEVENT    pfnEventProc)
{
    LONG         tr = LINEERR_NOMEM;
    CtspLine*    pLine = new CtspLine(htLine,
                                      pfnEventProc,
                                      dwDeviceID);
```

```
    if( pLine )
    {
      *phdLine = (HDRVLINE)pLine;
      tr = 0;
    }

    return tr;
  }
```

But suppose the line is opened with the intent of handling incoming calls, that is, with a call privilege of anything but LINECALLPRIVILEGE_NONE. Further, suppose TAPI hasn't already asked the TSP to detect calls of the media mode requested by the application. In this case, TAPI will call TSPI_lineSet-DefaultMediaDetection:

```
LONG
TSPI_lineSetDefaultMediaDetection(
    HDRVLINE     hdLine,
    DWORD        dwMediaModes)
```

This notifies the TSP that an application is interested in calls of the media modes specified in dwMediaModes and that if it should detect any such calls, please let TAPI know. A failure return from this function fails the lineOpen call as well. Since the WaveTSP does not support incoming calls, it implements TSPI_lineSetDefaultMediaDetection by simply returning LINEERR_OPERATIONUNAVAIL.[5]

When the line is no longer needed, the call to lineClose will be forwarded to the TSPI_lineClose function:

```
LONG
TSPI_lineClose(
    HDRVLINE     hdLine)
```

If there are any outstanding asynchronous functions, the implementation of TSPI_lineClose must post their results before it returns. Likewise, if the LINEDEVCAPS_CLOSEDROP bit is set in the LINEDEVCAPS structure, all

---

[5]Normally, a TSP call lets TAPI know to return LINEERR_OPERATIONUNAVAIL simply by not exposing that function. Unfortunately, the current implementation of TAPISRV crashes if this function is not exposed from the TSP.

active calls must be dropped at this time. Finally, when this function is called, no more events may be sent using the `HTAPILINE` value passed in on `TSPI_lineOpen`.

TSP Objects

Just as TAPI applications use line, call, and phone objects implemented by TAPI, TAPI relies on line, call, and phone objects implemented by the TSP. Because most telephony applications are very similar in structure, the TFX can provide a framework for building these kinds of applications and be generally useful. However, TSPs are far more specialized and specific. For ease of implementation, the WaveTSP declares two classes to represent the telephony objects it exposes: `CtspLine` and `CtspCall`. These classes are not generic framework classes but rather, are specific to the WaveTSP. Feel free to use these classes as a model for the development of your own TSPs, however.

Calls

Once the line has been opened, a TAPI application will often proceed to making a call via `lineMakeCall`, which is mapped to the TSP function `TSPI_lineMakeCall`:

```
LONG
TSPI_lineMakeCall(
    DRV_REQUESTID        dwRequestID,
    HDRVLINE             hdLine,
    HTAPICALL            htCall,
    LPHDRVCALL           phdCall,
    LPCWSTR              pszDestAddress,
    DWORD                dwCountryCode,
    LPLINECALLPARAMS     const pCallParams)
```

The `TSPI_lineMakeCall` function is a request from TAPI for the TSP to make a new outbound call. The TSP is provided with the destination address, the country code, and the optional `LINECALLPARAMS`, and TAPI expects a `HDRCALL` in return. The WaveTSP forwards the `MakeCall` request to the line indicated by the `HDRVLINE` parameter:

```
LONG TSPIAPI TSPI_lineMakeCall(
    DRV_REQUESTID        dwRequestID,
```

```
    HDRVLINE            hdLine,
    HTAPICALL           htCall,
    LPHDRVCALL          phdCall,
    LPCWSTR             pszDestAddress,
    DWORD               dwCountryCode,
    LPLINECALLPARAMS    const pCallParams)
{

    LONG      tr;
    CtspLine*  pLine = (CtspLine*)hdLine;
    tr = pLine->MakeCall(dwRequestID, htCall, phdCall,
                    pszDestAddress, dwCountryCode,
                    pCallParams);
    return tr;
}
```

If the call is started successfully, the `CtspLine` member function `Make-Call` will fill in the `phdCall` parameter with a new `CtspCall` pointer and return the `dwRequestID`. When the TSP has detected that the call has been successfully made (although not necessarily connected), it will signal TAPI via the asynchronous completion function. If the call cannot be made, the member function will fail immediately and never call the completion function. Asynchronous functions are discussed in more detail later in the chapter.

While `TSPI_lineMakeCall` signals the beginning of the life of the call, `TSPI_lineDrop` signals the end of the active life of the call. When the application is no longer interested in the call as a connection between two parties, it calls the `lineDrop` function. This function, in turn, is forwarded to the `TSPI_lineDrop` function:

```
LONG
TSPI_lineDrop(
    DRV_REQUESTID       dwRequestID,
    HDRVCALL            hdCall,
    LPCSTR              lpsUserUserInfo,
    DWORD               dwSize)
```

The `TSPI_lineDrop` function is a signal to terminate the physical connection represented by the call and transition the state of the call to idle. However, the status information associated with the call shouldn't be deallocated until after TAPI calls `TSPI_lineCloseCall`:

```
LONG
TSPI_lineCloseCall(
    HDRVCALL            hdCall)
```

This function is an indication that all of the call's resources should be deallocated. There is no guarantee, by the way, that `TSPI_lineDrop` will be called before `TSPI_lineCloseCall`, so `TSPI_lineCloseCall` should be prepared to drop an active call as well as reclaim the call's resources. The WaveTSP implements these two functions like this:

```
LONG TSPIAPI TSPI_lineDrop(
    DRV_REQUESTID    dwRequestID,
    HDRVCALL         hdCall,
    LPCSTR           psUserUserInfo,
    DWORD            dwSize)
{
    CtspCall*   pCall = (CtspCall*)hdCall;

    pCall->Drop();

    // TSPI_lineDrop is asynchronous, so
    // the result needs to be sent back
    // via the asynch. completion function.
    g_pfnCompletionProc(dwRequestID, 0);

    return dwRequestID;
}

LONG TSPIAPI TSPI_lineCloseCall(
    HDRVCALL     hdCall)
{
    CtspCall*   pCall = (CtspCall*)hdCall;

    // Drop the call if it wasn't
    // already dropped via TSPI_lineDrop
    pCall->Drop();
    delete pCall;

    return 0;
}
```

Asynchronous Functions

Two of the three call functions just discussed were asynchronous. An asynchronous function is supposed to either fail immediately or start an operation that can take arbitrarily long. When the operation has either completed successfully or failed, it's the TSP's job to notify TAPI using the proper request ID. For this scheme to work, it is the responsibility of every asynchronous function either to return a negative failure code immediately or to return a request identifier and endeavor somehow to be asynchronous.

Actually being asynchronous can be difficult, but TAPI can help. It does this in one way by assigning each asynchronous function a request ID and passing it as the first parameter to the TSPI function itself. When the asynchronous function has completed, either successfully or unsuccessfully, the TSP uses the request ID to call the asynchronous completion function pointer passed into `TSPI_providerInit`. The `ASYNC_COMPLETION` type is a `typedef` for a function that takes a `DWORD` request ID and a `LONG` result:

```
typedef void (CALLBACK * ASYNC_COMPLETION)(
    DRV_REQUESTID        dwRequestID,
    LONG                 lResult)
```

TAPI also helps with simulating asynchrony. It is not the TSP's responsibility to send asynchronous completion results asynchronously. By this I mean that if the asynchronous function succeeds synchronously, it may call the asynchronous completion function immediately. This saves the TSP from spinning a thread or pumping a message loop simply to pretend to be asynchronous. Whenever the asynchronous function calls the asynchronous completion function, TAPI queues the result until *after* the application has received the request ID as the result of the asynchronous function call.

For example, the `CtspLine` member function `MakeCall` consists mainly of creating a `CtspCall` object that will dial the `pszDestAddress` string. If the `pszDestAddress` is empty (which is legal), the `CtspCall` detects this. It then signals to TAPI, using the asynchronous completion function, that the `lineMakeCall` has completed successfully *before the call to lineMakeCall has returned.* TAPI will handle this by returning the `dwRequestID` to the application that has called `lineMakeCall` and following up immediately with a `LINE_REPLY` event.

Spontaneous Events

During the lifetime of any telephony object, the underlying device being modeled can change. It's the TSP's job to notice these changes and reflect them to TAPI via calls to the event procedure provided in the `pfnEventProc` parameter of the `TSPI_lineOpen` function. The TSP event procedure is a function with the following signature:

```
typedef void (CALLBACK * LINEEVENT)(
    HTAPILINE         htLine,
    HTAPICALL         htCall,
    DWORD             dwMsg,
    DWORD             dwParam1,
    DWORD             dwParam2,
    DWORD             dwParam3)
```

This should look familiar. It's almost exactly like the `LINECALLBACK` function that TAPI uses to signal an application of a telephony event. In fact, TAPI's implementation of the event procedure simply broadcasts the message to all interested applications.

The TSP should call the event procedure whenever it encounters a situation defined by any of the line messages, for example, `LINE_LINEDEVSTATE` and `LINE_CALLSTATE`. Notice that TAPI requires its identifier for the devices involved—the `HTAPILINE` and the `HTAPICALL`. It does not require the TSP's identifiers—the `HDRVLINE` and the `HDRVCALL`. For example, for a TSP to transition a call to idle in response to the `TSPI_lineDrop` function, it must fire a `LINE_CALLSTATE` event:

```
void DropCall(HTAPILINE htLine, HTAPICALL htCall)
{
    g_pfnEventProc(htLine,
                   htCall,
                   LINE_CALLSTATE,
                   LINECALLSTATE_IDLE,
                   0,
                   0);
}
```

New Calls

TSPs have another event for notifying TAPI of a new call in addition to all of the line events defined in `tapi.h`: LINE_NEWCALL:

```
LINE_NEWCALL
htLine = (HTAPILINE) hLineDevice;
htCall = (HTAPICALL) 0;
dwMsg = (DWORD) LINE_NEWCALL;
dwParam1 = (DWORD)(HDRVCALL) hdCall;
dwParam2 = (DWORD)(LPHTAPICALL) &htCall;
dwParam3 = (DWORD) 0;
```

A new call notification happens in the reverse order of a make call request. TAPI does not assign a HTAPICALL identifier for the call and ask for an HDRVCALL. Instead, the TSP, when firing the LINE_NEWCALL event, provides the HDRVCALL identifier and passes a pointer to an HTAPICALL to receive TAPI's identifier for the call. For example, to notify TAPI of a new call, a TSP would do this:

```
HTAPICALL NewCall(HTAPILINE htLine, HDRVCALL hdCall)
{
    HTAPICALL htCall;
    g_pfnEventProc(htLine,
                   0,
                   LINE_NEWCALL,
                   (DWORD)hdCall,
                   (DWORD)&htCall,
                   0);
    return htCall;
}
```

After the TSP has successfully received the htCall, it must follow up with the initial state of the call via a LINE_CALLSTATE event. Specifically, in the case of a new, unanswered inbound call, the initial call state should be LINECALL-STATE_OFFERING. This will often be followed by a LINE_LINEDEVSTATE message to indicate ringing. However, in the case of a new, outbound call, such as when the phone is picked up next to the computer and dialed manually, the initial call state is likely to be LINECALLSTATE_DIALING.

User Interface Functions

Under 16-bit Windows, the TSP DLLs were loaded directly into the address space of the application. If the DLL ever needed to interact with the user, for example, put up a dialog box to ask for input, it could do so without any trouble. However, now that TSPs are being loaded into TAPISRV, an executable without the capability to provide a UI,[6] TSPs are allowed to provide a UI only in specific functions. Calling these functions indicates that the TSP DLL has been loaded into the address space of the application and it is safe to provide a UI. The functions from which it is safe to provide a UI are those with the prefix `TUISPI` instead of the `TSPI` prefix seen so far. For example, the function called by `lineConfig-Dialog` is `TUISPI_lineConfigDialog`:

```
LONG TSPIAPI TUISPI_lineConfigDialog(
    TUISPIDLLCALLBACK    pfnUIDLLCallback,
    DWORD                dwDeviceID,
    HWND                 hwndOwner,
    LPCWSTR              pszDeviceClass)
```

The `dwDeviceID` identifies the line to configure, and the `pszDevice-Class` can be used to identify the "part" of the device to configure, if the device has multiple configuration dialogs. Of course, the `hwndOwner` is the parent window of the dialog. The interesting parameter is `pfnUIDLLCallback`, which is a pointer to a function. This function allows bidirectional communication between the part of the TSP that is loaded in the address space of TAPISRV and the part of the TSP that is loaded in the address space of the application. Under Win32, even if the same DLL is loaded into both address spaces, each gets its own copy of all global and static data (unless shared-memory arrangements are made). Figure 7.3 shows how a TSP is loaded into multiple address spaces when the UI functions are involved.

To determine which DLL the TSP would like to have loaded into the application's address space when a UI function is called, TAPI calls the `TSPI_pro-viderUIIdentify` function:

```
LONG
TSPI_providerUIIdentify(
    LPWSTR    pszUIDLLName)
```

---

[6] Under Windows NT, TAPISRV is an NT Service with its own desktop that is invisible to the user.

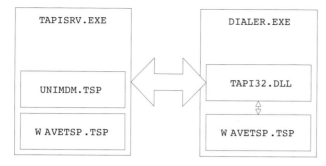

Figure 7.3: The TSP in multiple address spaces.

It's often convenient to expose both non-UI and UI functions in the same DLL. This can be accomplished with the following implementation of `TSPI_providerUIIdentify`:

```
LONG TSPIAPI TSPI_providerUIIdentify(
    LPWSTR    pszUIDLLName)
{
  char    szPath[MAX_PATH+1];
  GetModuleFileNameA(g_hinst, szPath, MAX_PATH);
  mbstowcs(pszUIDLLName, szPath, strlen(szPath) + 1);

  return 0;
}
```

To augment the use of the Win32 shared-memory functions, TAPI provides a callback function in every UI-allowed function. This function allows the UI portion of the TSP to make a request of the non-UI portion for data to display in the UI. The `pfnUIDLLCallback` parameter is a pointer to the callback function that has the following signature:

```
typedef LONG (CALLBACK * TUISPIDLLCALLBACK)(
    DWORD             dwObjectID,
    DWORD             dwObjectType,
    LPVOID            lpParams,
    DWORD             dwSize)
```

The `dwObjectID` parameter is either a line device ID, a phone device ID, a permanent provider ID, or an `HDRVDIALOGINSTANCE`, as specified by the value of `dwObjectType`. The kind of object identifier to pass is based on which UI function is being called. Provider-specific functions use provider IDs, line-specific functions use line device IDs and phone-specific functions use phone device IDs. The last one, `HDRVDIALOGINSTANCE`, is the backdoor for a non-UI function to generate a spontaneous UI, a process discussed shortly. Table 7.3 shows the TU-ISPI functions and the object types that are used.

The `lpParams` and `dwSize` parameters of the UI callback function describe the contents and size of the data to be sent from the UI portion of the TSP to the non-UI portion. The data will be copied by TAPI from one address space to the other, so be sure not to pass any address-space specific data, such as pointers. As much as I hate to say it, a TAPI-like VLS with offsets and sizes could be useful for sending complicated data between address spaces. While this kind of data structure isn't pretty, it's flexible and can be copied between address spaces without fear of mishap.

When the UI callback function is invoked, TAPI sends the copied data to the non-UI portion of the TSP and invokes the `TSPI_providerGeneric-DialogData` function:

```
LONG
TSPI_providerGenericDialogData(
    DWORD               dwObjectID,
    DWORD               dwObjectType,
    LPVOID              lpParams,
    DWORD               dwSize)
```

The UI portion of the TSP will block while the non-UI portion of the TSP is executing this function. Any modifications to the `lpParams` data will be copied back to the UI portion of the TSP when the `TSPI_providerGeneric-DialogData` function returns.

Table 7.3: TUISPI functions and `dwObjectType` values.

UI Function	`dwObjectType`
TUISPI_providerInstall TUISPI_providerConfig TUISPI_providerRemove	TUISPIDLL_OBJECT_PROVIDERID
TUISPI_lineConfigDialog TUISPI_lineConfigDialogEdit	TUISPIDLL_OBJECT_LINEID
TUISPI_phoneConfigDialog	TUISPIDLL_OBJECT_PHONEID
TUISPI_providerGenericDialog	TUISPIDLL_OBJECT_DIALOGINSTANCE

This bidirectional communications channel is useful because the UI portion of the TSP is separate from the non-UI portion. It is the job of the non-UI portion to do the real work with the telephony objects managed by the TSP. However, for the state of these telephony objects to be reflected in the UI portion of the TSP, the non-UI portion must be asked for the state of the telephony objects.

For example, changing the configuration of a line via the `TUISPI_line-ConfigDialog` while the line is open may not be possible for some TSPs. In the implementation of this function, the UI portion of the TSP can learn if a line is open by asking the non-UI portion. To do this, it uses the UI callback function and passes some data indicating the information needed. The non-UI portion of the TSP would implement `TSPI_providerGenericDialogData` and provide the open state of the particular line device back to the UI portion of the TSP. This UI portion can use this data to decide whether to allow the line to be configured. The following code shows how this could be implemented:

```cpp
// MyTsp.h
enum TSP_REQUEST_TYPE
{
    LINE_OPEN,
    ... // Other TSP request types here
};


struct TSP_REQUEST
{
    TSP_REQUEST_TYPE rt;
};


struct TSP_REQUEST_LINE_OPEN
{
    TSP_REQUEST_TYPE rt;
    bool             bLineOpen;
};


// MyTsp.cpp
#include "MyTsp.h"

// Called in the application's address space
LONG TSPIAPI TUISPI_lineConfigDialog(
    TUISPIDLLCALLBACK    pfnUIDLLCallback,
    DWORD                dwDeviceID,
    HWND                 hwndOwner,
```

```
    LPCWSTR               pszDeviceClass)
{
    long tr = 0;

    // Ask non-UI portion if line is open
    TSP_REQUEST_LINE_OPEN req = { LINE_OPEN };
    tr = pfnUIDLLCallback(dwDeviceID,
                          TUISPIDLL_OBJECT_LINEID,
                          &req,
                          sizeof(req));
    if( tr == 0 )
    {
        // Only show the dialog if the line is not open
        if( !req.bLineOpen )
        {
            DialogBox(g_hinst,
                      MAKEINTRESOURCE(IDD_CONFIG),
                      hwndOwner,
                      ConfigDlgProc);
        }
        else
        {
            tr = LINEERR_INUSE;
        }
    }

    return tr;
}

// Called in TAPISRV's address space
LONG TSPIAPI TSPI_providerGenericDialogData(
    DWORD   dwObjectID,
    DWORD   dwObjectType,
    LPVOID  pParams,
    DWORD   dwSize)
{
    if( dwObjectType == TUISPIDLL_OBJECT_LINEID )
    {
        switch( ((TSP_REQUEST*)pParams)->rt )
        {
```

```
    // Check to see if line is open
    case LINE_OPEN:
    {
        // Modify data to be sent back to UI portion
        TSP_REQUEST_LINE_OPEN* pReq = 0;
        pReq = (TSP_REQUEST_LINE_OPEN*)pParams;
        pReg->bLineOpen = IsLineOpen(dwObjectID);
    }
    break;

    ... // Handle other request types
    }
}

return 0;
}
```

Spontaneous UI

It is legal to provide TSP UI elements only during the processing of TUISPI functions. However, sometimes it is necessary for a TSP to show UI during the processing of a non-UI function. For example, before the WaveTSP can dial a phone number, it needs to let the user know to hold the phone near the computer speakers. So, during the processing of the `TSPI_lineMakeCall` function, it must show the dialog box shown in Figure 7.4.

Only when the user clicks the Dial button can the WaveTSP actually dial the

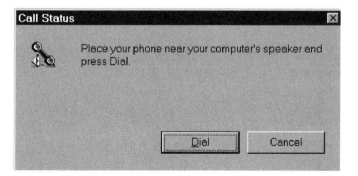

Figure 7.4: WaveTSP Call Status dialog.

phone number. Since `TSPI_lineMakeCall` is not allowed to generate any UI,[7] it must cause the UI portion of the TSP to be loaded into the application's address space and ask it to show the dialog box. For this reason, TAPI defines the `LINE_CREATEDIALOGINSTANCE` message:

```
htLine = (DWORD) hProvider;
htCall = (DWORD) 0;
dwMsg = LINE_CREATEDIALOGINSTANCE;
dwParam1 = (DWORD) lpTUISPICreateDialogInstanceParams;
dwParam2 = (DWORD) 0;
dwParam3 = (DWORD) 0;
```

The `hProvider` that is to be shoved into the spot normally reserved for the `htLine` is the same `hProvider` handed to the TSP in the `TSPI_providerEnumDevices` function. The `dwParam1` part of the message is meant to hold a pointer to a `TUISPICREATEDIALOGINSTANCEPARAMS` structure:

```
typedef struct tuispicreatedialoginstanceparams_tag {
    DRV_REQUESTID        dwRequestID;
    HDRVDIALOGINSTANCE   hdDlgInst;
    HTAPIDIALOGINSTANCE  htDlgInst;
    LPCWSTR              lpszUIDLLName;
    LPVOID               lpParams;
    DWORD                dwSize;
} TUISPICREATEDIALOGINSTANCEPARAMS,
    FAR *LP TUISPICREATEDIALOGINSTANCEPARAMS;
```

The `dwRequestID` parameter is the same `dwRequestID` that identifies the asynchronous function that the UI is being used to service. Since a UI is inherently asynchronous, TAPI doesn't allow synchronous functions to invoke the UI. This is done in the same way that the `hdLine` and `hdCall` values are assigned unique values by the TSP and `htLine` and `htCall` values are assigned by TAPI. The `hdDlgInst` member is assigned a unique value by the TSP, and the `htDlgInst` is assigned a unique value by TAPI should the UI message be received successfully by the UI portion of the TSP. The `lpszUIDLLName` should be set to the same value as set in the `TSPI_providerUIIdentify` function. Finally, the

---

[7] More precisely, if the non-UI portion of the TSP did show any UI, it would be on the same invisible desktop in which TAPISRV is running.

`lpParams` and `dwSize` parameters allow the non-UI portion of the TSP to send arbitrary, address space-independent data to the UI portion.

Once the `TUISPICREATEDIALOGINSTANCEPARAMS` structure is populated, the `LINE_CREATEDIALOGINSTANCE` message is sent to TAPI via the same event procedure used to send spontaneous events to interested applications. For example, in the WaveTSP's implementation of `TSPI_lineMakeCall`, it uses the following code to tell the UI portion know to put up a dialog box:

```cpp
// wavetsp.h
struct TSPUIDATA
{
    CtspCall*   pCall;          // Current call
    DWORD       dwRequestID;    // Asynch. ID
    LONG        tr;             // Asynch. result
    DWORD       nCallState;     // New call state
};


// tspcall.cpp
LONG CtspCall::StartDial(
    HINSTANCE               hinst,
    HPROVIDER               hProvider,
    DWORD                   dwRequestID,
    const wchar_t*          pwszAddress,
    const LINEDIALPARAMS&   dp)
{
    // Can't dial if we're already doing something else.
    if( (m_dwCallState != LINECALLSTATE_UNKNOWN) &&
        (m_dwCallState != LINECALLSTATE_CONNECTED) )
    {
        return LINEERR_OPERATIONUNAVAIL;
    }

    LONG        tr = 0;
    size_t      cbAddress = wcslen(pwszAddress) + 1;
    size_t      cbData = sizeof(TSPUIDATA) +
                         sizeof(LINEDIALPARAMS) +
                         cbAddress;
    TSPUIDATA*  pData = (TSPUIDATA*)(new BYTE[cbData]);
    if( pData )
    {
```

```
// Data is passed back from UI.
pData->dwRequestID = dwRequestID;
pData->pCall = this;

// Copy LINEDIALPARAMS for UI
LINEDIALPARAMS* pdp =
                (LINEDIALPARAMS*)((BYTE*)pData +
                 sizeof(*pData));
*pdp = dp;

// Copy dial string for UI.
char*   pszAddress = (char*)((BYTE*)pData +
                       sizeof(*pData) +
                       sizeof(LINEDIALPARAMS));
wcstombs(pszAddress, pwszAddress, cbAddress);

wchar_t pwszFileName[MAX_PATH+1];
TSPI_providerUIIdentify(pwszFileName);

TUISPICREATEDIALOGINSTANCEPARAMS     params;
params.dwRequestID = dwRequestID;
params.hdDlgInst = (HDRVDIALOGINSTANCE)this;
params.htDlgInst = 0;    // Set by TAPI
params.lpszUIDLLName = pwszFileName;
params.lpParams = (void*)pData;
params.dwSize = cbData;

// Send message to UI portion
m_pLine->Event((HTAPILINE)hProvider, 0,
              LINE_CREATEDIALOGINSTANCE,
              (DWORD)&params);

if( params.htDlgInst )
{
    m_pLine->m_nActiveCalls++;
}
else
{
    tr = LINEERR_OPERATIONFAILED;
}
```

```
    }
    else
    {
        tr = LINEERR_NOMEM;
    }

    delete[] pData;
    return tr;
}
```

When `tapi32.dll` receives this message, it doesn't forward it to the application. Rather, it loads the UI DLL into the application's address space and calls the `TUISPI_providerGenericDialog` function:

```
LONG
TUISPI_providerGenericDialog(
    TUISPIDLLCALLBACK      lpfnUIDLLCallback,
    HTAPIDIALOGINSTANCE    htDlgInst,
    LPVOID                 lpParams,
    DWORD                  dwSize,
    HANDLE                 hEvent)
```

The `lpfnUIDLCallback` parameter is the same as for every TUISPI function. The `htDlgInst`, `lpParams`, and `dwSize` parameters are those provided in the `TUISPICREATEDIALOGINSTANCEPARAMS` structure. The `hEvent` parameter is a handle to a Win32 event object. It should be set, using the Win32 `SetEvent` function, when the UI portion of the TSP has initialized the UI and is prepared to receive calls from the non-UI portion about updated UI information. The WaveTSP implements `TUISPI_providerGenericDialog` by pulling the information from the `lpParams` data and showing the dialog:

```
LONG TSPIAPI TUISPI_providerGenericDialog(
  TUISPIDLLCALLBACK      lpfnUIDLLCallback,
  HTAPIDIALOGINSTANCE    htDlgInst,
  LPVOID                 lpParams,
  DWORD                  dwSize,
  HANDLE                 hEvent)
{
  // Let TAPI know we're ready for more data
  // (can also be done in WM_INITDIALOG).
```

```
SetEvent(hEvent);

// Pull out extra data.
LINEDIALPARAMS* pdp =
              (LINEDIALPARAMS*)((BYTE*)lpParams +
                              sizeof(TSPUIDATA));
LPCSTR        pszAddress = (LPCSTR)((BYTE*)lpParams +
                          sizeof(TSPUIDATA) +
                          sizeof(LINEDIALPARAMS));

// Create a UI call object.
CuiCall call(htDlgInst,
            lpfnUIDLLCallback,
            pszAddress,
            pdp,
            (TSPUIDATA*)lpParams);

// Show the dialog, passing the UI call object.
DialogBoxParam(g_hinst,
            MAKEINTRESOURCE(IDD_CALL_STATUS),
            0,
            CallStatusProc,
            (LPARAM)&call);

    return 0;
}
```

After the event has been set, TAPI will forward any calls from the non-UI portion of the TSP on the `TUISPI_providerGenericDialogData` function (not to be confused with the `TSPI_providerGenericDialogData` function):

```
LONG
TUISPI_providerGenericDialogData(
    HTAPIDIALOGINSTANCE htDlgInst,
    LPVOID              lpParams,
    DWORD               dwSize)
```

The `TUISPI_providerGenericDialogData` function is called when the TSP has some data it would like to communicate with *existing* UI elements. The UI portion of the TSP is supposed to use calls to `TUISPI_providerGeneric-`

`DialogData` to update the UI it's showing to the user, for example, tearing down a dialog if the application has canceled the request. The TSP can cause the `TUISPI_providerGenericDialogData` function by sending the `LINE_SENDDIALOGINSTANCEDATA` event:

```
htLine = (DWORD) htDlgInst;
htCall = (DWORD) 0;
dwMsg = LINE_SENDDIALOGINSTANCEDATA;
dwParam1 = (DWORD) lpParams;
dwParam2 = (DWORD) dwSize;
dwParam3 = (DWORD) 0;
```

Finally, when the `TUISPI_providerGenericDialog` function returns, thereby indicating that the UI has been torn down, TAPI calls the non-UI portion of the TSP via the `TSPI_providerFreeDialogInstance` function:

```
LONG
TSPI_providerFreeDialogInstance(
    HDRVDIALOGINSTANCE hdDlgInst)
```

This function allows the TSP to clean up any resources associated with the UI request.[8]

Status

It's common for an application to want to know the status of one of the telephony devices it is using, such as lines, addresses, and calls. This can be supported via the following functions:

```
LONG
TSPI_lineGetLineDevStatus(
    HDRVLINE       hdLine,
    LPLINEDEVSTATUS plds)
```

---

[8] Even though the documentation states that implementation of the `TSPI_providerFree-DialogInstance` function is optional, the current implementation of TAPISRV will crash if that function is not provided and the TSP subsequently fires the `LINE_CREATEDIALOGINSTANCE` event.

```
LONG
TSPI_lineGetAddressStatus(
    HDRVLINE            hdLine,
    DWORD               dwAddressID,
    LPLINEADDRESSSTATUS pas)


LONG
TSPI_lineGetCallStatus(
    HDRVCALL            hdCall,
    LPLINECALLSTATUS    pls)


LONG
TSPI_lineGetCallInfo(
    HDRVCALL            hdCall,
    LPLINECALLINFO      pli)


LONG
TSPI_lineGetCallAddressID(
    HDRVCALL        hdCall,
    LPDWORD         pdwAddressID)
```

The implementations of these functions fill in the VLS (or a single DWORD in the case of `TSPI_lineGetCallAddressID`) based on the current telephony object status.

Installation

Once the TSP DLL is successfully compiled, it must be installed; otherwise, TAPISRV won't load it. Installation of a TSP is a two-stage process. First, the TSP is copied into the `system` (Win9x) or the `system32` (NT4+) directory. Second, TAPI must be informed of the new TSP via the `lineAddProvider` function:

```
LONG
lineAddProvider(
    LPCSTR              lpszProviderFilename,
    HWND                hwndOwner,
    LPDWORD             lpdwPermanentProviderID)
```

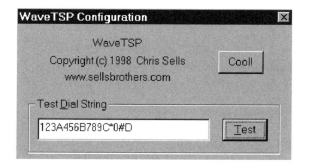

Figure 7.5: WaveTSP Configuration dialog.

If TAPI can find the TSP specified in the `lpszProviderFilename` argument, it will load it into the application's address space and call `TUISPI_provider-Install`:

```
LONG
TUISPI_providerInstall(
    TUISPIDLLCALLBACK      pfnUIDLLCallback,
    HWND                   hwndOwner,
    DWORD                  dwPermanentProviderID)
```

This is the TSP's chance to set up shop in its new home. Because it's a UI function, the TSP is allowed to gather installation options from the user. At the very least, the TSP should provide some UI to indicate it has been successfully configured. For example, the WaveTSP puts up a dialog box that allows the user to test using the computer's speakers as a means of dialing the phone, as shown in Figure 7.5. The `dwPermanentProviderID` argument to `TUISPI_provider-Install` is generated by TAPI and will be used as the provider's permanent ID until the provider is removed. This ID is especially important because it's possible for a single TSP to be installed multiple times. Each separate installation will be given its own provider ID. If your TSP does not wish to allow multiple instances of itself, it is responsible for detecting that it has already been installed and for returning `LINEERR_NOMULTIPLEINSTANCE` from `TUISPI_providerInstall`. Any error returned from `TUISPI_providerInstall` will abort the installation procedure.

After the provider has been installed, the user may wish to update the settings of the TSP. This is accomplished via the Telephony Control Panel,[9] which maintains a list of currently installed TSPs (as shown in Figure 7.6).

---

[9] The default installation of Windows 95 does not show the Telephony Control Panel in the list of available Control Panels. To show it, rename `telephon.cp$` to `telephon.cpl` in the System directory.

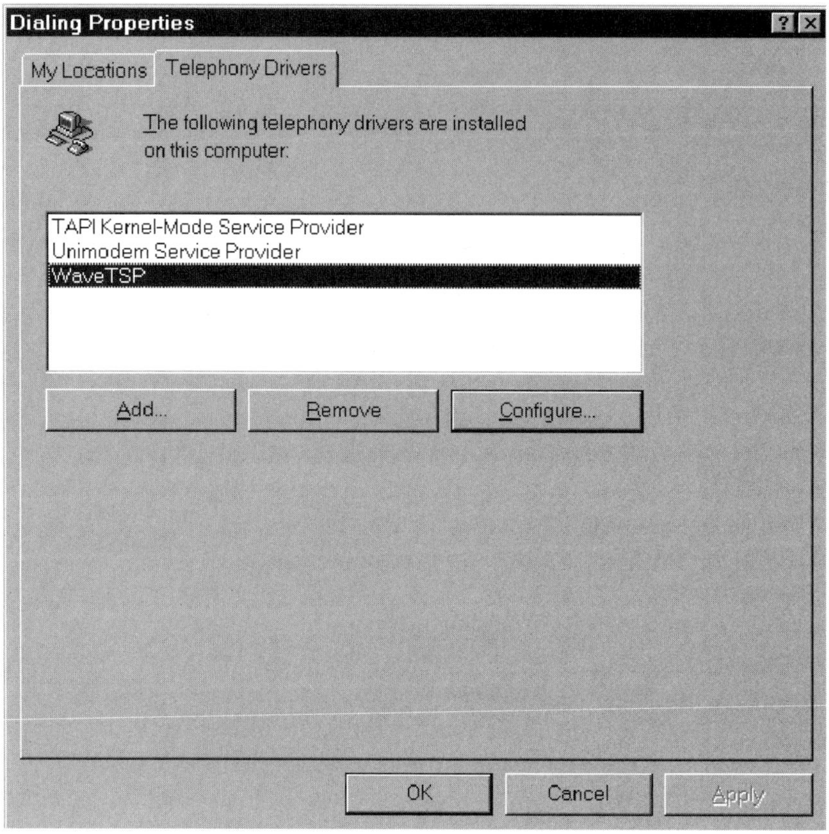

Figure 7.6: Configuring Telephony service providers.

By default, the filename of the TSP is listed in the Telephony Control Panel. If, however, a version information resource is provided in the TSP DLL, the `FileDescription` field will be used instead. When the user chooses to configure the currently selected TSP, the Telephony Control Panel calls the `TUISPI_providerConfig` function:

```
LONG
TUISPI_providerConfig(
    TUISPIDLLCALLBACK       pfnUIDLLCallback,
    HWND                    hwndOwner,
    DWORD                   dwPermanentProviderID)
```

To remove the currently selected TSP, the Telephony Control Panel calls the `lineRemoveProvider` function:

```
LONG
lineRemoveProvider(
     DWORD               dwPermanentProviderID,
     HWND                hwndOwner)
```

TAPI translates this call into a call to the TSP via the `TUISPI_provider-Remove` function:

```
LONG
TUISPI_providerRemove(
     TUISPIDLLCALLBACK    pfnUIDLLCallback,
     HWND                 hwndOwner,
     DWORD                dwPermanentProviderID)
```

`TUISPI_providerRemove` is the TSP's last chance to remove any installation residue and return the system to its state prior to the TSP's installation.

Supporting the Telephony Control Panel

Under TAPI 1.*x*, the Telephony Control Panel did not use the TUISPI functions to implement the Add, Remove, and Configure buttons of the Telephony Drivers property page. Instead, it used the following TSPI functions:

```
LONG
TSPI_providerInstall(
     HWND     hwndOwner,
     DWORD    dwPermanentProviderID)


LONG
TSPI_providerConfig(
     HWND     hwndOwner,
     DWORD    dwPermanentProviderID)


LONG
TSPI_providerRemove(
     HWND     hwndOwner,
     DWORD    dwPermanentProviderID)
```

Under TAPI 2.*x*, these functions are no longer used. However, the TSP still needs to see them exposed from the TSP; otherwise, the corresponding operations in the Control Panel are disabled. To enable this functionality, you must expose these functions from your TSP. Typical implementations of these functions do nothing and return success.

Debugging

Debugging TSPs is sometimes difficult, for a couple of reasons. First, the TSP is split into two pieces, that is, the UI and the non-UI pieces, and each piece runs in a different address space. Second, there are a couple of different "modes" in which the TSP is typically debugged. The first mode in which the TSP runs is the installation. Debugging the TSP in this mode requires the Control Panel applet to be started under debugger control. Since the Control Panel applet is itself a DLL, this can be a little tricky. The second mode that the TSP runs under is operation. So debugging the TSP often must occur in two different address spaces simultaneously: TAPISRV and a TAPI application. This also can be tricky. In this section, I discuss the procedures for both of these debugging modes.

Debugging a TSP During Installation

To debug a TSP during installation, you first install the TSP into the `System` directory (under Win9*x*) or the `System32` directory (under NT). So that the Telephony Control Panel can find the TSP, make sure your TSP has the `.tsp` file extension. Assuming your TSP project is open in your development environment, you're going to have to tell the debugger to debug the TSP file instead of (or in addition to) the normal project output. Under Visual C++ 5.*x* (VC5), this involves adding the TSP to the Additional DLLs list, as shown in Figure 7.7.

To start the Telephony Control Panel under debugger control, you must set `rundll32.exe` to be the executable to use for debugging. The `rundll32.exe` application provides a standalone address space for components packaged as DLLs. The `rundll32.exe` command line must be specified like this to start the Telephony Control Panel:

```
c:\nt4\rundll32.exe shell32.dll,Control_RunDLL telephon.cpl
```

Under VC5, the executable to use for debugging is set in the Settings dialog, as shown in Figure 7.8.

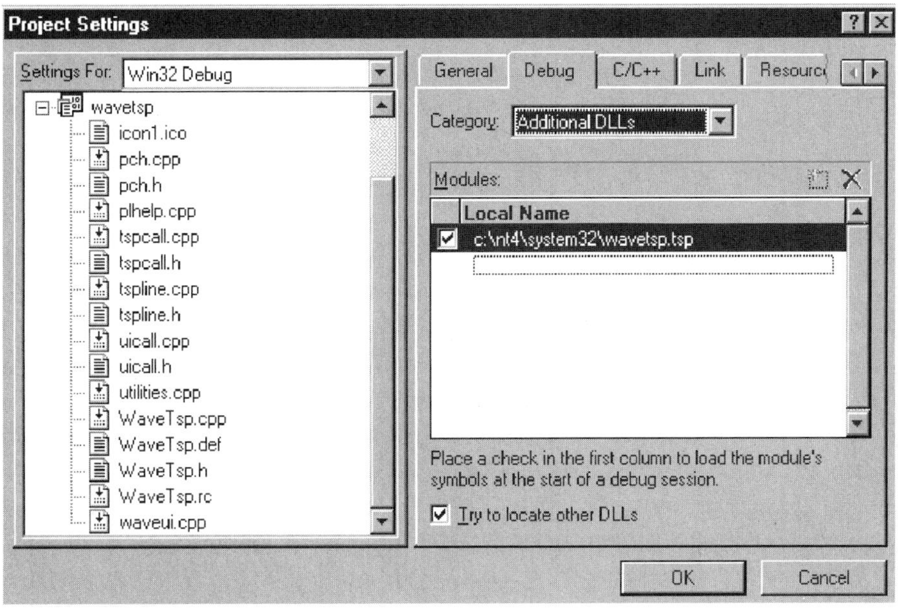

Figure 7.7: Setting additional DLLs in VC5.

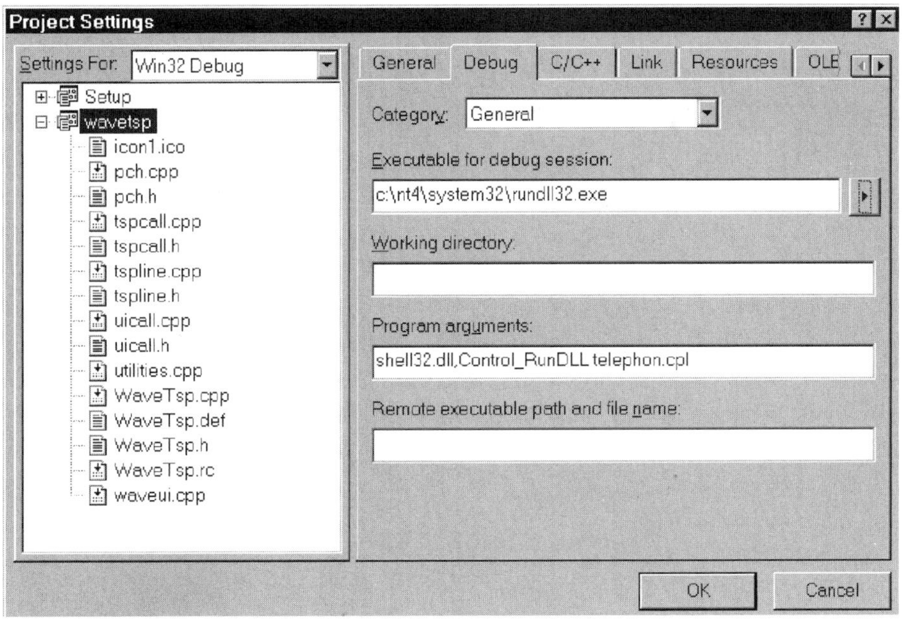

Figure 7.8: Setting the executable for debug in VC5.

Starting the debugging process will start the Telephony Control Panel. Click the Add button to show all of the TSPs. Choosing your TSP should call the `TUISPI_providerInstall` entry point and cause your breakpoints to be hit.[10]

Debugging a TSP under Normal Operation

Debugging a TSP under normal operation involves both the UI and the non-UI pieces of the TSP. Win32 restricts each debugging application to be in control of only a single address space at any given time. Since the UI and the non-UI portions of the TSP must run in two address spaces—TAPISRV and the TAPI application—you must have two debuggers running. One of the debuggers must have as the executable for debugging the TAPI application that will be making calls to your TSP. The other must be `TAPISRV.EXE`. Setting up the TAPI application as the executable for debug is just like setting up `rundll32.exe` as described. For example, Figure 7.9 shows the VC settings to use the tDial application to debug the UI portion of a TSP.

To debug TAPISRV, which is started automatically by `tapi32.dll` on the first TAPI call, you should attach a debugger to `TAPISRV.EXE` after it has been started. Under NT, this can be accomplished by right-clicking `TAPISRV.EXE` in the Process tab and choosing the Debug option. Under Win9*x,* you have to use other means to attach a debugger to TAPISRV. For example, VC5 has the command line argument –p that takes a process ID to which to attach a debugger. Once you've started your development environment in debug mode in control of TAPISRV, you can load your source code and set breakpoints.

Tracing TSP Operation

While it's often handy to step through exactly what is happening to your TSP while using the debugger, sometimes this is too labor-intensive. In these cases, you might like a log of what your TSP is doing that you can deconstruct in the event of a failure. The WaveTSP uses a technique inspired by the ATSP32 Win32 TSP sample to trace every TSP entry point and dump the log to a file (hardcoded to `c:\wave-tsp.out`). This file can then be used to discover the sequence of events that led up to a failure in your TSP and show you where to focus your debugging efforts. Following is an example trace of a typical installation of the WaveTSP:

```
TSPI_providerUIIdentify() from C:\WIN98\SYSTEM\TAPISRV.EXE
   in parameters:
```

[10] The procedure for starting a Control Panel Applet using `rundll32.exe` is documented in Microsoft Knowledge Base article Q135068. The Microsoft Knowledge Base is available as part of the Platform SDK as well as online at *http://www.microsoft.com/kb.*

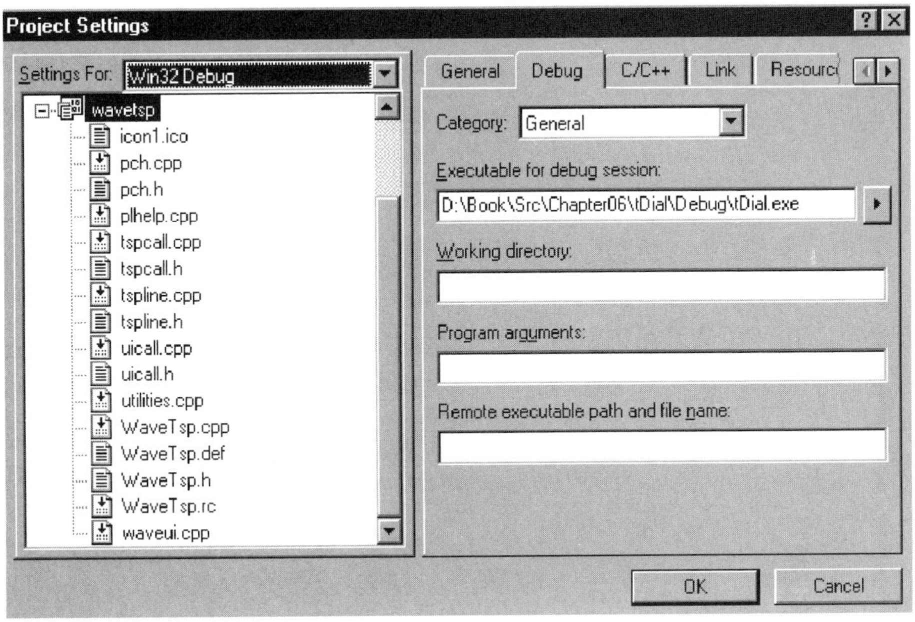

Figure 7.9: Using tDial to debug the UI portion of a TSP.

```
out parameters:
    pszUIDLLName= 0x420c2c 'C:\WIN98\SYSTEM\WAVETSP.TSP'
TSPI_providerUIIdentify() returning 0x0

TUISPI_providerInstall() from C:\NT4\SYSTEM32\RUNDLL32.EXE
  in parameters:
    pfnUIDLLCallback= 0x7f9b95c3
    hwndOwner= 0xbe8
    dwPermanentProviderID= 0x1003
  out parameters:
TUISPI_providerInstall() returning 0x0
```

Here's a somewhat more involved trace showing how the WaveTSP is used during the placing of a call:

```
TSPI_lineNegotiateTSPIVersion() from C:\NT4\system32\tapisrv.exe
  in parameters:
    dwDeviceID= 0xffffffff
    dwLowVersion= 0x10003
```

```
      dwHighVersion= 0x20000
    out parameters:
      pdwTSPIVersion= 0x148d48 '0x20000'
  TSPI_lineNegotiateTSPIVersion() returning 0x0


  TSPI_providerEnumDevices() from C:\NT4\system32\tapisrv.exe
    in parameters:
      dwPermanentProviderID= 0xe
      hProvider= 0x148d38
      pfnLineCreateProc= 0x24e7e9e
      pfnPhoneCreateProc= 0x24f138a
    out parameters:
      pdwNumLines= 0xf9faf8 '0x1'
      pdwNumPhones= 0xf9fb00 '0x0'
  TSPI_providerEnumDevices() returning 0x0


  TSPI_providerInit() from C:\NT4\system32\tapisrv.exe
    in parameters:
      dwTSPIVersion= 0x20000
      dwPermanentProviderID= 0xe
      dwLineDeviceIDBase= 0x1
      dwPhoneDeviceIDBase= 0x0
      dwNumLines= 0x1
      dwNumPhones= 0x0
      pfnCompletionProc= 0x24e2359
    out parameters:
      pdwTSPIOptions= 0x148d44 '0x1'
  TSPI_providerInit() returning 0x0


  TSPI_lineNegotiateTSPIVersion() from C:\NT4\system32\
  tapisrv.exe
    in parameters:
      dwDeviceID= 0x1
      dwLowVersion= 0x10003
      dwHighVersion= 0x20000
    out parameters:
      pdwTSPIVersion= 0xf9f96c '0x20000'
  TSPI_lineNegotiateTSPIVersion() returning 0x0


  TSPI_lineGetDevCaps() from C:\NT4\system32\tapisrv.exe
```

```
    in parameters:
      dwDeviceID= 0x1
      dwTSPIVersion= 0x20000
      dwExtVersion= 0x0
      pldc= 0x149908
    out parameters:
  TSPI_lineGetDevCaps() returning 0x0


  TSPI_lineGetDevCaps() from C:\NT4\system32\tapisrv.exe
    in parameters:
      dwDeviceID= 0x1
      dwTSPIVersion= 0x20000
      dwExtVersion= 0x0
      pldc= 0x149908
    out parameters:
  TSPI_lineGetDevCaps() returning 0x0


  TSPI_lineOpen() from C:\NT4\system32\tapisrv.exe
    in parameters:
      dwDeviceID= 0x1
      htLine= 0x1468e0
      dwTSPIVersion= 0x20000
      pfnEventProc= 0x24e7e9e
    out parameters:
      phdLine= 0x146914 '0x1640ad0'
  TSPI_lineOpen() returning 0x0


  TSPI_lineGetNumAddressIDs() from C:\NT4\system32\tapisrv.exe
    in parameters:
      hdLine= 0x1640ad0
    out parameters:
      pdwNumAddressIDs= 0x146928 '0x1'
  TSPI_lineGetNumAddressIDs() returning 0x0


  TSPI_lineMakeCall() from C:\NT4\system32\tapisrv.exe
    in parameters:
      dwRequestID= 0x149388
      hdLine= 0x1640ad0
      htCall= 0x1587c8
      pszDestAddress= 0x158588 'T 1 800 5551212'
```

```
      dwCountryCode= 0x0
      pCallParams= 0x158688
TSPI_providerUIIdentify() from C:\NT4\system32\tapisrv.exe
   in parameters:
   out parameters:
      pszUIDLLName= 0xf9f78c 'C:\NT4\system32\wavetsp.tsp'
TSPI_providerUIIdentify() returning 0x0

   out parameters:
      phdCall= 0x1587e4 '0x1640b10'
TSPI_lineMakeCall() returning 0x149388

TUISPI_providerGenericDialog() from C:\Program Files\Windows
NT\dialer.exe
   in parameters:
      lpfnUIDLLCallback= 0x74a18c9a
      htDlgInst= 0x158930
      lpParams= 0x841b0
      dwSize= 0x2f
      hEvent= 0x98
TSPI_providerGenericDialogData() from
C:\NT4\system32\tapisrv.exe
   in parameters:
      dwObjectID= 0x1640b10
      dwObjectType= 0x4
      pParams= 0x1588d0
      dwSize= 0x10
   out parameters:
TSPI_providerGenericDialogData() returning 0x0

TSPI_lineGetCallAddressID() from C:\NT4\system32\tapisrv.exe
   in parameters:
      hdCall= 0x1640b10
   out parameters:
      pdwAddressID= 0x1587ec '0x0'
TSPI_lineGetCallAddressID() returning 0x0

TSPI_providerGenericDialogData() from
C:\NT4\system32\tapisrv.exe
   in parameters:
```

```
      dwObjectID= 0x1640b10
      dwObjectType= 0x4
      pParams= 0x1588d0
      dwSize= 0x10
    out parameters:
TSPI_providerGenericDialogData() returning 0x0


    out parameters:
TUISPI_providerGenericDialog() returning 0x0


TSPI_providerFreeDialogInstance() from
C:\NT4\system32\tapisrv.exe
    in parameters:
      hdDlgInst= 0x1640b10
    out parameters:
TSPI_providerFreeDialogInstance() returning 0x0


TSPI_lineDrop() from C:\NT4\system32\tapisrv.exe
    in parameters:
      dwRequestID= 0x158898
      hdCall= 0x1640b10
      psUserUserInfo= 0x0
      dwSize= 0x0
    out parameters:
TSPI_lineDrop() returning 0x158898


TSPI_lineCloseCall() from C:\NT4\system32\tapisrv.exe
    in parameters:
      hdCall= 0x1640b10
    out parameters:
TSPI_lineCloseCall() returning 0x0


TSPI_lineClose() from C:\NT4\system32\tapisrv.exe
    in parameters:
      hdLine= 0x1640ad0
    out parameters:
TSPI_lineClose() returning 0x0


TSPI_providerShutdown() from C:\NT4\system32\tapisrv.exe
    in parameters:
```

```
            dwTSPIVersion= 0x20000
            dwPermanentProviderID= 0xe
        out parameters:
    TSPI_providerShutdown() returning 0x0
```

The tracing output is generated using a data structure that holds a set of function parameters. An instance of the data structure is built in every function and walked as every function is entered and left. I've also built a set of macros to make building and dumping the parameters slightly less painful. For example, here's what a typical entry point looks like:

```
LONG TSPIAPI TSPI_providerEnumDevices(
    DWORD        dwPermanentProviderID,
    LPDWORD      pdwNumLines,
    LPDWORD      pdwNumPhones,
    HPROVIDER    hProvider,
    LINEEVENT    pfnLineCreateProc,
    PHONEEVENT   pfnPhoneCreateProc)
{
    BEGIN_PARAM_TABLE("TSPI_providerEnumDevices")
        DWORD_IN_ENTRY(dwPermanentProviderID)
        DWORD_OUT_ENTRY(pdwNumLines)
        DWORD_OUT_ENTRY(pdwNumPhones)
        DWORD_IN_ENTRY(hProvider)
        DWORD_IN_ENTRY(pfnLineCreateProc)
        DWORD_IN_ENTRY(pfnPhoneCreateProc)
    END_PARAM_TABLE()

    g_hProvider = hProvider;
    *pdwNumLines = 1;
    *pdwNumPhones = 0;

    return EPILOG(0);
}
```

The BEGIN_PARAM_TABLE starts the initialization of the structure of parameters. Each entry in the table lists the kind of parameter (only DWORDs and strings are supported) as well as whether it's an input parameter or an output parameter. The END_PARAM_TABLE macro ends the data structure and dumps the name of the function, where it's being called from, and all of the input parameters. The

EPILOG macro takes the return value from the function and dumps it along with all of the output parameters. Of course, when the TSP is built in release mode, all of these macros fall away and the tracing code disappears. For your reference, these tracing macros are defined in `wavetsp.h` and the functions are implemented in `utilities.cpp`.

I believe this technique is generally useful for tracing non-UI components, and I'd like to thank the author of the ATSP32 sample, Dan Knudson, of Microsoft product support, for sharing it with us.

When Is a Lib Not a Lib?

The `tapi32.lib` looks like the import library for a dynamic link library. There's even a matching `tapi32.dll` that is shipped with every 32-bit operating system that Microsoft makes. However, `tapi32.lib` is not an import library, but rather a static library. I discovered this when I wanted to know the TSP calls that a TAPI application was attempting to make but couldn't because my TSP didn't expose them. I was using Matt Pietrek's excellent APISPY32 utility, but nothing was being dumped to the output stream. So, instead, I built my own `tapi32.dll` and replaced the one provided by Microsoft.

Before you become too impressed, my implementation of `tapi32.dll` just loads Microsoft's renamed implementation and forwards all calls directly by using `GetProcAddress`, very much like `tapi32.lib` does. But, as it forwards the calls, it also logs them and their results to a file, much like the trace file from WaveTSP. Using this technique, I was able to reverse-engineer exactly the functionality the TAPI application expected from my TSP and fix my TSP in about five minutes. Unfortunately, it took me all day to build my copy of `tapi32.dll`. Actually, it took me all day to write the perl code to generate the code for my copy of `tapi32.dll`. Fortunately, I've included a copy of the perl code as well as the source for my tracing version of `tapi32.dll` on the disk that accompanies this book, along with instructions for its use.[11]

`tapi32.lib` is a static library so that applications don't have to detect lower revisions of TAPI than they were programmed to be able to detect. `tapi32.lib` will call `GetProcAddress` so that any function that isn't available in the lower version will return a nice error code when called.

---

[11] After building my tracing version of `tapi32.dll`, I discovered the Repeater TSP for tracing of incoming calls as well as events across the TSPI. The Repeater TSP is mentioned in the Microsoft Knowledge Base Article Q167799.

Summary

Implementing a TSP is more than just exposing a few functions that perform the services of your TSP. It also requires supporting initialization, version negotiation, capability negotiation, and status information. Because of the UI limitations imposed by TAPI, even implementing the meat and potatoes functionality of your TSP may be more difficult than you had imagined. To help make this more manageable, this chapter presented a few debugging and tracing techniques. Now, I don't want to hear any more excuses from telephony device manufacturers that don't support NT.

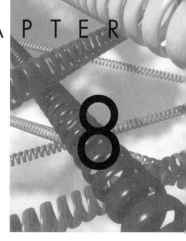

The Future of Windows Telephony

Dick: "What's your book about?"
Chris: "It's about computers and
telephones."
Dick: "Do you think either will ever
catch on?"
Dick Norman
Author's Stepfather
(he was kidding)

$\mathbf{A}$s wonderful as TAPI is, it's not quite perfect. Recall from Chapter 1 the goals that the TAPI architects had set for themselves:

1. Call control focus

2. Access to data via existing standard APIs

3. Network independence

4. Connection-model independence

5. Platform independence where possible

6. Sharing of lines between multiple applications

The architects of TAPI were, by and large, able to meet these goals. However, there is still some room for improvement[1] in the following areas:

1. **Improving Simplicity.** TAPI is a large and complicated part of the Win32 API. The large number of functions, events, and structures makes it extremely intimidating, especially for the average programmer who needs only a small part of it.

2. **Grouping Related Functions.** One aspect that makes TAPI complicated is that the functions are not logically grouped except in the sense of line versus phone. The address and call functions are indistinguishable from the line functions.

3. **Made for C.** TAPI was designed as a set of functions for C programmers. While it does model several telephony objects, the objects are hard to distinguish in the sea of handle-based functions. Because most programmers work in object-oriented languages of some form or another—for example, VB,

---

[1] As a wise man once said, "The largest room in the world is the room for improvement."

Java, Delphi, and C++—TAPI often must be wrapped in a set of explicit objects. For example, the TFX is a set of classes that wraps TAPI for C++ programmers. It's pretty easy to imagine building another wrapper for every language from which TAPI is used.

The problems of TAPI boil down to it's not being object-oriented. In short, TAPI is not based on Microsoft's Component Object Model (COM).

Features of TAPI 3.0

If you don't know what COM is, stop reading right now and read David Chappell's excellent book, *Understanding ActiveX and OLE,* from Microsoft Press. Once you've done that, and you've taken a short break to absorb what you read (say, a day or two),[2] you're ready to understand the beauty of combining Windows Telephony and COM, which occurs in the newest version of the Telephony API, TAPI 3.0.[3]

TAPI 3.0 provides several advantages over TAPI 2.*x:*

- **COM-based.** This means it's multilanguage and that the functionality is broken up into groups of logically related functions called *interfaces.* It also means that the objects are explicitly exposed as part of an object model (see Figure 8.1).

- **Simplicity.** Not only are the objects made explicit, but there are fewer of them. The entire object model consists of addresses, calls, terminals, call hubs (for managing groups of calls), and the TAPI object itself (for initialization and shutdown).

- **IP Telephony Support.** With the growing ubiquity of the Internet, many companies are jumping at the chance to take the traffic of the global telephony network and route it over the Internet. This results in much cheaper (often free) long distance phone calls. The downside is that instead of one

---

[2] If you *really* want to appreciate the beauty of COM from a C++ programmer's point of view, you need to read Don Box's excellent book, *Essential COM.* However, be prepared for a longer break after reading that one (say, a month or two).

[3] As of this writing, TAPI 3.0 is expected to eventually be available for Windows 95, Windows 98, Windows NT4.0, and Windows NT5.0. Currently, it is available only with the beta of NT5.0. Because TAPI 3.0 is not yet shipping, the details in this chapter are subject to wild and chaotic change. However, the central concepts are anticipated to remain the same.

worldwide telephony standard, there are hundreds of competing telephony protocols and data formats being spawned by the Internet. TAPI 3.0 attempts to unify the client/programming model so that IP telephony calls can be managed in the same way as PSTN telephony calls. This is especially important as the standardization process of IP telephony takes shape and TAPI 3.0 shields programmers from the shuffle of IP service providers at the TSP level.

- **Kernel-level Media Streaming.** For answering machine-type applications, the media control model of TAPI is adequate. However, for telephony servers, the inefficiencies of moving data back and forth using the Comm API or the Wave API between Kernel and User modes are too great and hamper scalability. TAPI 3.0 adds a model for providing Kernel-level media filters to prevent the mode-switch between Kernel and User modes.

- **NT5.0 Active Directory Support.** Phone numbers are pretty much the PSTN equivalent of dotted IP addresses, for example, 122.156.23.10. By this I mean that telephone numbers are long, meaningless, ever-changing, and easy to forget. The Internet provides a couple of partial solutions to this problem. Machines have names whose IP addresses can be obtained using the Internet Domain Name Service (DNS). Users have e-mail addresses that contain the machine name that knows how to contact the user. However, both machine names, for example, *sellsbrothers.com,* and e-mail addresses, for example, *csells@sellsbrothers.com,* are often hard to remember (although much easier than dotted IP addresses or phone numbers). To solve this problem, we often maintain a personal database of names of users we want to keep in contact with and their various phone numbers and e-mail addresses. The goal of the NT5.0 Active Directory is to make this available on a wider scale. Instead of having to update a person's various addresses in your PIM, the directory will provide an up-to-date mapping between a person's name and current addresses. The address and the type of address—for example, e-mail, machine name, or phone number—can then be used by the telephony application to establish a connection using the appropriate TSP.

Object Model

The TAPI 3.0 object model is designed for simplicity. The telephony application interrogates the system to find out the available address types, obtains an address from the user, and makes a call. The objects in the model are built to shield the user from the underlying mechanism used to perform these operations and to unify

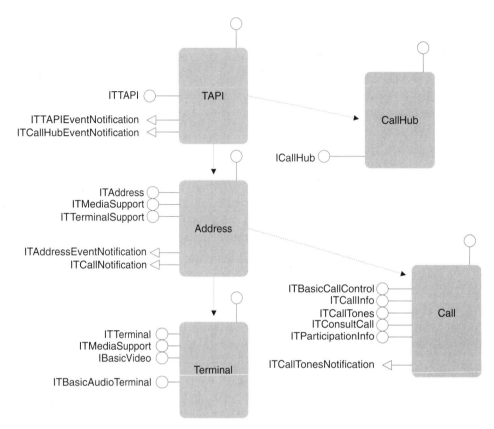

Figure 8.1: TAPI 3.0 object model.

the PSTN and IP telephony models. The object model consists of a single TAPI object that manages Address and CallHub objects. Each address object in turn manages associated Call and Terminal objects. These objects are discussed in the following list, and Figure 8.1 shows the TAPI 3.0 object model.

- **TAPI.** The TAPI object is the top of the object hierarchy and the programmer's entry point into telephony functionality. It is responsibile for holding all of the Address and CallHub objects.

- **Address.** The Address object is the TAPI 3.0 version of the line. It is where calls are created. Also, it masks the differences between address types, that is, PSTN and IP. The Address object holds the Terminal and Call objects.

- **Terminal.** The Terminal object represents a source or a sink for a media connection, for example, speaker, microphone, file, or video camera.

- **Call.** The Call object provides first-party control of a connection between two parties. Calls can be related to each other via the CallHub to provide third-party control.
- **CallHub.** The CallHub is a new abstraction for TAPI 3.0 and represents a collection of one or more Call objects for the purpose of providing third-party control. This object also simplifies the handling of multiparty calls.

Initialization and Shutdown

To give you a taste of TAPI 3.0, I'm going to take you through the typical parts of a TAPI 3.0 application, just as I've done in the rest of the book with previous versions of TAPI. In TAPI, initialization and shutdown happens via the `line-Initialize` and `lineShutdown` functions. Under TAPI 3.0, initialization and shutdown occur via member functions of the `ITTAPI` interface, implemented by the TAPI object:

```
interface ITTAPI : IDispatch {
  HRESULT Initialize();
  HRESULT Shutdown();

  [propget]
  HRESULT Addresses([out, retval] VARIANT* pVariant);
  HRESULT _EnumerateAddresses(
          [out, retval] IEnumAddress** ppea);

  HRESULT CreateMediaTerminal(
          [in] BSTR pMediaType,
          [in] ITTerminal* pTerminal,
          [out, retval] ITMediaTerminal** ppmt);
};
```

A VB programmer would create, initialize, and shut down the application's single TAPI object like so:

```
Dim g_tapi As ITTAPI

Private Sub Form_Load()
    Set g_tapi = New TAPI
```

```
        g_tapi.Initialize
End Sub


Private Sub Form_Unload()
        g_tapi.Shutdown
End Sub
```

TAPI 3.0 Collections

Once the TAPI object is constructed, it can be used to enumerate the addresses currently available to the system. As with any COM object model, the top-level object (the TAPI object, in this case) exposes the various contained objects via collections of zero or more subobjects. In the TAPI 3.0 object model, all collections are exposed in two ways. One is more convenient for programmers, and the other is more convenient for C++ programmers. All TAPI collections for VB programmers are objects that implement the `ITCollection` interface:

```
interface ITCollection : IDispatch {
  HRESULT Count([out, retval] long* lCount);

  [id(DISPID_VALUE), propget]
  HRESULT Item([in] long Index,
               [out, retval] VARIANT* pVariant);

  [id(DISID_NEWENUM), propget, restricted]
  HRESULT _NewEnum([out, retval] IUnknown** ppNewEnum);
};
```

This allows the VB programmer to write code like this:

```
' Use Count and Item
Private Sub EnumAddresses()
    Dim colAddresses As ITCollection
    Set colAddresses = g_tapi.Addresses

    Dim nAddresses As Long
    nAddresses = colAddresses.Count
```

```
        Dim n As Long
        For n = 1 To nAddresses
            Dim addr As ITAddress
            ' colAddresses(n) works, too
            Set addr = colAddresses.Item(n)
            ' Use addr
        Next n
    End Sub

    ' Use the For-Each syntax supported by _NewEnum
    Private Sub EnumAddresses()
        Dim colAddresses As ITCollection
        Set colAddresses = g_tapi.Addresses

        Dim var As Variant
        For Each var In colAddresses
            Dim addr As ITAddress
            Set addr = var
            ' Use addr
        Next var
    End Sub
```

VB has no trouble dealing in VARIANTs, a data type that is somewhat more troublesome for the C++ programmer. For the C++ programmer, TAPI 3.0 provides a set of collection interfaces, each typed specifically for the object being enumerated. For example, to enumerate the list of addresses, the C++ programmer would use the IEnumAddress interface:

```
interface IEnumAddress : IUnknown {
    HRESULT Next([in] unsigned long celt,
                 [out] ITAddress** ppElements,
                 [out] unsigned long* pceltFetched);
    HRESULT Reset();
    HRESULT Skip([in] unsigned long celt);
    HRESULT Clone([out, retval] IEnumAddress** ppEnum);
};
```

Using this interface, the C++ programmer would enumerate the collection of addresses like so:

```
HRESULT EnumAddresses()
{
    HRESULT         hr;
    IEnumAddresses* pea = 0;
    hr = g_pTapi->_EnumerateAddresses(&pea);
    if( FAILED(hr) ) return hr;

    enum { CHUNKSIZE = 100 };
    ITAddress*  rgp[CHUNKSIZE] = { 0 };

    do
    {
        ULONG cFetched;
        hr = pevar->Next(CHUNKSIZE, rgp, &cFetched);
        if( SUCCEEDED(hr) )
        {
            if( hr == S_OK ) cFetched = CHUNKSIZE;
            for( ULONG i = 0; i != cFetched; ++i )
            {
                // Use rgp[i]...
                rgp[i]->Release();
            }
        }
        while( hr == S_OK );
    }

    pea->Release();
    return hr;
}
```

While this code is not as neat and tidy as the VB equivalent, it is what C++ COM
programmers are used to and it is simpler than using _NewEnum as exposed from
ITCollection in C++.

Capabilities Discovery

Once the addresses have been discovered, one of them can be used to make a call.
An address is very much like a TAPI line. It represents a device (physical or logical) that can be used to place or answer a call. Each address object exposes basic
functionality by implementing the ITAddress interface:

```
interface ITAddress : IDispatch {
  [propget]
  HRESULT State(
          [out, retval] ADDRESS_STATE* pAddressState);

  [propget]
  HRESULT AddressName([out, retval] BSTR* ppName);

  [propget]
  HRESULT ServiceProviderName([out, retval] BSTR* ppName);

  [propget]
  HRESULT TAPIObject([out, retval] ITTAPI** ppTapiObject);
  HRESULT CreateCall(
          [in] BSTR pDestAddress,
          [out, retval] ITBasicCallControl** ppCall);
  [propget]
  HRESULT Calls([out, retval] VARIANT* pVariant);
  HRESULT _EnumerateCalls([out, retval] IEnumCall** ppec);

  [propget]
  HRESULT AddressTypes([out, retval] VARIANT* pVariant);
  HRESULT _EnumerateAddressType(
          [out, retval] IEnumAddressType** ppeat);

  HRESULT RegisterCallTypes([in] VARIANT_BOOL fOutgoing,
                            [in] VARIANT_BOOL fOwner,
                            [in] VARIANT_BOOL fMonitor,
                            [in] VARIANT MediaTypes);
};
```

However, before a call can be made, you must make sure that there is an address that supports both of the media types you're interested in, for example, audio or video, as well as the address type you have from the user, for example, e-mail address or phone number. To determine an address's supported media type, you need the address's `ITMediaSupport` interface:

```
interface ITMediaSupport : IDispatch {
  [propget]
  HRESULT MediaTypes([out, retval] VARIANT* pVariant);
  HRESULT _EnumerateMediaTypes(
          [out, retval] IEnumMediaType** ppemt);
```

Table 8.1: Media type string constants.	
Media Type	*Symbolic Constant*
Audio in	`TAPIMEDIATYPE_String_AudioOut`
Audio out	`TAPIMEDIATYPE_String_AudioIn`
Video in	`TAPIMEDIATYPE_String_VideoOut`
Video out	`TAPIMEDIATYPE_String_VideoIn`
Data modem	`TAPIMEDIATYPE_String_DataModem`
G3 Fax	`TAPIMEDIATYPE_String_G3Fax`

```
HRESULT QueryDirectShowSupport(
        [in] BSTR pMediaType,
        [out, retval] VARIANT_BOOL* pfSupport);


HRESULT QueryMediaType(
        [in] BSTR pMediaType,
        [out, retval] VARIANT_BOOL* pfSupport);
};
```

The QueryMediaType function takes one of several strings that uniquely identifies media types using Globally Unique Identifiers (GUIDs). Since raw GUIDs are hard to read, the TAPI type library provides a set of media type string constants, given in Table 8.1. For example, the following code checks whether an address supports voice phone call media types, that is, audio in and out:

```
Private Function SupportsVoice(addr As ITAddress) As Boolean
    ' Get ITMediaSupport interface.
    Dim ms As ITMediaSupport
    Set ms = addr

    ' Check for audio in/out.
    If ms.QueryMediaType(TAPIMEDIATYPE_String_AudioIn) And _
      ms.QueryMediaType(TAPIMEDIATYPE_String_AudioOut) Then
        SupportsVoice = True
    Else
        SupportsVoice = False
    End If
End Function
```

Table 8.2: Address types supported by TAPI 3.0.	
Address Type	*Symbolic Constant*
Phone number.	`ADDRESSTYPE_PHONENUMBER`
E-mail address.	`ADDRESSTYPE_EMAILNAME`
Machine name.	`ADDRESSTYPE_DOMAINNAME`
IP address.	`ADDRESSTYPE_IPADDRESS`
Conference name.	`ADDRESSTYPE_CONFERENCENAME`

The address types that TAPI 3.0 supports go far beyond just phone numbers, as shown in Table 8.2. Once the user has determined the type of address that will be used to establish the call, it's up to the application to determine if an address can support the given address type. This is done using the Address Types collection from the `ITAddress` interface, for example:

```
Private Function SupportsAddressType(addr As ITAddress, _
                                     nAddrType As Long) As
Boolean
    ' Get address types collection
    Dim colAddrTypes As ITCollection
    Set colAddrTypes = addr.AddressTypes

    ' Check for address type
    Dim varAddrType As Variant
    For Each varAddrType In colAddrTypes
        If varAddrType = nAddrType Then
            SupportsAddressType = True
            Exit For
        End If
    Next varAddrType
End Function
```

Putting this all together, you can likely see that to find an appropriate address to place a voice call consists of finding an address in the system that supports audio in and audio out as well as the user-selected address type, for example:

```
Private Function FirstVoiceAddress(nAddrType As Long) As Long
    ' Get address collection
```

```
    Dim colAddresses As ITCollection
    Set colAddresses = g_tapi.Addresses

    ' Find a suitable address
    Dim nAddresses As Long
    nAddresses = colAddresses.Count

    Dim n As Long
    For n = 1 To nAddresses
        Dim addr As ITAddress
        Set addr = colAddresses(n)
        If SupportsVoice(addr) And _
            SupportsAddressType(addr, nAddrType) Then
              FirstVoiceAddress = n
        End If
    Next n
End Function
```

Creating a Call

Once a suitable address has been found, a new call can be created using the
CreateCall member function of the ITAddress interface. The single input
parameter is a destination address, and the output is an interface of type IT-
BasicCallControl:

```
interface ITBasicCallControl : IDispatch {
    HRESULT SelectMediaTerminals(VARIANT MediaTerminals);
    HRESULT UnselectMediaTerminal(
            [in] ITMediaTerminal* pmt);
    HRESULT Connect([in] VARIANT_BOOL fSync);
    HRESULT Answer();
    HRESULT Disconnect([in] DISCONNECT_CODE code);
    HRESULT Hold([in] VARIANT_BOOL fHold);
    HRESULT Handoff([in] BSTR pApplicationName,
                    [in] BSTR pMediaType);
    HRESULT AddToConference(
            [in] BSTR pDestAddress,
            [in] VARIANT_BOOL fSync,
            [out, retval] ITConsultCall** ppcc);
    HRESULT SetupTransfer(
```

```
                    [in] BSTR pDestAddress,
                    [in] VARIANT_BOOL fSync,
                    [out, retval] ITConsultCall** ppcc);

        HRESULT GetDirectShowFilterGraph(
                    [out, retval] IDispatch** ppDirectShowFilter);
    };
```

The `ITBasicCallControl` interface is an interface implemented by all call objects. Unlike with TAPI 2.*x,* under TAPI 3.0 a newly created call is not a call that is in the process of connecting. Instead, for an application to establish a connection, the call object must be asked to connect using the Connect member function. Before that can happen, however, terminals must be set up to send and receive the input and output of the call, that is, audio, video, data, or fax.

Terminals

A terminal is where data goes to or comes from on a call. After a call is created, terminals can be added or subtracted as desired to route the media stream of the call. Terminals can be either static, for example, lines, phones, or video devices, or dynamic, for example, files. Each address can define and expose terminals via the `ITTerminalSupport` interface:

```
    interface ITTerminalSupport : IDispatch {
      [propget]
      HRESULT StaticTerminals([out, retval] VARIANT* pv);
      HRESULT _EnumerateStaticTerminals(
                [out, retval] IEnumTerminal** ppet);

      [propget]
      HRESULT DynamicTerminalClasses(
                [out, retval] VARIANT* pv);
      HRESULT _EnumerateDynamicTerminalClasses(
                [out, retval] IEnumTerminalClasses** ppetc);

      HRESULT CreateTerminal([in] BSTR pTerminalClass,
                             [out, retval] ITTerminal** ppt);
      HRESULT GetDefaultTerminal(
```

```
            [in] BSTR pMediaType,
            [out, retval] ITTerminal** ppt);
};
```

To associate terminals with a call, an application has several choices. It can enumerate the static terminals associated with the address. Or it can use the default terminal for a specific media type. Or it can create a new static terminal of a certain class or enumerate the dynamic terminal classes available for an address and create one of those. The possible terminal classes are listed in Table 8.3.

Once a terminal is created, it must be associated with the appropriate media type. This can be done with a MediaTerminal object, which is simply an association between media types and media terminals, that is, where does "audio out" go or where does "audio in" come from. MediaTerminal objects can be created using the `ITTAPI` interface member function `CreateMediaTerminal`.

Once the MediaTerminal objects are created, a variable-sized array of those objects is associated with a call using the `SetMediaTerminals` member function of `ITBasicCallControl`. For example, setting the default terminals for a voice call would look like this:

```
Private Sub SetDefaultVoiceTerminals( _
    addr As ITAddress, newCall As ITCall)

    ' Get ITTerminalSupport
    Dim ts As ITTerminalSupport
    Set ts = addr

    ' Get default audio terminals
    Dim termAudioIn As ITTerminal
    Dim termAudioOut As ITTerminal
    Set termAudioIn =
        ts.GetDefaultTerminal(TAPIMEDIATYPE_String_AudioIn)
    Set termAudioOut =
        ts.GetDefaultTerminal(TAPIMEDIATYPE_String_AudioOut)

    ' Create array of media terminals
    Dim rgmt(2) As ITMediaTerminal
    Set rgmt(1) =

g_tapi.CreateMediaTerminal(TAPIMEDIATYPE_String_AudioIn,
                           termAudioIn)
```

Table 8.3: Terminal classes.	
Terminal Class	*Symbolic Constant*
Video Output Window	`CLSID_String_VideoWindowTerm`
Video Capture Device	`CLSID_String_VideoInputTerminal`
Phone Handset	`CLSID_String_HandsetTerminal`
Phone Headset	`CLSID_String_HeadsetTerminal`
Speaker Phone	`CLSID_String_SpeakerphoneTerminal`
Microphone	`CLSID_String_MicrophoneTerminal`
Speakers	`CLSID_String_SpeakersTerminal`
File	`CLSID_String_FileTerminal`

```
    Set rgmt(2) =

  g_tapi.CreateMediaTerminal(TAPIMEDIATYPE_String_AudioOut,
                              termAudioOut)

    ' Select the media terminals
    newCall.SelectMediaTerminals rgmt
End Sub
```

Events

COM doesn't use callback functions, so the typical TAPI scheme of registering a callback function to receive events isn't going to work. Instead, COM uses callback interfaces—interfaces implemented on objects by the client to receive asynchronous notification of events. Under TAPI 3.0, these client-implemented event interfaces are registered with the telephony objects using the standard Connection Point mechanism. Under C++, this requires the client to use the `IConnection-PointContainer` and the `IConnectionPoint` interfaces. Under VB, however, this simply means using the `WithEvents` syntax (shown later in the chapter).

Instead of one function to filter all events, as with TAPI, each object defines an interface for firing events associated with that object. For example, to be notified of call status events, the associated address would fire events from the `ITCall-Notification` interface:

```
typedef enum {
    CET_CALLOWNER = 0,
    CET_CALLMONITOR = 1,
    CET_CALLSTATEEVENT = 2,
    CET_CALLMEDIAEVENT = 3
} CALL_EVENT_TYPE;

interface ITCallNotification : IUnknown {
  HRESULT CallEventNotification([in] ITAddress* pAddress,
                                [in] CALL_EVENT_TYPE cet,
                                [in] IDispatch* pEvent);
};
```

To filter events from an address to only those events the application is interested in, the address needs to know whether outgoing calls will be made, the media types the application is interested in, and whether the application wants to receive ownership and/or monitoring privileges on incoming calls. This information can be set using the `RegisterCallTypes` member function of `ITAddress`.

Making a Call

Now that we've got all the pieces, we can put them together to make a call. Here's how it's done using TAPI 3.0:

```
Dim WithEvents g_addr As Address

Private Function MakeCall( _
  sAddress As String, addr As ITAddress) as ITCall

    ' Create a call
    Dim newCall As ITCall
    Set newCall = addr.CreateCall(sAddress)

    ' Set the default terminals
    SetDefaltVoiceTerminals addr, newCall

    ' Register for outgoing call events
    Const bOutgoing As Boolean = False
```

```
        Const bOwner As Boolean = False
        Const bMonitor As Boolean = False

        Dim rgsMediaTypes(2) As String
        rgsMediaTypes(1) = TAPIMEDIATYPE_String_AudioIn
        rgsMediaTypes(2) = TAPIMEDIATYPE_String_AudioOut

    addr.RegisterCallTypes bOutgoing, bOwner, bMonitor,
MediaTypes
        Set g_addr = addr

        ' Connect the call
        newCall.Connect False ' Don't wait for call to connect or
fail

        ' Return the new call
        Set MakeCall = newCall
    End Sub
```

Answering a call is simply a matter of watching for the appropriate call event type (CET_CALLOWNER), pulling the `ITCall` interface from the `pEvent` parameter, and calling the `Answer` member function. Dropping a call is even more easily accomplished via the `Disconnect` member function.

Summary

This chapter has been a quick tour through the highlights of TAPI 3.0 as related to the functionality discussed in the rest of the book. TAPI 3.0 simplifies a lot of the basic call control programming chores (at least for the VB programmer). And because it is COM-based, the same explicit object model is exposed to programmers of all languages. TAPI 3.0 is conceptually very similar to TAPI 2.x, however. There are still lines (called addresses), calls, and terminals. In this release, the functionality of the addresses has been expanded to include multiple address types and the terminals have been beefed up to support video as well as audio. This added functionality allows IP telephony applications to be written using the same model as used for PSTN telephony. As IP telephony expands in the future, TAPI 3.0 will become more and more the overall telephony programming API of choice.

Telephony Device Classes

Table A.1 lists Microsoft-documented Telephony Device Classes. TSP developers are free to expose their own. The device classes supported by any given TAPI line, phone, or address can be discovered via the dwDeviceClassesSize and dwDeviceClassesOffset fields of the LINEDEVCAPS, PHONECAPS, and LINEADDRESSCAPS structures, respectively.

The tapi/terminal device class differs significantly based on whether it's used with lineGetID or phoneGetID. With lineGetID, the tapi/terminal device class is represented with an array of DWORDs, each presenting a phone device ID of a phone connected to the line. The number of elements in the array is specified by the dwNumTerminals member of the LINEDEVCAPS structure. If one of the elements is set to 0xFFFFFFFF (−1), this means the terminal at that offset in the array is not a phone device.

When used with phoneGetID, the tapi/terminal device class represents an array of DWORDs, one for each line as returned by lineInitialize or lineInitializeEx. Each entry in the array is a terminal device ID of the phone device associated with the line. An element value of 0xFFFFFFFF (−1) indicates a line without an attached phone.

Name	Description	Data Appended to VARSTRING
comm	Communications port.	LPCSTR pszName;
comm/datamodem	Modem through communications port.	HANDLE hComm; LPCSTR pszName;
comm/datamodem/portname	Name of the device to which the modem is connected.	LPCSTR pszName;
wave/in	Input-only wave audio device.	DWORD dwDevice;
wave/out	Output-only wave audio device.	DWORD dwDevice;
midi/in	Input-only MIDI sequencer.	DWORD dwDevice;
midi/out	Output-only MIDI sequencer.	DWORD dwDevice;
ndis	Network device.	HANDLE hDevice; LPCSTR pszType;
tapi/line	Line device.	DWORD dwDevice;
tapi/phone	Phone device.	DWORD dwDevice;
tapi/terminal	Terminal device.	(see below)

Table A.1: Telephony Device Classes.

TFX Reference

This appendix documents the classes of the Telephony Framework (TFX). For a tutorial of the intended usage of the classes in the TFX, see Chapter 4. The TFX class hierarchy is given in Figure B.1.

CtAddressCaps

The `CtAddressCaps` class is a wrapper around the TAPI `LINEADDRESSCAPS` structure as filled by the `lineGetAddressCaps` function. See the `LINE-ADDRESSCAPS` documentation for more information.

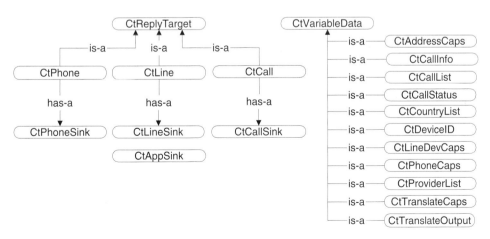

Figure B.1: TFX class hierarchy.

CtAddressCaps Class Members

Data Retrieval

```
TRESULT GetAddressCaps(DWORD nLineID, DWORD nAddressID);
```

Data Access

```
operator const LPLINEADDRESSCAPS() const;

DWORD    GetLineDeviceID() const;
LPCSTR   GetAddress() const;
DWORD    GetAddressSharing() const;
DWORD    GetAddressStates() const;
DWORD    GetCallInfoStates() const;
DWORD    GetCallerIDFlags() const;
DWORD    GetCalledIDFlags() const;
DWORD    GetConnectedIDFlags() const;
DWORD    GetRedirectionIDFlags() const;
DWORD    GetRedirectingIDFlags() const;
DWORD    GetCallStates() const;
DWORD    GetDialToneModes() const;
DWORD    GetBusyModes() const;
DWORD    GetSpecialInfo() const;
DWORD    GetDisconnectModes() const;
DWORD    GetMaxNumActiveCalls() const;
DWORD    GetMaxNumOnHoldCalls() const;
DWORD    GetMaxNumOnHoldPendingCalls() const;
DWORD    GetMaxNumConference() const;
DWORD    GetMaxNumTransConf() const;
DWORD    GetAddrCapFlags() const;
DWORD    GetCallFeatures() const;
DWORD    GetRemoveFromConfCaps() const;
DWORD    GetRemoveFromConfState() const;
DWORD    GetTransferModes() const;
DWORD    GetParkModes() const;
DWORD    GetForwardModes() const;
DWORD    GetMaxForwardEntries() const;
DWORD    GetMaxSpecificEntries() const;
DWORD    GetMinFwdNumRings() const;
DWORD    GetMaxFwdNumRings() const;
DWORD    GetMaxCallCompletions() const;
```

```
DWORD     GetCallCompletionConds() const;
DWORD     GetCallCompletionModes() const;
DWORD     GetNumCompletionMessages() const;
LPCSTR    GetCompletionMsgText(DWORD nMsg) const;
DWORD     GetAddressFeatures() const;
```

Data Access (TAPI 2.x)

```
DWORD     GetPredictiveAutoTransferStates() const;
DWORD     GetNumCallTreatments() const;
DWORD     GetCallTreatmentID(DWORD nCallTreatment) const;
LPCSTR    GetCallTreatmentName(DWORD nCallTreatment) const;
DWORD     GetNumDeviceClasses() const;
LPCSTR    GetDeviceClassName(DWORD nDeviceClass) const;
DWORD     GetMaxCallDataSize() const;
DWORD     GetCallFeatures2() const;
DWORD     GetMaxNoAnswerTimeout() const;
DWORD     GetConnectedModes() const;
DWORD     GetOfferingModes() const;
DWORD     GetAvailableMediaModes() const;
```

CtAppSink

The CtAppSink class is the base class for any class interested in application-specific TAPI events. The application sink object is provided in the call to Tfx-LineInitialize or TfxPhoneInitialize.

CtAppSink Class Members

These member functions are called when the associated TAPI event is received by the application. The associated TAPI event name can be calculated by removing the "On" and replacing the intercaps separator, for example, OnLineCreate = LINE_CREATE.

```
virtual void OnLineCreate(DWORD nLineID);
virtual void OnPhoneCreate(DWORD nPhoneID);
virtual void OnLineRequest(DWORD nRequestMode,
                           HWND hRequestWnd,
                           TREQUEST nRequestID);
```

CtCall

The CtCall class holds a TAPI HCALL data member and provides wrappers for accessing TAPI call-related functions. See the associated TAPI functions for more information.

CtCall Class Members

Operations

```
CtCall(CtLine* pLine);
CtCall(CtLine* pLine, HCALL hCall,
       CtCallSink* pInitialSink = 0);
virtual ~CtCall();

CtLine* GetLine() const;
HCALL   GetHandle() const;
HCALL   Attach(HCALL hCall, CtCallSink* pInitialSink = 0);
HCALL   Detach();
```

Asynchronous Request Management

```
void    AddSink(CtCallSink* pSink);
void    RemoveSink(CtCallSink* pSink);

BOOL    IsRequestPending(TREQUEST nRequestID = 0,
                         DWORD* pnRequestType = 0) const;
BOOL    IsRequestTypePending(DWORD nRequestType) const;

static CtCall*  FromHandle(HCALL hCall);
```

TAPI Wrappers

The associated TAPI function name can be calculated by appending "line" to each of the following member functions, for example, Accept = lineAccept.

```
tfxasync TRESULT
Accept(LPCSTR psUserUserInfo = 0, DWORD nSize = 0);

tfxasync TRESULT
Answer(LPCSTR psUserUserInfo = 0, DWORD nSize = 0);
```

```
tfxasync TRESULT
Dial(LPCSTR szDestAddress, DWORD dwCountryCode = 0);

tfxasync TRESULT
Drop(LPCSTR psUserUserInfo = 0, DWORD nSize = 0);

tfxasync TRESULT
GenerateDigits(LPCSTR szDigits, DWORD nDuration = 0,
               DWORD nDigitMode = LINEDIGITMODE_DTMF);

TRESULT
GenerateTone(DWORD nToneMode, DWORD nDuration,
             DWORD nCustomTones = 0,
             LINEGENERATETONE* pCustomTones = 0);

TRESULT Deallocate();

TRESULT
GatherDigits(LPSTR pszDigits, DWORD nDigits,
             LPCSTR pszTerminationDigits = 0,
             DWORD nFirstDigitTimeout = 5000,
             DWORD nInterDigitTimeout = 5000,
             DWORD nDigitModes = LINEDIGITMODE_DTMF);

TRESULT Handoff(LPCSTR szFileName);
TRESULT Handoff(DWORD nMediaMode);

tfxasync TRESULT
MakeCall(LPCSTR szDestAddress = 0,
         DWORD nCountryCode = 0,
         CtCallSink* pInitialSink = 0,
         LINECALLPARAMS* pCallParams = 0);

TRESULT
MonitorDigits(DWORD dwDigitModes = LINEDIGITMODE_DTMF);
```

CtCallInfo

The CtCallInfo class is a wrapper around the TAPI LINECALLINFO structure as filled by the lineGetCallInfo function. See the LINECALLINFO
documentation for more information.

CtCallInfo Class Members

Data Retrieval

```
TRESULT GetCallInfo(const CtCall* pCall);
TRESULT GetCallInfo(const HCALL hCall);
```

Data Access

```
operator const LPLINECALLINFO() const;

HLINE    GetLineHandle() const;
DWORD    GetLineID() const;
DWORD    GetAddressID() const;
DWORD    GetBearerMode() const;
DWORD    GetRate() const;
DWORD    GetMediaMode() const;
DWORD    GetAppSpecific() const;

DWORD    GetCallID() const;
DWORD    GetRelatedCallID() const;
DWORD    GetCallParamFlags() const;
DWORD    GetCallStates() const;
DWORD    GetMonitorDigitModes() const;
DWORD    GetMonitorMediaModes() const;

const LPLINEDIALPARAMS  GetDialParams() const;

DWORD    GetOrigin() const;
DWORD    GetReason() const;
DWORD    GetCompletionID() const;

DWORD    GetNumOwners() const;
DWORD    GetNumMonitors() const;
```

```
DWORD      GetCountryCode() const;
DWORD      GetTrunk() const;

DWORD      GetCallerIDFlags() const;
LPCSTR     GetCallerID() const;
LPCSTR     GetCallerIDName() const;

DWORD      GetCalledIDFlags() const;
LPCSTR     GetCalledID() const;
LPCSTR     GetCalledIDName() const;

DWORD      GetConnectedIDFlags() const;
LPCSTR     GetConnectedID() const;
LPCSTR     GetConnectedIDName() const;

DWORD      GetRedirectionIDFlags() const;
LPCSTR     GetRedirectionID() const;
LPCSTR     GetRedirectionIDName() const;

DWORD      GetRedirectingIDFlags() const;
LPCSTR     GetRedirectingID() const;
LPCSTR     GetRedirectingIDName() const;

LPCSTR     GetAppName() const;
LPCSTR     GetDisplayableAddress() const;
LPCSTR     GetCalledParty() const;
LPCSTR     GetComment() const;
LPCSTR     GetDisplay() const;

DWORD      GetUserUserInfoSize() const;
void*      GetUserUserInfo() const;

DWORD      GetHighLevelCompSize() const;
void*      GetHighLevelComp() const;

DWORD      GetLowLevelCompSize() const;
void*      GetLowLevelComp() const;

DWORD      GetChargingInfoSize() const;
void*      GetChargingInfo() const;
```

```
DWORD    GetNumTerminals() const;
DWORD    GetTerminalModes(DWORD nTermID);

DWORD    GetDevSpecificSize() const;
void*    GetDevSpecificInfo() const;
```

CtCallList

The `CtCallList` class is a wrapper around the TAPI `LINECALLLIST` structure as filled by the `lineGetCallList` function. See the `LINECALLLIST` documentation for more information.

CtCallList Class Members

Data Retrieval

```
TRESULT GetNewCalls(HLINE hLine);
TRESULT GetNewCalls(DWORD dwAddress);
```

Data Access

```
operator const LPLINECALLLIST() const;

DWORD    GetNumCalls() const;
HCALL    GetCall(DWORD nCall) const;
```

CtCallSink

The `CtCallSink` class is the base class for any class interested in call-specific TAPI events. The call sink object is provided in the call to the `CtCall` constructor or the `CtCall` member functions `MakeCall` or `AddSink`.

CtCallSink Class Members

These member functions are called when the associated TAPI event is received by the call. The associated TAPI event name can be calculated by replacing "On" with "LINE_" or "LINE_CALL", for example, `OnCallInfo = LINE_CALLINFO` and `OnCallGatherDigits = LINE_GATHERDIGITS`.

```
virtual void OnCallInfo(CtCall* pCall, DWORD nCallInfo);
virtual void OnCallState(CtCall* pCall, DWORD nCallState,
                         DWORD dwParam2,
                         DWORD nCallPrivilege);
virtual void OnCallGatherDigits(CtCall* pCall,
                                DWORD nGatherTerm);
virtual void OnCallGenerate(CtCall* pCall,
                            DWORD nGenerateTerm);
virtual void OnCallMonitorDigits(CtCall* pCall,
                                 char cDigit,
                                 DWORD nDigitMode);
virtual void OnCallMonitorMedia(CtCall* pCall,
                                DWORD nMediaMode);
virtual void OnCallMonitorTone(CtCall* pCall,
                               DWORD dwAppSpecific);
virtual void OnCallReply(CtCall* pCall,
                         TREQUEST nRequestID,
                         TRESULT tr, DWORD nRequestType);
```

CtCallStatus

The CtCallStatus class is a wrapper around the TAPI LINECALLSTATUS structure as filled by the lineGetCallStatus function. See the LINECALL-STATUS documentation for more information.

CtCallStatus Class Members

Data Retrieval

```
TRESULT GetCallStatus(const CtCall* pCall);
TRESULT GetCallStatus(const HCALL hCall);
```

Data Access

```
operator const LPLINECALLSTATUS() const;

DWORD   GetCallState() const;
DWORD   GetCallStateMode() const;
DWORD   GetCallPrivilege() const;
```

```
DWORD     GetCallFeatures() const;

DWORD     GetDevSpecificSize() const;
void*     GetDevSpecificInfo() const;
```

Data Access (TAPI 2.x)

```
DWORD        GetCallFeatures2() const;
SYSTEMTIME   GetStateEntryTime() const;
```

CtCountryList

The `CtCountryList` class is a wrapper around the TAPI `LINECOUNTRYLIST` structure as filled by the `lineGetCountry` function. See the `LINECOUNTRY-LIST` documentation for more information.

CtCountryList Class Members

Data Retrieval

```
TRESULT GetCountryList();
```

Data Access

```
operator const LPLINECOUNTRYLIST() const;

DWORD     GetNumCountries() const;
DWORD     GetCountryCode(DWORD nCountry) const;
LPCSTR    GetCountryName(DWORD nCountry) const;
LPCSTR    GetSameAreaRule(DWORD nCountry) const;
LPCSTR    GetLongDistanceRule(DWORD nCountry) const;
LPCSTR    GetInternationalRule(DWORD nCountry) const;
```

CtDeviceID

The `CtDeviceID` class is a wrapper around the TAPI `VARSTRING` structure as filled by the `lineGetID` and `phoneGetID` functions. See Appendix A, Telephony Device Classes, for more information.

CtDeviceID Class Members

Data Retrieval

```
TRESULT GetID(LPCSTR szDeviceClass, HPHONE hPhone);
TRESULT GetID(LPCSTR szDeviceClass, HLINE hLine);
TRESULT GetID(LPCSTR szDeviceClass, HLINE hLine,
              DWORD nAddressID);
TRESULT GetID(LPCSTR szDeviceClass, HCALL hCall);
```

Data Access

```
LPCSTR  GetString();
LPCSTR  GetHandleAndString(HANDLE* ph);
DWORD   GetDeviceID();
DWORD*  GetDeviceIDs();
```

CtLine

The CtLine class holds a TAPI HLINE data member and provides wrappers for accessing TAPI line-related functions. See the associated TAPI functions for more information.

CtLine Class Members

Operations

```
CtLine();
virtual ~CtLine();

HLINE   GetHandle() const;
DWORD   GetDeviceID() const;
```

Asynchronous Request Management

```
void    AddSink(CtLineSink* pSink);
void    RemoveSink(CtLineSink* pSink);

BOOL    IsRequestPending(TREQUEST nRequestID = 0,
                         DWORD* pnRequestType = 0) const;
```

```
BOOL      IsRequestTypePending(DWORD nRequestType) const;


static CtLine*    FromHandle(HLINE hLine);
```

Static Line and Application Information

```
static DWORD      GetNumDevs();
static HLINEAPP GetAppHandle();
static DWORD      GetAppVersion();
static void       SetAppVersion(DWORD dwLoVersion,
                                DWORD dwHiVersion);
static DWORD      GetApiVersion(DWORD nLineID);
```

Static TAPI Wrappers

The associated TAPI function name can be calculated by appending "line" to
each of the following static member functions, for example, `Initialize` =
`lineInitialize`. Most of these functions are wrapped by global TFX helper
functions as described later.

```
static TRESULT
Initialize(CtAppSink* pAppSink, LPCSTR szAppName,
           HINSTANCE hInst);


static TRESULT Shutdown();


static TRESULT
GetMakeCallRequest(LPLINEREQMAKECALL plmc);


static TRESULT
GetMediaCallRequest(LPLINEREQMEDIACALL plmc);


static TRESULT
RegisterRequestRecipient(DWORD dwRegisterMode,
                         BOOL bEnable);


static TRESULT
TranslateDialog(DWORD nLineID, HWND hwndOwner,
                LPCSTR szAddressIn);
```

```
static TRESULT
ConfigDialog(DWORD nLineID, HWND hwndOwner,
             LPCSTR pszDeviceClass = 0);

static TRESULT
GetIcon(DWORD nLineID, LPHICON phicon,
        LPCSTR pszDeviceClass = 0);

static TRESULT SetCurrentLocation(DWORD nLocationID);
```

TAPI Wrappers

The associated TAPI function name can be calculated by appending "line" to each of the following member functions, for example, `Accept = lineAccept`.

```
TRESULT
Open(DWORD nLineID, CtLineSink* pInitialSink = 0,
     DWORD dwPrivileges = LINECALLPRIVILEGE_NONE,
     DWORD dwMediaModes = LINEMEDIAMODE_INTERACTIVEVOICE);

TRESULT Close();

TRESULT GetAddressID(LPDWORD pdwAddressID,
                     DWORD nAddressMode,
                     LPCSTR pszAddress,
                     DWORD nSize) const;

TRESULT GetNumRings(DWORD nAddressID, DWORD* pnRings);
TRESULT SetNumRings(DWORD nAddressID, DWORD nRings);

tfxasync TRESULT
ForwardAll(LPLINEFORWARDLIST const plfl, DWORD nRings);

tfxasync TRESULT
ForwardAddress(DWORD nAddressID,
               LPLINEFORWARDLIST const plfl,
               DWORD nRings);
```

CtLineDevCaps

The `CtLineDevCaps` class is a wrapper around the TAPI `LINEDEVCAPS` structure as filled by the `lineGetDevCaps` function. See the `LINEDEVCAPS` documentation for more information.

CtLineDevCaps Class Members

Data Retrieval

```
TRESULT GetDevCaps(DWORD nLineID);
```

Data Access

```
operator const LPLINEDEVCAPS() const;

LPCSTR   GetProviderInfo() const;
LPCSTR   GetSwitchInfo() const;
DWORD    GetPermanentLineID() const;
LPCSTR   GetLineName() const;

DWORD    GetAddressModes() const;
DWORD    GetNumAddresses() const;
DWORD    GetBearerModes() const;
DWORD    GetMaxRate() const;
DWORD    GetMediaModes() const;

DWORD    GetGenerateToneModes() const;
DWORD    GetGenerateToneMaxNumFreq() const;
DWORD    GetGenerateDigitModes() const;
DWORD    GetMonitorToneMaxNumFreq() const;
DWORD    GetMonitorToneMaxNumEntries() const;
DWORD    GetMonitorDigitModes() const;
DWORD    GetGatherDigitsMinTimeout() const;
DWORD    GetGatherDigitsMaxTimeout() const;

DWORD    GetMedCtlDigitMaxListSize() const;
DWORD    GetMedCtlMediaMaxListSize() const;
DWORD    GetMedCtlToneMaxListSize() const;
DWORD    GetMedCtlCallStateMaxListSize() const;
```

```
DWORD    GetDevCapFlags() const;
DWORD    GetMaxNumActiveCalls() const;
DWORD    GetAnswerMode() const;
DWORD    GetRingModes() const;
DWORD    GetLineStates() const;


DWORD    GetUUIAcceptSize() const;
DWORD    GetUUIAnswerSize() const;
DWORD    GetUUIMakeCallSize() const;
DWORD    GetUUIDropSize() const;
DWORD    GetUUISendUserUserInfoSize() const;
DWORD    GetUUICallInfoSize() const;

const LPLINEDIALPARAMS   GetMinDialParams() const;
const LPLINEDIALPARAMS   GetMaxDialParams() const;
const LPLINEDIALPARAMS   GetDefaultDialParams() const;


DWORD    GetNumTerminals() const;
LPCSTR   GetTerminalText(DWORD nTermID) const;
const LPLINETERMCAPS    GetTermCaps(DWORD nTermID) const;


DWORD    GetLineFeatures() const;
```

Data Access (TAPI 2.x)

```
DWORD    GetSettableDevStatus() const;
DWORD    GetNumDeviceClasses() const;
LPCSTR   GetDeviceClassName(DWORD nDeviceClass) const;
```

CtLineSink

The CtLineSink class is the base class for any class interested in line-specific
TAPI events. The line sink object is provided in the call to the CtLine member
functions Open or AddSink.

CtLineSink Class Members

These member functions are called when the associated TAPI event is received by the line. The associated TAPI event name can be calculated by replacing "On" with "LINE_", for example, `OnLineAddressState = LINE_ADDRESSSTATE`.

TAPI 1.x+ Events

```
virtual void
OnLineAddressState(CtLine* pLine, DWORD nAddressID,
                   DWORD nAddressState);

virtual void
OnLineNewCall(CtLine* pLine, HCALL hCall,
              DWORD nAddressID, DWORD nCallPrivilege);

virtual void
OnLineClose(CtLine* pLine);

virtual void
OnLineDevSpecific(CtLine* pLine, DWORD dwDevice,
                  DWORD dwParam1, DWORD dwParam2,
                  DWORD dwParam3);

virtual void
OnLineDevSpecificFeature(CtLine* pLine, DWORD dwDevice,
                         DWORD dwParam1, DWORD dwParam2,
                         DWORD dwParam3);

virtual void
OnLineDevState(CtLine* pLine, DWORD nDevState,
               DWORD dwParam2, DWORD dwParam3);

virtual void
OnLineReply(CtLine* pLine, TREQUEST nRequestID,
            TRESULT nResult, DWORD dwRequestType);
```

TAPI 2.x+ Events

```
virtual void
OnLineAgentSpecific(CtLine* pLine,
                    DWORD dwAgentExtensionIDIndex,
```

```
                              DWORD dwHandlerSpecific1,
                              DWORD dwHandlerSpecific2);

    virtual void
    OnLineAgentStatus(CtLine* pLine, DWORD nAddressID,
                      DWORD nAgentStatus,
                      DWORD dwAgentStatusDetail);

    virtual void
    OnLineProxyRequest(CtLine* pLine,
                       LINEPROXYREQUEST* pProxyRequest);

    virtual void
    OnLineRemove(CtLine* pLine, DWORD dwDeviceID);
```

CtPhone

The `CtPhone` class holds a TAPI `HPHONE` data member and provides wrappers for accessing TAPI phone-related functions. See the associated TAPI functions for more information.

CtPhone Class Members

Operations

```
    CtPhone();
    virtual ~CtPhone();

    HPHONE  GetHandle() const;
    DWORD   GetDeviceID() const;
```

Asynchronous Request Management

```
    void    AddSink(CtPhoneSink* pSink);
    void    RemoveSink(CtPhoneSink* pSink);

    BOOL    IsRequestPending(TREQUEST nRequestID,
                             DWORD* pnRequestType = 0) const;
```

```
BOOL      IsRequestTypePending(DWORD nRequestType) const;

static CtPhone*      FromHandle(HPHONE hPhone);
```

Static Phone and Application Information

```
static DWORD      GetNumDevs();
static HPHONEAPP GetAppHandle();
static DWORD      GetAppVersion();
static void       SetAppVersion(DWORD dwLoVersion,
                                DWORD dwHiVersion);
static DWORD      GetApiVersion(DWORD nLineID);
```

Static TAPI Wrappers

The associated TAPI function name can be calculated by appending "phone" to each of the following static member functions, for example, `Initialize = phoneInitialize`. Most of these functions are wrapped by global TFX helper functions as described later.

```
static TRESULT
Initialize(CtAppSink* pAppSink, LPCSTR szAppName,
           HINSTANCE hInst);

static TRESULT   Shutdown();
static TRESULT
GetIcon(DWORD nPhoneID, LPHICON phicon,
        LPCSTR pszDeviceClass);
```

TAPI Wrappers

The associated TAPI function name can be calculated by appending "phone" to each of the following member functions, for example, `Open = phoneOpen`.

```
TRESULT
Open(DWORD nLineID, CtPhoneSink* pInitialSink = 0,
     DWORD dwPrivileges = PHONEPRIVILEGE_OWNER);

TRESULT Close();
TRESULT SetHookSwitch(DWORD dwHookSwitchDevs,
                      DWORD nHookSwitchMode);
```

CtPhoneCaps

The `CtPhoneCaps` class is a wrapper around the TAPI `PHONECAPS` structure as filled by the `phoneGetDevCaps` function. See the `PHONECAPS` documentation for more information.

CtPhoneCaps Class Members

Data Retrieval

```
TRESULT GetDevCaps(DWORD nPhoneID);
```

Data Access

```
operator const LPPHONECAPS() const;
LPCSTR   GetProviderInfo() const;
LPCSTR   GetPhoneInfo() const;
DWORD    GetPermanentPhoneID() const;
LPCSTR   GetPhoneName() const;

DWORD    GetPhoneStates() const;
DWORD    GetHookSwitchDevs() const;
DWORD    GetHandsetHookSwitchModes() const;
DWORD    GetSpeakerHookSwitchModes() const;
DWORD    GetHeadsetHookSwitchModes() const;
DWORD    GetVolumeFlags() const;
DWORD    GetGainFlags() const;

DWORD    GetDisplayNumRows() const;
DWORD    GetDisplayNumColumns() const;
DWORD    GetNumRingModes() const;
DWORD    GetNumButtonLamps() const;
DWORD    GetButtonModes(DWORD nButton) const;
DWORD    GetButtonFunction(DWORD nButton) const;
DWORD    GetLampModes(DWORD nLamp) const;

DWORD    GetNumSetData() const;
DWORD    GetSetData(DWORD nDatum) const;
DWORD    GetNumGetData() const;
```

```
DWORD     GetGetData(DWORD nDatum) const;

DWORD     GetDevSpecificSize() const;
void*     GetDevSpecificData() const;
```

CtPhoneSink

The CtPhoneSink class is the base class for any class interested in phone-specific TAPI events. The phone sink object is provided in the call to the CtPhone member functions Open or AddSink.

CtPhoneSink Class Members

These member functions are called when the associated TAPI event is received by the phone. The associated TAPI event name can be calculated by replacing "On" with "PHONE_", for example, OnPhoneButton = PHONE_BUTTON.

TAPI 1.x+ Events

```
virtual void
OnPhoneButton(CtPhone* pPhone, DWORD nButtonOrLampID,
              DWORD nButtonMode, DWORD nButtonState);

virtual void
OnPhoneClose(CtPhone* pPhone);

virtual void
OnPhoneDevSpecific(CtPhone* pPhone, DWORD dwDevice,
                   DWORD dwParam1, DWORD dwParam2,
                   DWORD dwParam3);

virtual void
OnPhoneReply(CtPhone* pPhone, TREQUEST nRequestID,
             TRESULT nResult, DWORD dwRequestType);

virtual void
OnPhoneState(CtPhone* pPhone, DWORD dwPhoneStates,
             DWORD dwPhoneStateDetails);
```

TAPI 2.*x*+ Events

```
virtual void
OnPhoneRemove(CtPhone* pPhone, DWORD dwDeviceID);
```

CtProviderList

The `CtProviderList` class is a wrapper around the TAPI `LINEPROVIDER-LIST` structure as filled by the `lineGetProviderList` function. See the `LINEPROVIDERLIST` documentation for more information.

CtProviderList Class Members

Data Retrieval

```
LONG      GetProviderList();
```

Data Access

```
DWORD    GetNumProviders() const;
DWORD    GetProviderPermanentID(DWORD nProvider) const;
LPCSTR   GetProviderFilename(DWORD nProvider) const;
```

CtReplyTarget

`CtReplyTarget` serves as the base class for all classes that can receive telephony reply events via `LINE_REPLY` and `PHONE_REPLY`.

CtReplyTarget Class Members

```
virtual void OnReply(
  TREQUEST nRequestID,// Async. request ID
  TRESULT nResult,    // TAPI result
  DWORD nRequestType) // Async. request type
```

Each asynchronous function wrapped by the TFX has its own `nRequestType`, as shown in Table B.1.

TFX Class	Member Function	nRequestType
CtLine	ForwardAll	LINEREQUEST_FORWARD
CtLine	ForwardAddress	LINEREQUEST_FORWARD
CtCall	Accept	CALLREQUEST_ACCEPT
CtCall	Answer	CALLREQUEST_ANSWER
CtCall	Dial	CALLREQUEST_DIAL
CtCall	Drop	CALLREQUEST_DROP
CtCall	GenerateDigits	CALLREQUEST_GENERATEDIGITS
CtCall	MakeCall	CALLREQUEST_MAKECALL
None	Asynch. TAPI function not made by the TFX.	CALLREQUEST_UNKNOWN LINEREQUEST_UNKNOWN

Table B.1: nRequestTypes.

CtTranslateCaps

The `CtTranslateCaps` class is a wrapper around the TAPI `LINETRANS-LATECAPS` structure as filled by the `lineGetTranslateCaps` function. See the `LINETRANSLATECAPS` documentation for more information.

CtTranslateCaps Class Members

Data Retrieval

```
TRESULT GetTranslateCaps();
```

Data Access

```
DWORD    GetCurrentLocationID() const;
DWORD    GetNumLocations() const;

DWORD    GetPermanentLocationID(DWORD nLocation) const;
LPCSTR   GetLocationName(DWORD nLocation) const;
DWORD    GetCountryCode(DWORD nLocation) const;
LPCSTR   GetAreaCode(DWORD nLocation) const;
LPCSTR   GetCityCode(DWORD nLocation) const;
```

```
DWORD     GetPreferredCardID(DWORD nLocation) const;
LPCSTR    GetLocalAccessCode(DWORD nLocation) const;
LPCSTR    GetLongDistanceAccessCode(DWORD nLocation) const;
LPCSTR    GetTollPrefixList(DWORD nLocation) const;
DWORD     GetCountryID(DWORD nLocation) const;
DWORD     GetLocationOptions(DWORD nLocation) const;
LPCSTR    GetCancelCallWaiting(DWORD nLocation) const;

DWORD     GetCurrentPreferredCardID() const;
DWORD     GetNumCards() const;

DWORD     GetPermanentCardID(DWORD nCard) const;
LPCSTR    GetCardName(DWORD nCard) const;
DWORD     GetCardNumberDigits(DWORD nCard) const;
LPCSTR    GetSameAreaRule(DWORD nCard) const;
LPCSTR    GetLongDistanceRule(DWORD nCard) const;
LPCSTR    GetInternationalRule(DWORD nCard) const;
DWORD     GetCardOptions(DWORD nCard) const;
```

CtTranslateOutput

The CtTranslateOutput class is a wrapper around the TAPI LINETRANS-
LATEOUTPUT structure as filled by the lineTranslateAddress function.
See the LINETRANSLATEOUTPUT documentation for more information.

CtTranslateOutput Class Members

Data Retrieval

```
TRESULT
TranslateAddress(DWORD nLineID, LPCSTR pszAddressIn,
                 DWORD nCardID = 0,
                 DWORD dwTranslateOptions = 0);
```

Data Access

```
operator const LPLINETRANSLATEOUTPUT() const;

LPCSTR    GetDialableString() const;
LPCSTR    GetDisplayableString() const;
```

```
DWORD     GetCurrentCountry() const;
DWORD     GetDestCountry() const;
DWORD     GetTranslateResults() const;
```

CtVariableData

The CtVariableData class is the base class for all TAPI VLS wrappers, for example, CtAddressCaps. Classes derived from CtVariableData must implement the FillBuffer function:

```
virtual TRESULT FillBuffer() =0;
```

CtVariableData Class Members

These class members are available only to classes derived from CtVariable-Data.

```
TRESULT UpdateData();


LPCSTR
GetStringPtr(DWORD nOffset, DWORD nSize,
        DWORD dwStringFormat = STRINGFORMAT_ASCII) const;


void*   GetDataPtr(DWORD nOffset) const;
```

TFX Helper Functions

Line-related Helpers

The following functions call the associated static CtLine member functions.

```
DWORD TfxGetNumLines();
TRESULT TfxLineInitialize(CtAppSink* pAppSink = 0,
                          LPCSTR szAppName = 0,
                          HINSTANCE hInst = 0);
void TfxLineShutdown();
```

```
TRESULT
TfxRegisterRequestRecipient(
  DWORD dwRequestMode = LINEREQUESTMODE_MAKECALL);

void
TfxUnregisterRequestRecipient(
  DWORD dwRequestMode = LINEREQUESTMODE_MAKECALL);

TRESULT
TfxGetAppPriority(
  DWORD nMediaMode,
  LPDWORD pnPriority,
  LPLINEEXTENSIONID const pExtID = 0,
  DWORD nRequestMode = LINEREQUESTMODE_MAKECALL,
  LPVARSTRING pvsExtName = 0);

TRESULT
TfxSetAppPriority(
  DWORD nMediaMode,
  DWORD nPriority,
  LPLINEEXTENSIONID const pExtID = 0,
  DWORD nRequestMode = LINEREQUESTMODE_MAKECALL,
  LPCSTR pszExtName = 0);

TRESULT TfxGetMakeCallRequest(LPLINEREQMAKECALL plmc);
TRESULT TfxGetMediaCallRequest(LPLINEREQMEDIACALL plmc);

TRESULT
TfxLineConfigDialog(DWORD nLineID, HWND hwndOwner,
                    LPCSTR szDeviceClass = 0);

TRESULT
TfxLineTranslateDialog(DWORD nLineID, HWND hwndOwner,
                       LPCSTR szAddressIn = 0);

TRESULT
TfxLineGetIcon(DWORD nLineID, LPHICON phicon,
               LPCSTR pszDeviceClass = 0);

TRESULT TfxSetCurrentLocation(DWORD nLocationID);
```

Phone-related Helpers

The following functions call the associated static `CtPhone` member functions.

```
DWORD TfxGetNumPhones();

TRESULT
TfxPhoneInitialize(CtAppSink* pAppSink = 0,
                   LPCSTR szAppName = 0,
                   HINSTANCE hInst = 0);

void TfxPhoneShutdown();

TRESULT TfxPhoneGetIcon(DWORD nPhoneID,
                        LPHICON phicon,
                        LPCSTR pszDeviceClass = 0);
```

CtPhoneNo

The `CtPhoneNo` class encapsulates a phone number. It is not part of the compiled TFX libraries.

CtPhoneNo Class Members

Construction

```
CtPhoneNo();
CtPhoneNo(LPCSTR szWholePhoneNo);
CtPhoneNo(LPCSTR szCountryCode, LPCSTR szAreaCode,
          LPCSTR szPhoneNo);
CtPhoneNo(DWORD nCountryCode, LPCSTR szAreaCode,
          LPCSTR szPhoneNo);

CtPhoneNo(const CtPhoneNo& pno);
CtPhoneNo& operator=(const CtPhoneNo& pno);

virtual ~CtPhoneNo();
```

Accessors

```
LPCSTR   GetCountryCode();
DWORD    GetCountryCodeNum();
```

```
LPCSTR   GetAreaCode();
LPCSTR   GetPhoneNo();

virtual LPCSTR   GetCanonical();
virtual LPCSTR   GetDisplayable();

virtual LPCSTR
GetTranslatable(
  LPCSTR pszMap = "2223334445555666777788889999");
```

Mutators

```
virtual void SetWholePhoneNo(LPCSTR szWholePhoneNo);
virtual void SetCanonical(LPCSTR szCanonical);
virtual void SetCanonical(LPCSTR szCountryCode,
                          LPCSTR szAreaCode,
                          LPCSTR szPhoneNo);
virtual void SetCanonical(DWORD nCountryCode,
                          LPCSTR szAreaCode,
                          LPCSTR szPhoneNo);

void     ResetToLocation();

void     SetCountryCode(LPCSTR szCountryCode);
void     SetCountryCode(DWORD nCountryCode);
void     SetAreaCode(LPCSTR szAreaCode);
void     SetPhoneNo(LPCSTR szPhoneNo);
```

CtWave

The CtWave class encapsulates a WAVE file. It is not part of the compiled TFX libraries. This class will load, save, or play WAVE files in any format but will record only PCM format in mono at 8kHz, 8 bits/sample.

CtWave Class Members

```
CtWave(CtWaveSink* pSink = 0);
~CtWave();
```

```
bool Load(HINSTANCE hinst, UINT nID);
bool Load(HINSTANCE hinst, LPCTSTR pszID);

bool Load(LPCSTR pszFileName);
bool Save(LPCSTR pszFileName);

bool Play(UINT nWaveOut, bool bLoop = false);
bool Record(UINT nWaveIn, UINT nSecs);
bool Stop();
bool Close();
```

CtWaveSink

The `CtPhoneSink` class is the base class for any class interested in wave events. The wave sink object is provided in the call to the `CtWave` constructor.

CtWaveSink Class Members

Wave Out Events (Playing)

```
virtual void OnWaveOutOpen();
virtual void OnWaveOutDone();
virtual void OnWaveOutClose();
```

Wave In Events (Recording)

```
virtual void OnWaveInOpen();
virtual void OnWaveInData();
virtual void OnWaveInClose();
```

Using the TFX

- To use the line part of the TFX, include `tfxLine.h`.
- To use the phone part of the TFX, include `tfxPhone.h`.
- To use the `CtPhoneNo` class, include `tPhoneNo.h` and, in exactly one place, `tPhoneNo.cpp`.

- To use the `CtWave` class, include `tWave.h` and, in exactly one place, `tWave.cpp` and `tInvisibleWindow.cpp`.

Building the TFX

To build the TFX libraries, open the TFX project using Visual C++ 5.0 or better and choose Batch Build from the Build menu. Building all four targets will yield the TFX static libraries for TAPI 1.4 and TAPI 2.0 in both Debug and Release versions.

Index

MFC Programming
Alan R. Feuer

This book provides an in-depth introduction to writing 32-bit Windows applications using C++ and the Microsoft Foundation Class (MFC) library. The text builds from the ground up, first describing the Windows architecture and showing how MFC works with that architecture; then covering the document/view framework that simplifies the creation of industrial-strength programs; and finally illustrating advanced concepts like the usage of dynamic link libraries (DLL), creating Internet clients, and building form-based applications. *MFC Programming* answers the hard questions, diving below the surface presented in the Reference Manual by building comprehensive, detailed chapters on all types of controls, all of the common dialogs (along with the various methods of customization), serialization, printing and previewing, and customization of the Page Setup dialog. The accompanying CD-ROM contains source code for all programs in the book.

0-201-63358-2 • Hardcover • 480 pages • ©1997

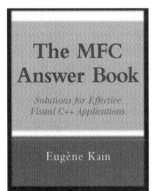

The MFC Answer Book
Solutions for Effective Visual C++ Applications
Eugène Kain

Microsoft Foundation Class (MFC) Library is becoming increasingly popular among Windows programmers—more than one million developers use MFC. Although there are many tutorials covering MFC programming, there are few texts that teach you to build sophisticated and professional user interfaces that go beyond Wizard-supplied functionality. *The MFC Answer Book* is specifically designed to help programmers solve their MFC programming problems in the most efficient way possible, both immediately in answer form and through detailed explanations. The techniques covered in this book will save the MFC programmer hours or even days of frustration looking for the right answer to a pressing question. The accompanying CD-ROM contains more than 100 sample programs demonstrating the various solutions discussed in the book, enabling the programmer to immediately reuse those proven techniques in their own projects.

0-201-18537-7 • Paperback • 752 pages • ©1998

Extending the MFC Library
Add Useful Reusable Features to the Microsoft® Foundation Class Library
David A. Schmitt

MFC allows you to code for new or customized capabilities by extending the application framework and creating your own reusable classes. *Extending the MFC Library* brings C and C++ programmers quickly up to speed on MFC's implementation of traditional C++ features, then presents numerous extension projects, discussing how they are created and used, and how to further customize them for use in your own projects. The extension projects are included ready-to-run on disk.

0-201-48946-5 • Paperback • 384 pages • ©1996

MFC Internals
Inside the Microsoft® Foundation Class Architecture
George Shepherd and Scot Wingo

According to Dean McCrory, Microsoft's MFC Development Lead, "Quite simply, this book is a must-have for any serious MFC developer." This guide to the inner workings of the Microsoft Foundation Classes gives you in-depth information on undocumented MFC classes, utility functions and data members, useful coding techniques, and analyses of the way MFC classes work together. The book covers both graphical user interface classes and extensions to the basic Windows support. You will learn about specific topics such as MFC's document/view architecture, undocumented aspects of MFC serialization and classes, implementation of OLE controls, and more.

0-201-40721-3 • Paperback • 736 pages • ©1996

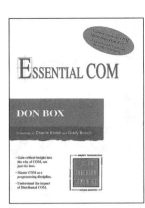

Essential COM
Don Box

Essential COM helps developers go beyond simplistic applications of COM and become truly effective COM programmers. You will find comprehensive coverage of the core concepts of Distributed COM (interfaces, classes, apartments, and applications), including detailed descriptions of COM theory, the C++ language mapping, COM IDL (Interface Definition Language), the remoting architecture, IUnknown, monikers, threads, marshalers, security, and more. Written by the premier authority on the COM architecture, this book offers a thorough explanation of COM's basic vocabulary, provides a complete Distributed COM application to illustrate programming techniques, and includes the author's test library of COM utility code. By showing you the why of COM, not just the how, Don Box teaches you to apply the model creatively and effectively to everyday programming problems.

0-201-63446-5 • Paperback • 464 pages • ©1998

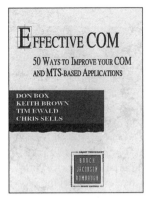

Effective COM
50 Ways to Improve Your COM and MTS-based Applications
Don Box, Keith Brown, Tim Ewald, and Chris Sells

Written by *Essential COM* author Don Box in conjunction with three other trainers at DevelopMentor, *Effective COM* offers fifty concrete guidelines for COM based on the communal wisdom that has formed over the past five years of COM-based development. This book is targeted at developers who are living and breathing COM, humbled by its complexity and challenged by the breadth of distributed object computing. Although the book is written for developers who work in C++, many of the topics (e.g., interface design, security) are approachable by developers who work in Visual Basic, Java, or Object Pascal. *Effective COM* takes a practical approach to COM, offering guidelines developers can use immediately to become more effective, efficient COM programmers.

0-201-37968-6 • Paperback • 208 pages • Available late fall 1998

Multithreading Applications in Win32®
The Complete Guide to Threads
Jim Beveridge and Robert Wiener

Windows® 95 and Windows NT™ allow software developers to use the powerful programming technique of multithreading: dividing a single application into multiple "threads" that execute separately and get their own CPU time. This can result in significant performance gains, but also in programming headaches. Multithreading is difficult to do well, and previous coverage of the subject in Windows has been incomplete. This book provides hands-on experience about when and how to use multithreading, expert advice, and working examples in C++ and MFC. The CD-ROM contains the code and sample applications from the book, including code that works with Internet Winsock.

0-201-44234-5 • Paperback • 400 pages • ©1997

Win32® Network Programming
Windows® 95 and Windows NT™ Network Programming Using MFC
Ralph Davis

As a developer of applications that must communicate across Windows® 95 and Windows NT™, you need to know what network capabilities have been implemented across both platforms. *Win32® Network Programming* is a guide to building networked applications for both Windows 95 and Windows NT 4.0, focusing on overlapped I/O, Windows Sockets 2.0, the Registration Service API, RPC, and Named Pipes. The disk accompanying the book contains the example code cast as a C++/MFC class library that extends MFC to support overlapped I/O, I/O completion ports, the Windows Sockets Service Registration API, and related functionality.

0-201-48930-9 • Paperback • 832 pages • ©1996

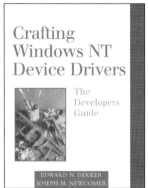

Crafting Windows NT Device Drivers
The Developers Guide
Edward N. Dekker and Joseph M. Newcomer

Device drivers are a necessary evil, connecting the operating system with its peripherals. There is not always a need for a custom device driver, but it is difficult to determine when one is necessary until driver fundamentals are clear. This book emphasizes the core techniques of programming device drivers. Without this core knowledge, all of the "advanced" driver techniques (layered drivers, WDM, File System Filters, File System Drivers) are inaccessible. This book covers the components of a Kernel mode device driver for Windows NT. There is also background on the bus interfaces the driver programmer will use, the ISA and the PCI. The authors tackle both existing drivers (the ISA bus and the PCI bus, the primary buses in today's computers).

0-201-69590-1 • Hardcover • 704 pages • Available fall 1998

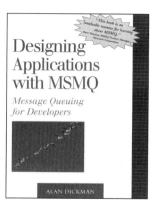

Designing Applications with MSMQ
Message Queuing for Developers
Alan Dickman

Using Web technology effectively to access a vast number of potential customers while keeping customer service levels high is a difficult task. MSMQ (Microsoft Message Queuing) works with MTS (Microsoft Transaction Server) to connect databases and automate responses to external customers (e.g., order processing, customer service issues via email). *Designing Applications with MSMQ* offers a resource for understanding the fundamentals of distributed transactional objects or components. Developing and deploying TP applications has historically been a highly complex task. Microsoft's transaction-processing products, now integrated with Windows NT, make development of mission-critical applications simpler. This book addresses the needs of both Window developers and UNIX TP developers, including software and examples to support the correct design of distributed transactional object systems using MS products, through detailed coverage of online retailing applications.

0-201-32581-0 • Paperback • 432 pages • Available fall 1998

Win32 System Programming
Johnson M. Hart

With this book you can capitalize on your knowledge of high-end operating systems such as Unix, MVS, or VMS to learn Windows system programming quickly. *Win32 System Programming* focuses on the core operating system services of Win32, the common API for the Windows 95 and Windows NT operating systems. The book offers extensive coverage of I/O, security, memory management, processes, threads, and synchronization. You will also find discussions of other advanced topics, including file locking, DLLs, asynchronous I/O, fibers, and the registry. Other features include numerous practical examples and comparisons of Win32 and UNIX functions. The accompanying CD-ROM contains all of the code examples found in the text, a suite of programs for testing system performance, and a collection of UNIX-like utilities.

0-201-63465-1 • Hardcover • 384 pages • ©1997

Windows™ Sockets Network Programming
Bob Quinn and Dave Shute

Windows Sockets (WinSock), a standard network API for use with Windows®, UNIX®, and TCP/IP networking environments, is an extraordinary resource for network programmers. This book shows you how to reap WinSock's full benefits to create network-ready applications. In addition to comprehensive coverage of WinSock 1.1 and 2.0 function calls, you will find information on porting existing BSD Sockets source code to Windows, debugging techniques and tools, common traps and pitfalls to avoid, and the many different operating system platforms that currently incorporate WinSock.

0-201-63372-8 • Hardcover • 656 pages • ©1996

Win32 Programming

Brent E. Rector and Joseph M. Newcomer

Win32 Programming covers all the material necessary to understand and write 32-bit Windows® applications for both Windows® 95 and Windows NT™ 3.5.1. The book details Win32 application programming concepts, approaches, and techniques for the common Application Programming Interface of Windows 95 and Windows NT. It covers basic methods of Windows message handling, advances in mouse and keyboard input handling, and graphical output using the Graphics Device Interface. The CD-ROM is a gold mine of useful programs, with a C template to create your own Windows applications and dozens of other programs.

0-201-63492-9 • Hardcover • 1568 pages • ©1997

Windows NT™ Security Guide

Stephen A. Sutton

Weak links in a security system leave the door open to data tampering, virus attacks, and numerous other unpleasant scenarios. This book shows system administrators how to protect their networks from intruders. It contains information on critical security issues by providing practical examples and tutorials on configuring and managing a leak-proof network. Perhaps most crucial, the *Windows NT™ Security Guide* provides guidelines for assessing the effectiveness of a network's defense system.

0-201-41969-6 • Paperback • 384 pages • ©1997

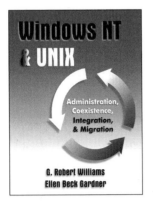

Windows NT & UNIX

Administration, Coexistence, Integration, & Migration
G. Robert Williams and Ellen Beck Gardner

This book is a guidebook for managing a smoothly running system that incorporates both UNIX and Windows NT. It clarifies the key issues you are likely to encounter in dealing with the two operating systems, focusing on the three specific areas of interaction: coexistence, integration, and migration. Planning and implementing the introduction of Windows NT into a UNIX environment is discussed in depth, from selecting a topological model and assessing hardware requirements to rollout and training. The book also addresses such topics as accessing data across platforms; user interface emulators; running Windows applications under UNIX and vice versa; ported POSIX commands and utilities; and SNMP. In addition, it presents available tools for porting UNIX applications to Win32, discusses retrofitting UNIX CPUs, and examines CORBA and DCOM interoperability issues.

0-201-18536-9 • Paperback • 768 pages • ©1998